Let Us Eat Cake

ReganBooks

An Imprint of HarperCollins*Publishers*

Let Us Eat Cake

*Adventures in Food
and Friendship*

SHARON BOORSTIN

In memory of Mary Ann, who always knew the recipe.

To Paul, my secret ingredient.

Contents

Part III: Getting Serious About Life and Turkeys

Part IV: Connections and Reconnections

Introduction

The Long-Lost Recipe Notebook

'm the opposite of a pack rat. When things are no longer useful, I trash them. In fact, my husband says that I'm so quick to throw things away, he won't give me the power to pull the plug if—God forbid—he should ever be on life support.

But there is a desk in our house that I've never cleaned out, a burnished antique Federal desk with dusty cubbyholes and worn drawer pulls that come off in your hand. It was our first major purchase after Paul and I got married thirty-three years ago. If furniture can be haunted, the Federal desk holds the ghosts of our blissful, newlywed years past.

Here's a partial inventory of what's in it:

- the rattle from the rattlesnake that Paul slew in front of our house on the hot summer night we moved in, in 1973
- a hundred *New Yorker* magazine covers, circa 1972–1985, with which I planned one day to wallpaper a bathroom but never did

- the last of the formal ivory—now yellowed—Crane sta-
  tionery I used to write thank-you notes for our wedding gifts

It was under the thank-you notes in the bottom drawer of the
Federal desk that I discovered the inspiration for this book—a
loose-leaf notebook of recipes that I had gathered from girlfriends
and relatives when I was a newlywed. Among the recipes:

> Irma's Tandoori Chicken
> Aunt Hannah's Chocolate Cheesecake
> Mary Ann's Grapes Brûlée
> Mom's Egg-Bread Stuffing

Each recipe brought back memories of the woman who gave it
to me, of the occasions when we made and enjoyed the dish, and of
the friendship we shared.

I wrote an article about the discovery of the notebook—and the
old times and old friends it brought to mind—for *More* magazine.
In doing so, I realized just how important food, recipes, and cooking are in connecting women of different generations in a family,
and in connecting friends. Fathers and grandfathers teach their sons
and grandsons how to throw a baseball. Mothers and grandmothers
teach their daughters and granddaughters how to cook. You could
even say that women bond over food the way men do over sports.
With women it's not, "So, how do you like those Mets?" but "How
do you like the chocolate mousse?"

It also dawned on me how much my friendships have changed
over the years. When I was a newlywed, I devoted so much emotional energy to my husband that I gave short shrift to my childhood
and college girlfriends. My husband became my best friend;
together we had "couples" friends. This was true for many young
married women at the time. Later, when my children were toddlers,
I became friends with their playmates' mothers. But because so

much of my energy—emotional *and* physical—went to my kids, I did not develop any new female friendships that existed apart from my husband and my children. I was also working as my husband's screenwriting partner. Who had time for girlfriends?

Eventually my children grew into adolescents. Once they started driving, I was free. I gave up screenwriting with my husband to concentrate on food writing and journalism. In my new, independent state, I began to find more time for girlfriends, and I discovered that it's easier to have girlfriends now. When I was younger, friendship could be undermined by competitive feelings—about men, looks, career. Not anymore. Ask any woman over forty if she agrees. Most likely she'll nod, laugh, and say, *"Competition?* We're too old for that!"

I also realized that now, even more so than when we were younger, my friends and I share an interest in food—cooking, recipes, dining out. Unlike our mothers, we don't cook just because it is expected of us as wives and mothers. And unlike our former unliberated single selves, we don't find comfort in food when we can't find a man, or use cooking to find one. When we entertain now, we do it with less effort, and we cook—and savor food—because we find it enjoyable, nurturing, and creative.

While I was writing the article for *More,* I contacted a girlfriend whose recipe for tandoori chicken I discovered in my old recipe notebook—a girlfriend I hadn't seen or heard from in over twenty years. In the late sixties, Irma and I carpooled to the high school in Watts where we taught, picketed together in the teachers' strike, and had dinner at each other's apartments. I was a bridesmaid at Irma's wedding, but Paul and I never took to her husband, Bill. When they moved away shortly after their marriage, Irma disappeared off my radar screen. Thanks to the Internet, I found her; she was running a bookstore in Laguna Beach, not far from where I live in L.A. A perfect job, I thought, for one of the best-read women I've known.

Walking the picket line in miniskirts:
Irma, me, and Sue.

The minute I heard Irma's voice on the phone, it was as if twenty years had peeled away. I filled her in on my career ups and downs. She filled me in on her divorce from Bill (I wasn't surprised) and her triumph over breast cancer. And of course we talked about our kids. She has a boy and a girl, like me, and coincidentally, we both named our daughters Julia. It was as if the two of us were gabbing away in my faded red un-air-conditioned stick-shift Volvo, stuck in traffic on the 405 freeway on a smoggy school day.

"Remember that chicken recipe we used to make?" I asked.

As bubbly as ever, Irma broke in: "I make it all the time! I know it by heart!" But the recipe she proceeded to recite wasn't the one for tandoori chicken that she had given me. It was for Chicken La Cassine, a recipe that I had given *her*—and one I had long since forgotten.

Since that call, Irma and I have seen each other often and remain in close touch. We talk about our children, our work, our lives. We also share secrets—one of the benefits, I've rediscovered, of having a trusted girlfriend. When Irma comes to my house we inevitably end up in the kitchen. I'm always amazed at how much conversation we can pack in while whipping up dinner.

Rediscovering Irma made me feel as if I'd found a treasured gift I had lost, and it inspired me to reconnect with other long-lost friends. In each case, my friends and I shared the joyous—and painful—experiences we've gone through since we last met. We also discussed our delicious shared food memories: what we ate (sometimes with guilt for pigging out), what we cooked, and what was going on in our lives at the time. Girlfriends, I discovered, never forget these things.

This book turned out to be more autobiographical than I had planned, but in many ways my changing sense of myself as a woman—and my relationships with my girlfriends and my family—is like that of others born during or just after World War II. We were at the tail end of the generation of women who were raised with old-fashioned notions about what constitutes "respectable" behavior and our place in society, yet we were just ahead of those who grew up with the freedoms afforded by the women's lib movement.

Food is one way all women connect, and I have included not just my own food memories but those of others as well. Some are family or friends; others are food professionals I have met through the years. I hope that recounting their experiences sheds light on attitudes about food and friendship shared by women not only from my generation but from other generations and other parts of the world.

While I was writing this book, I was struck by an article in *The New York Times Magazine* about English club kids who get high on Ecstasy. The author explains that the drug turns these usually sullen teenagers into weepy sentimentalists who spout off about how much they love their fellow man. (*"Hey, mate, y'know I love you!?"*) What an ironic twist for kids whose parents, in stiff-upper-lip British fashion, rarely use the *l* word.

The article got me thinking: When I was growing up in the

fifties, my parents, though loving, rarely said, "I love you" to me. I recently asked my mother why. Her answer: "Why say what's obvious?" To that I say, why *not*?

The fact is, I never said, "I love you" to my high school and college girlfriends, though what I felt for them was deep, unconditional love. Those three magic words were reserved for the most intimate moments between a woman and a man. Every relationship women of my generation had with the opposite sex before marriage seemed to hinge on whether or not these words were spoken. If we were fortunate, as I was, we married men who continued to say them after the honeymoon was over.

After I became a mother, I found myself saying, "I love you" to my children even before they knew what it meant. Just looking at their faces filled my heart with love—as if I were high on Ecstasy. I read in a book by Penelope Leach, my child-rearing guru, that parents can never say, "I love you" too often to their children. As a result of hearing the words from me, my kids grew up saying them back—and saying them to their grandparents. I was moved when I found my mother and father saying, "I love you!" in return to my kids—without feeling embarrassed about it. They even started saying it to me.

Now, when I'm with my mother, my sisters, or my grown-up children—or on the phone with them—it's pro forma for us to say, "Love you" instead of "Good-bye." When I told this to a friend of mine, a man who's a decade older than me, he growled, "Those words get thrown around too easily. They lose their meaning." Sorry. Not in the case of my family. They come from the heart.

Today I say "Love you" to my girlfriends too, and they say it back. Why not? We really *do* love each other. Having reached middle age, we have learned that we may fall in and out of love with men, but we never stop loving our parents, our children—and our girlfriends. And that when it comes right down to it, a woman really is the sum of all the friends she has had in her life.

Part I

Age of Innocence
and Frozen Marshmallows

*I*n the fifties, our mothers led simpler lives. The Depression and the war were behind them, and as their husbands prospered, they drove their children to and from school in their two-tone Oldsmobiles with Patti Page singing "How Much Is That Doggie in the Window?" on the radio. While the kids were in class, they cleaned the house and did the laundry. If they could afford it, they hired someone to help so that they would have time to play golf and bridge with their friends. Most of them cooked because it was part of their job description, not for pleasure. Steak and roast beef starred at dinner—and not just because they were easy to prepare. Expensive cuts of red meat symbolized the affluence that their own mothers had lacked.

Daughters had it easy too. Society expected only that we be good girls and model ourselves after our mothers. We watched—and sometimes helped—them in the kitchen and looked forward to one day getting married and being housewives just like them. When we played with our girlfriends, our games included "grown-up," "wedding," and "mommy."

The attitudes of the fifties spilled over into the early sixties. In high school we maintained our virginity while dancing the twist and the mashed potato with boys who ranged from cute but conceited, to fun but irresponsible, to solid but boring. The goal was to learn to spot good husband material by the time we hit twenty. In the meantime, we practiced our homemaking skills by baking chocolate cakes and chocolate chip cookies.

In college our childhood illusions of a secure and predictable future were shaken by the blast from Lee Harvey Oswald's rifle and napalmed in Vietnam. We danced frenziedly to the music of the Beatles, protested the war, and began to embrace—albeit more slowly than girls younger than us—women's lib. Cheap student charter flights whisked us to Europe, where we celebrated our new independence and, for the first time, tasted real food. There was no turning back.

Chapter 1

The Fish Family

The most beautiful girl at Garfield" is how more than one man who knew my mother in high school described her. A gifted violinist as well as a beauty, with wavy black hair and a figure that made men's heads turn, Fannie Horowitz became the concertmistress in the University of Washington orchestra, but she was too nervous when performing to pursue a career as a professional musician. At the age of twenty she stowed away her violin, married my father, and devoted herself to being Mrs. Robert E. Silver, the perfect housewife and, later, mother.

My mother was a good cook and she was proud of what she made, but she didn't *love* cooking. Like most women of her generation, she cooked because it was her responsibility in the family, like washing clothes or buying new saddle shoes for my two sisters and me before school started each fall. When I helped her cook for a special holiday dinner or a party, she didn't play opera, gossip, or discuss the meaning of life with me, the way I do today when I'm cooking with my daughter, Julia. My mother was all business in the kitchen, and she rarely followed a recipe. The only cookbook she owned—*The Settlement Cookbook*—collected dust on the shelf. She was a self-described *shiterein* cook—that's Yiddish for "she just threw stuff in."

Somehow, my mother knew the correct number of onions to chop for the casseroles she threw together for weekday dinners, and the amount of sugar needed to sweeten the jam she made from the tart purple plums my sisters and I picked in our backyard. My mother called it jam, but since she didn't use pectin, it was runny, more like sauce. She liked it that way; I liked the chunks of plum I could fish out with a fork. Even though my mother's plum whatever didn't need to be frozen, she stored it in the freezer.

In our house, just about every food that didn't come in a can— from Dungeness crab legs to Milky Ways to marshmallows—was stashed in the freezer. The freezer also contained ice cream in big commercial cartons and oversized oatmeal-raisin cookies that were baked by my mother's brothers, Harry and Norman, who sold them wholesale.

Other families made do with a freezer compartment at the top of their refrigerator. Ours was a twenty-cubic-foot Sears chest freezer that was nearly as big as our kitchen table and stood within arm's reach of it. The gleaming white treasure chest was a symbol of just how important a role food played in our household, a role that bordered on obsession. Perhaps it was because my mother and father had grown up during the Depression, when their parents could barely put enough food on the table to feed their families. Or because my father was the vice president of a fish company and brought home canned tuna, salmon, and crab by the case. Whatever the reason, the thought and energy that other families focused on sports and hobbies, ours focused on food. Even the nickname my parents gave me had a food reference: not Sherry for Sharon, but Cherry.

When the whim hit her, my mother would cook a big pot of borscht and store it in jars in the freezer. One summer, Dorothy, our teenage live-in baby-sitter, mistook a jar of frozen borscht for frozen plum sauce and baked what turned out to be a borscht pie. When the pie was baking, cabbage stink pervaded the house. Dorothy was embarrassed. She was just a farmer's daughter, she told my mother—what did *she* know?

Dorothy had moved to Seattle from Montana so she could experience *life in the big city*. A thin brunette with freckles who looked like Veronica in the Archie comics, Dorothy traded baby-sitting and light cleaning for a room in our basement. She wore bobby pins to hold her spit curls in place, a thin gold ankle bracelet, and straight skirts that hit midcalf and were so tight that she had difficulty walking in them. I was around eight at the time, and I dreamed of looking just like her when I was a teenager.

My father helped Dorothy with her high school homework; she never would have graduated without him. He also kept her boyfriend, Vito, a James Dean wannabe with a ducktail, at bay. Vito was only allowed to come over when my parents were home, so he wasn't around the night our pet chicken was killed. It was just my two sisters, Dorothy, and me. As often happened at our house, food played a part in the story.

My father, who had studied food chemistry in college, often tested new pet foods—by-products of his company's canned fish—on our pets. By pets I mean two German shepherds, a neurotic mother-and-son duo named Blickendorf and Wolfgang; a mutt named Lucky; and two cats who for practical reasons we called Biggie and Littlie. Collectively, the pets were referred to as "the animals."

My father would bring home cans of pet food marked X, Y, and Z and plunk them down in front of the animals. The can they favored became the next Kitty Cat Food or Happy Dog Food. Since my father made good use of our animals, I figured I might as well add a chicken to the brood. Especially since it was free.

We lived on the outskirts of Seattle, so far out of town that when one car-pool mom drove kids home, she took all the others to their houses and then dropped me off at a bus stop. One benefit of living in the boonies, though, was that near our house were fields overgrown with wildflowers, stands of evergreen trees, and a small farm. My younger sister, Sheila, and I walked past the farm on our way home from elementary school.

Once a month or so a hatchery dumped a pile of rotten fertilized eggs in front of the barn for the farmer's compost heap. It became a game for the kids walking home from school to stop and dig through the heap of slimy eggshells, hoping to find the rare, newly hatched chick that was still breathing. One day I got lucky. Though bits of rotten eggshell were clinging to its half-dead body, I wrapped the chick in Sheila's sweater, tucked it inside her Howdy Doody lunch box (the perks of being the big sister), and brought it home.

My mother took one glance at the pathetic critter and said that since the chick was surely going to die anyway, we should trash it. I begged for a reprieve. Dorothy grew up on a farm, I argued. She would know how to save a chick. The minute Dorothy and Vito pulled up in Vito's '49 Chevy, Dorothy sitting so close to him that you could have fit two more adults in the front seat beside her, I pleaded for help.

Proof that Dorothy was more down-to-earth than the sultry Veronica persona she exuded around Vito, she brushed off her boyfriend and set to work. She warmed up the oven to a low heat, then turned it off. Next, she cradled the chick in a coffee mug and slid it inside. Voilà—an instant incubator. The next hurdle was getting the creature to eat. She tried scrambled eggs, then oatmeal. The chick wouldn't bite. It was my idea to try Kitty Cat Food. Using a toothpick, Dorothy inserted the sticky stuff into the chick's beak. The chick swallowed it and peeped. We now had a pet chicken. I dubbed it Chicken Little.

After a few days on Kitty Cat Food, the chick was strong enough to move outside. My father was proud that the animal had survived thanks to his pet food, and he set about training our three dogs and two cats not to eat the fluffy morsel. Given what a generally quiet and gentle man my father was, his training method came as a surprise: Hold chick up to dog's or cat's jaws. Smack said canine/feline on snout. Repeat several times.

My father's behavior-modification technique worked. After several days of repetition, whenever Chicken Little came near our dogs and cats, they fled. Thus, the chick was free to roam our big, grassy yard. I say "he" because soon the chick began to exhibit the orange comb and cocky attitude of a rooster.

On Fridays, Louie, a seemingly ancient man, tended our yard for four dollars and all he could eat. Chicken Little rode on his rake as he gardened. Louie got a kick out of digging up worms for the chicken, which it would devour in one gulp. My sisters and I were grossed out when a minute later the chicken produced an excrement the same length as the worm.

On a diet of worms, Kitty Cat Food, and leftover table scraps, Chicken Little was fast becoming Chicken Big. My father commented that one day we would roast him for dinner. I never got to find out if he was joking.

One summer night my parents went to their golf-and-country club to play bridge and Dorothy broiled lamb chops for dinner. I considered lamb chops a treat because we only had them when my father wasn't home. My father hated the smell of lamb—it reminded him of the cheap mutton his mother had cooked during the Depression when their family of ten was so poor, he slept on two chairs pushed together because there weren't enough beds in the house. On this balmy night, it was my turn to feed the animals, a task that required opening nine cans of pet food and dumping them, along with dry kibble and table scraps, into bowls lined up near the carport. I tossed the lamb-chop bones on top.

Chicken Little lacked teeth, but he grabbed a bone and dragged it to his cage. The three dogs were too busy chewing on their own bones to notice. Chicken Little confiscated another lamb-chop bone. This time Lucky snarled at him. Deciding it was time to lock up our cocky prepubescent rooster before he became dog food, I grabbed him and stuffed him into his cage, but before I could get the door latched, he escaped in a flurry of feathers and scurried back to the pile of bones.

The next few moments were a blur. The chick snatched a bone out of Lucky's jaws. The mutt growled. Chicken Little was suddenly in his face again, pinching another bone. This time Lucky snapped at him. Chicken Little crumpled to the ground without a peep. Dorothy's diagnosis: a broken neck.

My sisters and I wept over the demise of Chicken Little. Dorothy tried to calm us down—"*It's just a chicken.*" She also helped us give him a proper burial in the garden, where, perhaps, the worms he might one day have eaten ate him.

Dorothy was like a kind, loving big sister to me, unlike my real older sister, Susan, who either tortured or ignored me. When Dorothy graduated from high school, I was sad to see her move out and get a *real* job. She had learned shorthand in high school *(remember shorthand?)*, and she became a junior secretary in an insurance office. For a few months she called to check in with us. Then, silence. I fantasized that she had gotten pregnant and been forced to marry Vito and was embarrassed to tell us. While I was writing this book, I thought of trying to track Dorothy down, but I realized I never knew her last name—or Vito's.

My mother also missed Dorothy, though she complained that no matter how hard she tried, she was never able to teach Dorothy how to cook. The borscht pie was proof.

I, however, was a devoted student in my mother's kitchen because I sensed it was a way of winning her love. Sheila, my younger sister, did so by excelling at the piano. Susan did it by painting, playing viola, looking beautiful—and just getting up in the morning. My mother seemed more focused on Susan than on Sheila or me. When Susan was an infant, my mother once told me, she came down with rheumatic fever and nearly died. Perhaps that was the reason my mother always kept a close watch over her. It wasn't until years later that our family realized Susan had a deep-seated problem that couldn't be solved by mother love.

Since my mother had three daughters, she tended to think of us as "the girls." We even had the same initials, S.J.S.—for Susan Jeanette, Sharon Judith, and Sheila Jane. (If my parents had had a boy, they said, they would have named him Steven Joseph.) I wore monogrammed blouses and shirtwaist dresses that were hand-me-downs from Susan, and if they were still in one piece by the time I outgrew them, Sheila wore them. With first names so similar, my mother often mixed them up. I grew so accustomed to being called Susan that to this day I still turn around if I hear someone call that name.

Most of the time, it was my mother and the girls doing errands, my mother and the girls riding in the car, or my mother and the girls modeling matching outfits at the annual mother-daughter charity luncheon she cochaired. About the only time I wasn't just one of the girls and I had my mother all to myself was when she was cooking. So after school I helped her make dinner. When my father walked into the house at six on the dot, he expected the food to be on the table.

Mother's dinner repertoire revolved around the following dishes:

- roast beef
- pot roast
- chicken baked with Lipton's dry onion-soup mix
- tongue
- liver
- tuna-noodle casserole made with my father's canned tuna fish

- salmon loaf made with my father's canned salmon
- top round steak tenderized with Accent (aka MSG; my father sprinkled it on everything he ate) or occasionally top sirloin
- meat loaf
- ground-beef casseroles

All of these were served with ketchup.

My mother improvised variations on the theme of the ground-beef casserole. Sometimes she prepared it with elbow macaroni or kidney beans or both. She threw in chopped onions and/or chopped tomatoes, canned corn, and whatever vegetables she could scrounge up in the freezer. Ketchup was not only served on the side, it was sometimes a key ingredient.

She also prepared spaghetti casserole-style. The noodles were boiled well in advance, then mixed with the meat sauce and dumped into a Pyrex dish. The final touch was a shower of Parmesan cheese from a shiny green Kraft container. She heated the spaghetti casserole in the oven just before dinner. By the time it was served, the noodles were as mushy as the sauce.

In the summertime my father brought home fresh salmon from his office, which was located across the street from the Seattle waterfront where the fishing boats came in. My mother was proud that she got fresher salmon than any of her friends—and that she didn't have to pay for it. She baked salmon simply, with salt, pepper, and a squirt of lemon juice. I found it bland unless it was slathered with the Thousand Island dressing she made with Miracle Whip and ketchup—two staples in our house—along with pickle relish, lemon juice, chopped hard-boiled eggs, and a dash of horseradish.

Regardless of whether the main course was salmon or tongue, on the side my mother served frozen peas or frozen string beans that she "doctored up" with condensed Campbell's cream of mushroom soup. Sometimes she served mashed or baked potatoes, and she always tossed an iceberg-lettuce salad with either bottled Wishbone Italian dressing, her Thousand Island dressing, or Green Goddess dressing she made in our Sears blender from handfuls of chopped green onions and equal parts sour cream and Miracle Whip.

Kraft Miracle Whip was a key ingredient not only in my mother's Thousand Island and Green Goddess dressings but in the tuna fish sandwiches that she made for just about every lunch I brought to school in my Archie & Veronica lunch pail. My mother used Miracle Whip in every recipe that called for mayonnaise. Maybe it was a West Coast thing, because the women I know who grew up on the East Coast were raised on Hellmann's.

The canned tuna fish in our house was white-meat albacore—the best. Along with the canned salmon my father brought home from the office, and the jars of borscht and plum sauce/jam that didn't fit into the freezer, my mother stored it in a small basement storage room that had a wooden door six inches thick and no windows. Since this was the height of the cold war, I dubbed the storage room the "bomb shelter."

I was the Silver sister who experienced separation anxiety when our mother was late picking us up from school, and who hid under the bed when it was time to go to the doctor's. My fear of nuclear devastation was no less acute—especially because I could see one of the Boeing airplane plants from my bedroom window. Everyone knew that Boeing crews were working around the clock building B-52 bombers. It followed that if the Russians attacked, Boeing would be one of their first targets. I added a few necessities to the bomb shelter just in case: a can opener for the cans, several rolls of toilet paper, bottled water, and my father's U.S. Navy dress sword.

My bedroom, which I had decorated in pink and black, the colors I would have picked for a two-tone Cadillac if I could have had one, was on the third floor of my family's peak-roofed brick house overlooking Lake Washington. On a clear day, beyond the south end of the lake, I could see Mount Rainier floating in the sky like an image projected on an invisible movie screen. "The mountain is out," people in Seattle say when Rainier looms magically larger than life-sized like that, the foothills below it disappearing in the clouds.

Behind the house, an acre of land sloped down to the lake. My father couldn't afford to buy this choice waterfront property, but for most of my youth it remained undeveloped and was overgrown with blackberries. When the berries ripened, my sisters and I helped our mother pick them. The juicy ones that didn't end up in our mouths she poured into the kitchen sink, which she filled with water until they floated. It was my job to pick out the worms, the shriveled berries, and the occasional thorn before she dumped the berries into a big pot, added sugar, and turned them into blackberry jam. Like her plum jam/sauce, it was runny but contained chunks of blackberries that I enjoyed fishing out with a fork and eating. She stored the blackberry jam/sauce in the freezer.

On the waterfront, a weather-beaten dock jutted out into the lake. My father bought fishing poles and taught us how to fish there. We caught the occasional trout, which my mother fried for dinner. Most of the time, however, all we pulled in were six-inch-long bullheads that were all bone and gristle. My sisters and I were forbidden to walk onto the dock unless an adult was present because a few of the planks were missing. After I learned to swim, I ignored my parents' rule.

Here's how I learned to swim: When I was five and a half, my uncle Merle, a tall, handsome, bigger-than-life guy who was married to my mother's younger sister, Rosie, threw me into the lake and yelled, "Swim!" If I'd been older, I might have realized that Uncle Merle's behavior hinted at a dark side to his usual charming self. Years later Rosie caught him in bed with one of her girlfriends. Soon afterward Merle became my ex-uncle.

Next-door to our house was a public beach where I hung out with my sisters on summer days when it wasn't raining. We came home only for lunch, which consisted of tuna fish sandwiches and milk. In our house, peanut-butter-and-jelly sandwiches, a staple of most kids' diets, were considered exotic.

On the Fourth of July our family hosted an annual backyard barbecue. Among the guests were our closest family friends, Mary and Harry Brown and their two children, and Edith and Bill Warshal and their four kids.

Mary and Edith were my mother's best friends, and I learned a lot about friendship by watching them together. They did volunteer work for charities and often went to luncheons to support one cause or another. For ladies' luncheons, they wore wool suits with skirts that came just below the knee, cloche hats with little veils that they left up rather than pulled down over their faces, and white cotton gloves with little ridges on the fingers. My mother and her friends felt it was important to always look their best.

Mary was the only one of my mother's friends who worked. During college she had been a journalist; now she helped her husband, Harry, in their drugstore. The other women in their social circle devoted all their time to their husbands and children. When the kids were in school, the women played golf or bridge. My mother and Edith excelled at both, and I found it fascinating that as close as they were, they were always competing against each other on the golf course. Even when they were vying for the women's club championship—my mother beat Edith in the finals three times—they were mutually supportive. To this day, my mother insists that when it came right down to it, Edith was a better golfer than she was.

The Browns, the Warshals, and the Silvers got together for family parties several times throughout the year. My mother was the best cook among the three women, but the menu varied little regardless of who was the hostess, in part because they shared recipes for such standards as brisket of beef, lasagna, and spaghetti

Thanksgiving 1955. My mother's egg-bread stuffing was already legendary.

casserole, and because each woman always brought one of her signature dishes. My mother's were crab legs, salmon, and blintzes.

With cocktails, they served crackers and a dip made from sour cream and marinated artichoke hearts mixed together and topped with caviar (the inexpensive kind made from lumpfish). There was always a fresh fruit platter with neat rows of cantaloupe and honeydew slices, pineapple wedges displayed in the shell, and clusters of Thompson seedless grapes. Maybe it was because they lived in rainy Seattle, where it was difficult to get fresh fruit off-season, or because they grew up during the Depression, but my mother and her friends were big on fruit platters. They always complimented one another on the freshness of the fruit and the attractive presentation.

Dessert was often a devil's food or lemon sheet cake served right out of the baking tin. My mother and her friends didn't make cakes from scratch—not after Duncan Hines and Betty Crocker mixes came on the market. My mother preferred Duncan Hines, but if it was her turn to bake a cake for a party, she bought whichever brand was on sale.

Because Mary worked, she was the only one of the three women who had a full-time cook/housekeeper. When she hosted a party, however, she prepared the main course herself, usually a chicken-and-rice casserole containing Campbell's cream of celery soup, carrots, onions, and paprika. Mary, Edith, and my mother sprinkled paprika on just about every nonsweet dish they served—for the orange-red color, not the flavor.

Edith was known for making layered Jell-O molds, perhaps with a strawberry layer bejeweled with fruit cocktail (I searched for a maraschino cherry), and a lemon-lime layer that was milky with cream cheese. Her other specialty was potato pancakes that were crisp and lacy around the edges. The secret, she said, was to not squeeze out the water from the potatoes after she grated them, contrary to what most cooks did. This was in the days before Cuisinarts, so Edith grated all the potatoes by hand.

My mother rarely made potato pancakes because she ended up grating her knuckles along with the potatoes, and because she couldn't stand the odor of frying food. She said it smelled up the house and clung to her clothes and hair. She preferred turning potatoes into luscious, chunky potato salad that she made with chopped hard-boiled eggs, cut-up celery, green onions, plenty of salt, and Miracle Whip.

Just as Mary and Edith were my mother's best friends, their daughters, Gloria and Laurie, were mine. What makes "best friends" when you're eight, nine, ten, or eleven years old? You enjoy playing the same games, I suppose, and have similar interests. You are considerate of each other's feelings and don't get bogged down in petty jealousies. I considered Brenda, a freckled blonde at my elementary school, to be my best

Gloria and Laurie, my best friends, do Marilyn Monroe.

friend—until the day she beat me up in my own front yard. She said it was because her grandmother had told her my ancestors killed Christ. That was the first I'd heard of it. (I wasn't surprised when, in the eighth grade, Brenda was sent to live with an aunt east of the Cascade Mountains. In those days in Seattle, that was a euphemistic way of saying she'd been sent to a home for unwed mothers.)

Gloria, Laurie, and I took ballet and horseback riding lessons together, and we played hide-and-seek at the country club when our parents were out on the golf course. "Simple." That was the word we used to describe girls who were perfectly nice but didn't have the zest, the imagination, or the smarts to attract us as friends. The three of us were far from "simple."

Gloria had her mother's big, deep-set eyes and outgoing personality, and I preferred playing at her house instead of mine because I had a crush on her brother, Chester, who was four years older than me. Chester was dark and handsome and had a killer smile—he joked that he'd be great in a Crest toothpaste commercial.

Even at thirteen, Chester had charisma. In 1954, when the Crew Cuts came out with the first rock-and-roll hit, "Sh-Boom," Chester taught all the Brown, Warshal, and Silver kids to sing it in harmony. It was on a road trip our three families took to Las Vegas. In those days, desert sand still blew across the Strip, and instead of going to video arcades while their parents gambled, kids were stuck in day care centers run by what I was convinced were mobsters' molls. I can still picture Chester in his starched chinos and immaculate white buck shoes (the following year, dirty white bucks were in), his crew cut stiffened with hair wax, leading our little choir in the Sands Hotel while the binging slot machines in the background provided counterpoint.

Chester was a prince in his family, the golden boy who could charm his way out of just about any sticky situation. It was a talent he thought would get him through life, I suppose. Decades later, it was a tragedy when that talent failed him.

Laurie Warshal was soft-spoken and had a good sense of humor like her mother; she was a picky eater, something that was unheard-of in my family. I preferred playing at Laurie's house instead of mine because I had a crush on her brother, Steve, who was a year older than me. Steve lacked Chester's magnetism, but he was cute and funny and—bottom line—he was a boy, something that was sorely lacking in my house.

Every New Year's Eve my parents, the Browns, the Warshals, and their other friends celebrated at the country club. One year they even took a month of dance lessons at Arthur Murray in preparation. I eagerly volunteered to be my mother's partner when she practiced in our living room. Clasped to her bosom, I awkwardly followed her lead in the rhumba, the mambo, the samba, and the cha-cha, dances that I still know by heart.

Though my mother ordinarily wore only lipstick—Revlon Fire and Ice—on New Year's Eve she went all out to look glamorous. I sat at her elbow, trying on her dangly rhinestone earrings while she applied mascara to her long eyelashes and dabbed sparkly blue shadow on her eyelids. She needed my help when it came time to squeeze into her black, strapless corset, called a merry widow. Then she poured herself into a silky black sheath that revealed her cleavage, and slipped on high-heeled sandals with clear plastic tops that showcased her red-painted toenails. My father, looking handsome and pleased with himself in his rented tux, gave her the once-over and claimed she'd be the most beautiful woman at the club that night. No doubt she was.

Before the festivities began, my parents' friends stopped for cocktails at our house. Gloria and Laurie came along for a sleepover. This was the one night of the year when we were allowed to stay up until midnight, so after our parents left we intended to play "cocktail party."

Just before the guests arrived, my mother lit the candles on the dining room table, poured miniature hot dogs into a chafing dish, drowned them in Hunt's cocktail sauce, and pulled a tray of deviled eggs from the fridge. The main attraction was an array of fresh Dungeness crab legs and shrimp that my father had brought home from the office, heaped on the silver platters my mother had won in golf tournaments.

Gloria, Laurie, and I knew that the adults would pass on the mini hot dogs and deviled eggs but demolish the crab and shrimp. We looked forward to biting into the juicy little wieners and licking the yolk filling out of the eggs—who needed the whites? My mother made luscious deviled eggs. Her secret ingredient for the mashed yolks was Miracle Whip instead of mayo, of course, plus chopped olives, a dash of French's mustard, and lots of salt.

Once the crab and shrimp were eaten, the silver platters so bare you could read SEATTLE WOMEN'S GOLF CHAMPIONSHIP—1955 engraved on one, the women donned their fur coats. In those days, there was no stigma attached to owning a fur coat; it was a proud badge of prosperity. My mother had a beaver-skin coat that my father's uncle Max, the furrier, had made for her—wholesale. I remember hugging my mother in that milk-chocolate-colored coat, the beaver so soft and silky that I wanted to lose myself in it. Instead of "Good night," this was the one night she said, "See you next year!" before she stepped out into the night. Somehow, that made my separation anxiety sting all the more.

Chapter 2

Chocolate Bears and
Cheese Blintzes

My younger sister, Sheila, admits that she hated me until the day I got married. I don't blame her. From the day she was old enough to crawl into my space, I did everything to make her life miserable. *Why?* She pulled a double whammy on me. Not only was she born, displacing me in my parents' affections. She was born on my second birthday.

Throughout our childhood, Sheila was always in my face, outdoing me with her boundless energy and smarts. Furthermore, on the one day of the year that was supposed to be all mine, there she was, the other birthday girl at the other end of the party table. When it came time for us to blow out the candles together, I could feel Sheila's breath outblowing mine.

Every year our mutual birthday-party lunch consisted of tuna fish and egg salad sandwiches—with some tuna-and-egg combos thrown in—plus a few token peanut-butter-and-jelly sandwiches for the girls who wouldn't eat any other kind. When I was in fifth grade I convinced my mother that since Sheila and I were forced to share our birthday party, at least we should be allowed to each have our own birthday cake. Mother agreed for one reason: She could get the cakes wholesale.

The problem was choosing—a chocolate cake in the shape of a bear or a white cake in the shape of a rabbit. To outsmart Sheila, I chose the rabbit. Even though it was a white cake instead of the obvious favorite, chocolate, I figured that since a rabbit has long ears, my cake would be bigger. When my mother slid the cakes out of their pink cartons on our birthday, I felt jealous and stupid; my rabbit cake was indeed longer than Sheila's bear. But the bear had a nose that was a good three inches high and four inches across—and it was all chocolate frosting! The following year, my mother ordered the same two cakes, only this time I made sure that my name was on the chocolate bear and Sheila's was on the white rabbit.

Gloria and Laurie were always at our mutual birthday party, but since they were family friends, I couldn't claim them as my guests alone. They sat toward the middle of the table, between my friends and Sheila's. I was grateful that Sheila's best friend, Judy Kessler, was there to divert Sheila's attention so that I could have Gloria and Laurie to myself.

Judy's family was almost as food-obsessed as ours. Her uncle Charlie owned the fish company where my father worked, so the Kesslers' house, like ours, was stocked with free cases of canned tuna and salmon. Because Judy's grandfather was a baker—the first in Seattle to bake bagels—they also had pastries galore, whereas we had only our uncles' oatmeal-raisin cookies.

I paid little attention to Judy in those days. I was more eager to be friends with her sister, Leida, who was a year older than me. Leida, however, was my sister Susan's best friend. They only allowed me to join their imaginary games if I played the witch or the horse. I never would have guessed that when I grew up, I would become as close friends with Judy—well, *almost* as close—as Sheila still is.

Both Sheila and Judy were short and plump, and they did

naughty things like sneak into our freezer late at night and devour all the frozen marshmallows. They took piano lessons from the same teacher and played duets at their annual recital. Sheila always played the hard part, for Judy only took piano lessons because Sheila did, while for Sheila piano was a passion.

Sheila practiced piano for two hours every morning and again after school. On the day of her weekly lesson, I hung out with my mother until it was time to pick Sheila up. "Hanging out" consisted of going grocery shopping and visiting my grandparents. My mother stopped in to see them nearly every day. Looking after her elderly parents was another one of her familial responsibilities, and she was a dutiful, gentle caretaker.

The clearest memory I have of my Grandma Ann, who died when I was fourteen, is of a short, stubby woman—no taller than five feet, and all breasts—standing in her kitchen holding a butcher knife. She is wearing a faded cotton housedress with a frayed collar and black lace-up "granny" shoes with turned-down hose. Her face is soft and round and has few wrinkles—she was only seventy-two when she died—yet she looks ancient to me. And messy. Her wire-rimmed glasses are smudged from where she pushed them up on her tiny nose with greasy fingers, and her long, salt-and-pepper hair is falling in wisps out of a bun.

At least one of my grandmother's fingers was usually bandaged because she had cut herself while chopping onions for the chicken soup she seemed to make on a daily basis. And there was often a burn on her chubby forearm. My grandma was careless when cooking. I'm convinced it was because when she was in the kitchen, she usually was engaged in a Yiddish shouting match with my grandfather, who sat in the adjoining dining room, praying.

Because I didn't understand Yiddish, I never knew what my grandparents were arguing about. One day it dawned on me that

A rare photo of my grandparents together.
Usually Grandma Ann was in the kitchen.

since they quarreled so often, they didn't love each other. I suggested this to my mother. "Of course they do!" was her response. "They're *married*!" She went on: "Dad was very handsome when he was a young man." Even as an old man, my grandfather still had a gorgeous, full head of steel-gray hair. "And Ma was very beautiful." I found it hard to imagine my grandmother as the lovely young woman in their wedding photo. They were matched up shortly after my grandfather arrived in Seattle from Russia, which he had fled to avoid serving in the army. "They were a good couple. They respected each other and worked hard to raise their family." My mother spoke of those traits as if they were more important than love. Perhaps in those days they were.

My mother used to tell me how she learned to cook from my grandmother after my aunt Rosie was born, when their family lived on a farm outside of Seattle. Like all of my grandmother's six children, Rosie was delivered at home and my grandmother was required to recuperate in bed for ten days. Since my grandfather worked in a scrap-metal junkyard in the city, my mother was expected to do the cooking until my grandmother was back on her feet. My mother was nine years old at the time.

"Your grandma would yell from her bed and tell me what to put in the pot," my mother remembered. "Vegetables from the garden, a chicken that had to be plucked, and butter that she'd made from our cow's milk. I did what Ma said. Pretty soon I figured it out for myself."

A few years later the family sold the farm and moved to a modest house in Seattle. My mother had one dress—she washed and ironed it every day after school so that it would look nice the next morning—and she shared a bed with her sister Rosie, who was nine years younger, until the day she got married. "Rosie was so happy on the day of my wedding," recalled my mother. "Finally she would have the bed all to herself."

By the time I was born, my grandparents had moved to a two-bedroom clapboard house with a cherry tree in the backyard that bore sour cherries. When I visited my grandparents after school with my mother, there was nothing for me to do, and since they didn't speak much English, it was hard for me to communicate with them. I figured out a way to bond with my grandmother, at least: I helped her in the kitchen.

Grandma Ann made blintzes by the dozen. Most were cheese blintzes, but she also filled the thin, eggy pancakes with a mixture of sautéed onions and ground beef, or sautéed onions and chopped hard-boiled eggs. I recently tried to duplicate her meat and egg blintzes, for I hadn't tasted them—hadn't seen them on restaurant menus—since then. A dozen eggs and a stick of butter later, I had a few paltry blintzes to show for it. They were not as tasty as my grandmother's, but they brought back memories of the afternoons I stood next to her in her cramped kitchen. With my little girl's hands next to her chubby, wrinkled ones, we scooped the meat, egg, or cheese filling—always with the fingers, never a spoon—onto the delicate pancakes and folded the dough over them. While we worked side by side, we didn't talk—we didn't speak the same language—but like many immigrants with their New World grandchildren, she taught me how to make the same dishes that she'd learned from her grandmother when she was my age. If there were bits of blintz filling left on the cutting board when we were finished, she put them into my mouth.

For special occasions—religious holidays, a birthday—my mother's family congregated at my grandparents' house. Everyone sat around the long, lace-covered table that was jury-rigged to fit the ten, twelve, or twenty relatives who showed up. My grandmother was always the last to sit down—sometimes she didn't join us until dessert—because she was busy cooking and serving.

Like my mother, my grandmother was a good cook and she took pride in the results, but I doubt that she enjoyed it—or, if she did, that she was aware of that fact. For the women of her generation who cooked before dishwashers, electric mixers, and Cuisinarts were invented, cooking was a chore.

My aunt Rosie, who was the youngest of my grandmother's children, remembers her as a sweet and gentle woman: "I never realized until she was old what a hard life Ma had," she said. Rosie reminded me that my grandmother's first daughter, Hannah, had been born with brain damage from a botched forceps delivery and was severely disabled. Still, my grandmother insisted on caring for her at home. It wasn't until Hannah was thirteen that she agreed to send her to an institution. "It was a heartbreaking decision for Ma," said Rosie, "but I think she realized that because she was devoting so much time to Hannah, she was neglecting her other children." For years after, on Sundays, my grandfather drove my grandmother for hours in his Model T Ford, to visit Hannah. "When I was little, I went with them," recalled Rosie. "Hannah didn't even recognize us."

Looking back, my mother says that my grandmother seemed happiest when they lived on the farm and she could pick vegetables from her garden and milk her cow. My mother remembers her humming while she made butter in a wooden churn. Butter, no doubt, that she used when frying blintzes.

Grandma's Blintzes

MAKES 12 TO 15 BLINTZES

It takes practice to get the hang of making blintz pancakes, so be prepared to dump your first batch—they may be too thick, too thin, or uneven. Once you get it down, though, you should be able to turn out one pancake every couple of minutes. My mother is so good at it that she always has two pans going at once. Blintzes freeze well, so if you're going to the trouble of making them, double the recipe and freeze half.

FOR THE PANCAKES

> 4 eggs
> ½ cup milk
> ½ cup water
> 3 tablespoons butter, melted and cooled to room temperature
> Scant teaspoon salt
> 1 cup sifted flour
> Butter or butter-flavor cooking-oil spray for putting on top of blintzes when baking

FOR THE FILLING

> ½ cup farmer cheese
> ½ cup cottage or ricotta cheese
> 2 eggs
> 1 tablespoon butter, melted and cooled to room temperature
> 2 tablespoons sugar
> Scant teaspoon salt
> Juice of half a lemon
> ½ teaspoon cinnamon and ¼ teaspoon fresh grated nutmeg (optional)
> Sour cream, strawberry jam, and/or applesauce

1. Make the pancakes: In a food processor or with a whisk, beat the eggs and mix in all the ingredients except the flour. Add the flour ½ cup at a time, mixing constantly. When the batter is well blended (no lumps), place it in the refrigerator for 10 minutes, or until the foam subsides.

2. While the batter is in the refrigerator, make the filling: In a bowl, blend all the ingredients by hand. Do not use a food processor or it will become runny. Refrigerate the batter until ready to fill the pancakes.

3. Brush an 8-inch nonstick pan with vegetable oil and heat over medium-high heat until a drop of water sizzles on the surface. Stir the pancake batter, then take the pan off the burner and move it next to the batter bowl. With a ladle, quickly add a little more than 1 tablespoon of batter to the pan—just enough to cover the bottom—and swirl it around so that it is evenly distributed. The pancakes should be very thin. Return the pan to the heat, and with a nonstick spatula, loosen the edges of the pancake all around as it cooks—about 45 seconds to 1 minute. Do not let the bottom of the pancake burn, and remove the pan from the heat before the pancake top is fully cooked.

4. Slide the pancake, uncooked side up, onto a plate. (Have two plates ready for this.) Wipe any bits of leftover pancake from the pan, regrease the pan, and repeat the process, sliding the next pancake onto the other plate. When the finished pancakes have cooled a bit, transfer them to a piece of waxed paper. Stack them using pieces of waxed paper in between. Let the pancakes cool to room temperature before filling them.

5. Preheat the oven to 350°F. Grease a baking pan with butter or cooking-oil spray. Working on a waxed-paper surface, lay out a pancake and place approximately 2 teaspoons of filling toward one end, then roll up the pancake and tuck in the ends, so that it is tubular in shape. Place the blintz, seam side down, in the greased pan. Continue filling the pan with the blintzes.

6. Cut butter into small pieces and sprinkle a few on top of each blintz, or spray them with the butter-flavor cooking-oil spray. Bake the blintzes for 20 to 30 minutes, or until they are plumped up, heated through, and lightly brown on top. If they start to burn, cover them with tinfoil.

7. When serving, pass around the sour cream, jam, and applesauce.

VARIATIONS

A fattening but delicious alternative to baking blintzes is to fry them in butter, a few at a time, like my grandmother did. To make them less fattening, cut the melted butter in the batter recipe to 1½ teaspoons and use nonfat milk. In the filling, eliminate the melted butter and use egg whites and nonfat ricotta cheese.

Chapter 3

Friends, Food, and Sex

Robin and I became best friends during junior high school when we took home economics together, a required course for girls, along with sewing. (The boys took auto shop and wood-working.) I liked the playhouselike kitchenettes in the home ec classroom, but it was hard to take the class seriously. Our teacher, Miss Thompson, a Betty Crocker look-alike without the warm, fuzzy quality you'd expect from America's favorite baker, taught us how to squeeze orange juice and make such obvious dishes as scrambled eggs, cinnamon toast, and bacon. I became a pro at everything except the bacon. To this day, I avoid frying bacon; it always ends up burnt.

Robin and I also attended after-school charm school, where our teacher, Miss Fathergill, a reed-thin woman with permanently pursed lips, told us that we shouldn't wear patent leather shoes because they reflected our panties. She also taught us such etiquette basics as . . .

- When getting into or out of a car, keep your legs tightly together so that your panties don't show (Miss Fathergill had a thing about panties).
- Shake hands firmly as opposed to like a dead fish.
- Apply makeup for a natural as opposed to a harlot look.

The makeup lessons were our favorite part of charm school because we were given pink vinyl makeup kits containing all the essentials: turquoise eye shadow regardless of whether our eyes were blue or brown; frosted pink lipstick regardless of whether our complexion was pale or dark; black mascara; an eyebrow pencil; a comb; and a compact mirror. When we practiced at home, despite what Miss Fathergill had said, Robin and I went for the harlot look.

Robin was taller than me and seemed more mature and self-confident. She had reddish blond hair, and when she got embarrassed, her peaches-and-cream cheeks blushed crimson. She was one of the most popular girls in school, not just because of her outgoing personality, but because she had an ability to concentrate her attention on whatever friend she was with at the time. Everyone loved Robin, and I was jealous. I wanted her all to myself.

In tenth grade, thanks to my sister Susan, who was one of the most beautiful and popular senior girls, Robin and I were invited to pledge her sorority. We were thrilled that we had been deemed socially acceptable—until we got the gist of what pledging entailed.

For weeks that fall we were forbidden to wear makeup, and our daily uniform consisted of a navy blue stitched-down pleated skirt with a white sailor-style blouse called a middy. We carried around "goodie boxes" full of chocolate chip cookies, candy, and gum for our sorority sisters to choose from when they were hungry. To keep our goodie boxes stocked, once a week after school Robin and I baked chocolate chip cookies together when we should have been doing homework. We made some batches with nuts and some without because our sorority sisters demanded a choice. One time we made a batch containing coconut as well. We liked their chewy texture and flavor so much, they never made it into our goodie boxes.

As for the gum and candy, if our sorority sisters didn't like our selection, we were forced to walk across the street from school and restock at the Beanery, a fifties version of a 7-Eleven where the teenage lowlifes hung out and smoked. I dreaded running the gauntlet of Elvis wannabes and future car thieves who snickered at my pledge outfit when I stepped inside.

Hell Night was the culmination of our sorority-pledge ordeal. I was terrified, for from what Susan hinted, it was a lesson in just how sadistic the most popular girls in high school can be. And food was part of the torture.

Joyce, a bitch of a junior, blindfolded me, shoved my head into a bowl of what she said were worms, and commanded me to eat. In my heart I knew the "worms" were only cold, wet noodles, but I was far from rational and I nearly choked. Next, a girl cracked an egg on top of my head and made me rub the sticky stuff in my hair. Then she cracked one into my mouth and made me swallow it. I gagged.

The final humiliation came when a whole raw onion was shoved between my jaws and I was told to chomp away. I burst out sobbing. In a small act of kindness, Susan told the girl to lay off and dragged me away.

Robin and I were both so turned off by Hell Night that we considered quitting the sorority. At least Robin did—she always was more outspoken about such things. But we feared being social outcasts, so we stuck it out until senior year.

Robin's stepfather, Gene, was the owner, director, and sometimes star of the local theater-in-the-round. Her mother, Janice, helped out and occasionally acted herself. They were a flamboyant, theatrical couple, and I found them a lot more fun than my parents. When Robin came to my house, my father tutored us in algebra.

Sweet Sixteen party, 1960. I'm with dark and handsome Chester,
plus Laurie and Robin and their dates.

When I went to Robin's house, we played. For example, when
Teahouse of the August Moon was running at Gene's theater, Robin
and I loaded the goat from the show into the backseat of Gene's
Plymouth and drove to Burgermaster, a drive-in restaurant where
the high school kids hung out, eating cheeseburgers and sipping
chocolate milk shakes from a tray that hooked onto their car doors.
The goat was an instant boy magnet. We were sad when the show
closed and Gene sent the goat back to a petting zoo.

Robin and I threw a joint Sweet Sixteen party with our mutual
friend Laurie Winston. We decorated Gene's theater-in-the-round
with pink balloons and used the central stage as a dance floor. Our
parents chaperoned and made sure that no one poured vodka into
the bowl of cherry-red punch.

My date was Chester, Gloria's big brother. He had taken a romantic interest in me the summer after tenth grade when our families went on a joint vacation. "Vacation" consisted of spending the weekend at a motel with a swimming pool and access to a golf course in eastern Washington, where it was guaranteed to be sunnier than in Seattle. On the way there, we stopped at a cherry orchard and picked cherries for fifteen cents a pound and "all you can eat." My mother still tells the story of how when she couldn't find me—I was up in a tree, picking and eating away—she went wandering through the cherry orchard calling, "Cherry! Cherry!" and the other pickers looked at her like she was crazy.

Sparks flew between Chester and me that weekend despite the fact that I was fifteen and he was nineteen. If he'd been any other boy that much older than me, my parents would have forbidden us to date. But since Chester was Mary and Harry's son, they gave us their blessing. If it had been fifty years earlier, the two families would have arranged our marriage.

For our Sweet Sixteen party, I "ratted" (back-combed) my hair into a bouffant and lacquered it with hairspray. My dress was a chiffon formal with a delicate green-and-white floral pattern, one of several hand-me-down formals from Susan. Since Susan had more on top to hold up a strapless dress than I did, my mother sewed little white straps to the bodice for me. I wore sparkly green eye shadow and $9.95 dyed green satin pumps to match the formal, and to give the skirt extra body, I donned four crinolines—each of which I had soaked in a liquid starch solution and dried until it was stiff. A formal required a strapless merry widow underneath, like the one my mother wore on New Year's Eve. Just as I'd done for her when I was a little girl, my mother helped me squeeze into mine before the party.

That night, sixty or so of our teenage friends fast-danced to songs like "Itsy Bitsy Teeny Weeny Yellow Polka Dot Bikini" and "Alley-Oop," and slow-danced to songs like Bobby Darin's "Beyond the Sea." Wearing a merry widow meant that I had little room for the chips, hot dogs, and birthday cake—chocolate, of course—served at the party. Neither did Laurie or Robin, for the same reason. Later, back at my house, the three of us unhooked one another from our corsets and converged on the kitchen. My mother had already wrapped the leftover birthday cake in tinfoil and stowed it in the freezer. We tore open the package and finished off the cake with our fingers. It tasted even better frozen.

Like most of the girls I knew, I had a love-hate relationship with food. None of us were fat, though we often *felt* fat and from time to time bordered on what my mother called "chunky." Still, we were always watching our weight and trying new diet fads. That didn't stop us from making a beeline for the fridge (or at my house the freezer) the minute we felt anxious, depressed, or bored. The only natural appetite suppressant was falling in love. Unfortunately, that didn't happen very often, and when it did, it didn't last very long. But there was an *un*natural appetite suppressant that proved effective.

In our social circle, it was considered so important to have a slim figure that family doctors freely doled out Preludin to us. The tiny orange pill killed our appetites and revved us up to the point where we had the constant urge to smoke. I didn't take Preludin as often as other girls I knew, but when I did, I pinched my mother's Parliaments. What I know now is that Preludin was an amphetamine. It amazes me that our doctors—and our parents—didn't worry about us getting hooked.

Laurie Winston, my Sweet Sixteen–party cohostess, was petite but busty and had the world's longest eyelashes. Her mother had died when she was an infant, and her father and a succession of nannies had raised her. As a result, Laurie had even more insecurities than I did. She enjoyed the cozy family feeling at my house; I liked the freedom at hers, for her father was rarely there. In the summertime we hung out by her swimming pool, sometimes with Robin and our other good friend, Shelley, snacking on chocolate chip cookies that we baked and singing along with the Barbra Streisand, Ella Fitzgerald, and Judy Garland records that blared over the outdoor speakers. We learned all the lyrics to "People," "A Foggy Day in London Town," and "Somewhere Over the Rainbow." When the sun went down, we jumped into Laurie's red compact Buick and headed to Burgermaster for burgers, shakes, and—we hoped—boys.

Unlike my other girlfriends, Shelley had a rebellious streak that sometimes got her into trouble. I was attracted to her boldness—something I was short on—and I discovered that beneath her tough façade, she was a loving and sensitive friend. I was not as emotionally tied to Shelley as I was to Robin or Laurie because I hadn't known her as long. It allowed us to have a friendship that in some ways was easier than mine was with Robin and Laurie.

Laurie, Robin, Shelley, and I never competed for the same boys. Perhaps that's one of the reasons the four of us were such close friends throughout high school. Chester was my first *true love,* but as handsome, smart, fun, and affectionate as he was, after six months I grew tired of waiting for him to show up for a date, only to have him call and say that he was stuck on the golf course or at the beach. Chester wasn't lying. He had the best tan in town.

I had other boyfriends before and after Chester, some for a few months, most for a few weeks. Just as I sometimes wore Susan's hand-me-down dresses, I dated a few boys who were hand-me-down boyfriends of hers. I even passed a boyfriend or two of mine down to Sheila. I admit to briefly making out with one of them once, however, just to get back at her. I had discovered in junior high school that even though Sheila was two years younger than me, she had much bigger breasts.

Like my friends, I was most attracted to boys who were good-looking, popular, and fun. Smart was a plus, as was having a letterman's jacket or a car. Unfortunately, boys who had all of the above tended to be self-centered. Unlike my daughter and her friends today, we had few "guy friends," boys with whom sex was not an issue. Because everyone dated—rarely did kids go out in mixed groups, Dutch treat, as they do now—most of our relationships with boys included at least the potential for romance.

In high school, my girlfriends and I abided by unspoken rules about sex. "Going all the way" was the common euphemism for the act itself, and it was something that only "fast" girls did. If you were a "good" girl, which my girlfriends and I were, there was a limited range of sexual activities that you were allowed without "losing your reputation." The first and foremost was "making out," what earlier generations called "necking."

Making out usually took place in the boy's car late at night at the end of a date. What happened inside the car was between the girl and the boy—and all the boy's friends, to whom he would describe it in exaggerated detail the next day. This was why a good girl had to be careful about who she made out with and where she let him put his hands (breasts and crotches were off-limits). Making out— or even permitting a good-night kiss—on a first date would mark a girl as fast; accepting a first date to a drive-in movie theater would definitely have that effect. Everyone knew that the purpose of going to a drive-in was for some hot and heavy action, and that the car windows would be too steamed-up for you to see the movie.

If you were "going" with a boy—that is, you were boyfriend and girlfriend—it was acceptable to make out lying down. This was done fully clothed in the front or back seat of the boy's car. Orgasms might result, though my girlfriends and I never discussed the o-word and I'm not even sure I knew one when I had one. As for oral sex, we had never heard of it.

As close as we were, Laurie, Robin, Shelley, and I didn't discuss the details of our (pre-)sex lives. Our conversations were limited to whether or not the boys we dated were "good kissers." This was in contrast to what my mother and her girlfriends talked about when they dated. According to my mother, their discussions were limited to whether or not a boy was a good *dancer*.

Robin, Shelley, Laurie, and I never argued over petty concerns, and we respected one another's differences. One thing the four of us shared was a longing, a kind of yearning that the plaintive songs of Barbra, Ella, and Judy embodied. Whether we were hanging out around Laurie's swimming pool or in my kitchen, fishing frozen marshmallows out of the freezer, as much as we joked and laughed, melancholy clung to us like faded perfume. I'm not sure what we were yearning for. Romance? True love? That's what they called it in the Technicolor Doris Day–Rock Hudson movies we grew up on.

Perhaps we just longed to be finished with high school so that we could move on to the next, grown-up phase of our lives.

Chapter 4

Moving Out

I knew by the time I was halfway through high school that I would need to leave home—and my hometown—before I truly could grow up. One motivating factor was the crisis in the family after my sister Susan's nervous breakdown.

Recently I read in my diary from that time (I was fanatical about keeping a diary in high school) that I missed my "big sister" when she lived in a sorority during her freshman year at the University of Washington. We had become close during our teenage years, and I was glad when she moved back home for her sophomore year. One misty winter night, when my parents were out playing bridge, Susan anxiously reported to Sheila and me that a car was driving up and down the neighboring driveway and the driver was out to harm her. She wouldn't let us call our parents, so Sheila phoned her friend Andy, a macho football player, who sped over in his Chevy. I pulled my father's Sears BB gun from its hiding place under my parents' bed, and Andy loaded it.

We stood watch at the window. An occasional car drove up or down the neighboring driveway, but Susan's fears seemed unfounded. We couldn't convince her. The next morning she would not—*could* not—get out of bed. She had refused to get up for school occasionally in the past, but my mother had always persuaded her. Not this time. Susan was confused and frightened, and my mother called our family doctor. He paid a rare house call and phoned for an ambulance. The paramedics whisked Susan off to the mental ward of the university hospital.

Susan had been the beauty of the three Silver sisters, the one with the most voluptuous figure. In high school she had dated a handsome boy from one of the wealthiest families in town; in college they became "pinned," which meant "engaged to be engaged." Susan was sweet and gentle as well as a knockout, so it had been no surprise when the members of a UW fraternity crowned her as their "sweetheart." I was at the dance the night they placed the rhinestone tiara on her head and draped the shiny purple ribbon emblazoned with her new title across her chest. Susan looked resplendent in a strapless white chiffon gown. The next time I'll see Susan in a long white dress, I thought at the time, will be at her wedding.

My sister Susan, sweetheart of ZBT.

There was never to be a wedding. After Susan recovered enough from her nervous breakdown to leave the hospital, she began a life's struggle with what was diagnosed as schizophrenia. Some years she was well enough to live in New York and work in fashion retailing. Others she was so distraught that she attempted suicide.

In retrospect, I can look back and pinpoint symptoms of Susan's illness earlier in her life, like when she was thirteen and her fear of germs cut short a family vacation, or later when some days she stayed in bed with the lights off and the window shades pulled down. In the fifties and early sixties, however, in our close-knit community, mental illness was something that wasn't discussed—or even considered.

The morning that Susan was taken to the hospital, I went to school in a daze—how could something so horrible have happened to my sister, and so out of the blue? Robin read the pain on my face and knew that something was wrong. I revealed what could not be kept as a dark family secret. Robin understood. Perhaps it was because, as I learned years later, Robin's family had a terrible, dark secret as well.

Laurie was determined to go to Mills College, in Oakland, California. Mills was where her late mother had gone, and everything Laurie knew about her came from the diaries she had kept during her four years there. Since Laurie and I shared dreams of going away to college, her interest in Mills rubbed off on me. My father tried to talk me into staying in Seattle and attending the University of Washington—that's what kids I knew did if their grades were good enough—but my mind was made up. I convinced him that I'd do better at Mills because it was a women's college, and I wouldn't be distracted by boys. My father relented, and somehow managed to come up with the $2500 tuition.

My last summer at home was emotionally wrenching (I gained

ten pounds as a result). On the one hand, I was eager to move on with my life. On the other, separation anxiety plagued me. Added to the whirlwind of feelings was guilt: I had always suspected that my mother loved Susan more than me, but now Susan was sick—and I was the survivor, along with Sheila.

Though we didn't discuss it, my mother understood that I needed to leave and she didn't try to stop me. She didn't try to make me feel guilty about it, either. When she took me to the airport for my flight to the Bay Area, it wasn't the season to wear that soft beaver fur coat of hers (which had since been replaced by a mink, anyway), but I clung to her, weeping, as I did when I was a child on New Year's Eve.

I arrived at Mills College in 1962 with an Olivetti portable type-writer and my father's old U.S. Navy footlocker. It was packed with cotton shirtwaist dresses, matching wool-skirt-and-angora-sweater outfits in jade green and coral, penny loafers, a muumuu, a few pairs of Capri pants, and a turquoise cocktail dress that my mother had made on her Sears sewing machine, with dyed-to-match turquoise satin pumps.

Laurie and I roomed two doors away from each other in Ethel Moore Hall, which looked more like a Mediterranean-style mansion than a dormitory. There was one telephone per floor, and when girls' dates arrived to pick them up, they waited in the foyer until the girls made their grand entrances down a tiled staircase. Men were not allowed into our rooms except from two to four on Sunday afternoons—and then only if the door remained open. Security guards disguised as janitors pushed brooms around, looking out for our safety.

At Mills my shirtwaist dresses and skirts and sweaters came in handy, for we were not allowed to wear pants to dinner. There were no cafeteria lines, no plastic trays in the dining room. Students at

Mills were considered "young ladies," and we ate off of china plates and were served by waitresses. If we woke up too late for breakfast, Laurie and I scarfed down a handful of red licorice vines before class.

As a women's college, Mills was intent on instilling in us notions of strength and independence, but its view of women's role in society was an old-fashioned one. An example was the cherished ritual surrounding the announcement of an engagement. We all knew that one was coming when they

Laurie and me as Mills girls. What's with Laurie's leopard-print muumuu?

dimmed the lights during dinner and passed around a cupcake with a candle in it. We held our breaths to see who had bagged a husband. When the cupcake arrived at the lucky new bride-to-be, she blew out the candle to much delighted screaming and applause.

The first thing I learned at Mills was that going to a women's college did not make it easier for me to concentrate on my studies, as I had hoped. Just the opposite. Laurie and I spent every spare moment looking for guys. Every few weeks, Ethel Moore Hall invited fraternity boys from Stanford, an hour's drive away, to a mixer in our dining hall; by the time they arrived they were tanked. At one dance a drunk Sigma Nu peed in the crystal punch bowl and another told Laurie that Stanford guys (Stanford had four boys to every girl in those days) thought of Mills as a "women's zoo" where the "animals" were just waiting for them, panting.

It wasn't until second semester that I learned the second important thing about Mills: The real action was at UC Berkeley, a half-hour drive away. Laurie and I went there several times a week. On

Saturday nights we often returned just moments before Mills's iron gates clanked shut for the night at 2 A.M. How convenient for us that we began dating two fraternity brothers.

Justin was a funny, bright, and cute guy from L.A., and we were like two playful puppies. We cuddled and joked and constantly had to be close to each other. Partly because of Justin and partly because I hated Mills, I transferred to Berkeley for my sophomore year. So did Laurie. We lived in adjoining dorms and had dinner together any night that we weren't with our boyfriends—which wasn't very often. I spent so much time with Justin, I made no new girlfriends who weren't part of the couples with whom we socialized. Laurie was not just my best girlfriend; she was just about my *only* girl-friend.

I met Justin's high-school-age sister, Ellen, when she visited at Berkeley. A dark-haired, zaftig beauty with dark flashing eyes and permanent dimples, Ellen wore all her emotions on her face. She stood very close to people as if she were trying to read their karma, and she sucked up life as if she were starving. Ellen looked up to me as the older sister she never had, and I was crazy about her. There was not an ounce of jealousy between us even though she wor-shipped her big brother and I was in love with him.

During vacation, Justin took me to Los Angeles to meet his par-ents. It was obvious that he was the apple of their eye, the golden boy who could do no wrong. (In that way he reminded me of Chester, only Justin wasn't as handsome or as charismatic.) Justin's parents expected him to become a doctor like his father, and Justin planned to go one step further. His father lamented that he was a mere Beverly Hills doctor-to-the-stars and not a psychoanalyst. Justin intended to live out his father's dream.

Dorothy, his mother, was a journalist who had brought down the wrath of the McCarthyites in the fifties by campaigning for public schools having the right to teach students about the United Nations. Not only was Dorothy more sophisticated about food than my mother or any of her friends, but she was the first woman I ever met who found true joy in cooking. I was eager to move beyond the basics that I'd picked up in my mother's kitchen, and Dorothy was a patient, upbeat teacher. I was thrilled to find myself learning from a gourmet cook.

I helped Dorothy prepare steak tartare—who ate raw chopped beef in Seattle?—and duck (and who ate *duck*?) that she roasted on a rotisserie until the skin was crisp, the meat succulent. She made French fries in a big cast-iron pot—she knew the oil was hot enough when she threw in a piece of bread and it cooked. On Sunday mornings she whipped up puffy soufflélike German pancakes and served them dusted with powdered sugar. Dorothy loved the color purple, and she garnished her dishes with candied violets and purple grapes that she coated with sugar. She always smelled of Estée Lauder's classic perfume, and she always wore pearls—even when she was cooking.

The next fall Justin went east to medical school. I returned to Seattle and moved back in with my parents, so that I could cram my junior and senior years into one at the University of Washington. Justin and I had discussed the possibility of getting married after his first year, and I wanted to have my B.A. under my belt, just in case.

I remember very little of that year at home except that I was lonely. I had that damn longing, that yearning that I had felt in high school, yet again. Justin was on the other side of the country, Laurie was still at Berkeley, and Robin and Shelley had moved to San Francisco to work in fashion retailing. My father said, "Don't put all your eggs in one basket," but I didn't date and I nurtured no new girlfriends. I was determined to maintain my relationship with Justin despite our separation. Perhaps one reason was that I had been raised at the end of the era when a "respectable" woman didn't sleep with a man unless she was married to him. Since I had broken that rule with Justin, I felt compelled to make things right.

During Christmas vacation, Justin and I announced our engagement. He was twenty-two and I was twenty, the age my mother had been when she married my father.

Ellen was ecstatic—soon we would be sisters-in-law. Justin's parents threw a festive engagement party at their house high above Sunset Strip in Los Angeles. Dorothy did all the cooking and laid out a sumptuous buffet. My parents flew down from Seattle for the occasion, bearing fresh Dungeness crab legs.

By summer, however, our separation had taken a toll on Justin and me. I suspected that he was seeing another woman—okay, I *knew* he was. But the wedding invitations were in the mail, my wedding gown was ordered, and the gifts were trickling in. As part of his medical training, Justin had gone into therapy. With less than three weeks to go until the big day, his psychoanalyst called me from Los Angeles and came right to the point: "I'm afraid Justin is not ready to get married."

How many women have their weddings called off by a shrink?

I wept. My mother agonized over how to call off the wedding without losing face. My father said to hell with face—return the gifts, cancel the wedding dress, and tell the guests the wedding has been postponed indefinitely. My mother enlisted my aunt Rosie to help her make calls, and within two days the deed was done. Justin offered to let me keep my diamond engagement ring, but I mailed it back to him. The only trace that I had ever been engaged was a toaster oven from a cousin who insisted I keep it. I toasted bagels in it for the next twenty years.

To help me pick up the pieces of my life, my father got on the phone and by some miracle—and a little begging—arranged for me to return to UC Berkeley and enter the Graduate School of Education. Laurie offered to let me share her apartment. Two weeks later, in the fall of 1965, I was back in the place that I most associated with my happiness. To celebrate, I coaxed Laurie into climbing up the fire escape to the roof of our apartment building, from where we could glimpse the Golden Gate Bridge far across San Francisco Bay. The atmosphere in the Western Hemisphere that year contained more dust particles than usual because of a volcanic eruption somewhere in the South Pacific. As a result, since the sun's rays reflected off the dust particles, the sunsets were particularly vivid. My first night back in Berkeley, the sunset, indeed, turned the Golden Gate Bridge golden.

Berkeley had been transformed during the year I was away. Mario Savio had led rowdy antiwar protests, and students had taken to wearing their hair long and sandals instead of loafers. On Telegraph Avenue hippies in love beads passed out political pamphlets and sold incense and patchouli oil. I had never seen a joint during my first two years in college, but now smoking marijuana was de rigueur.

Laurie and I, however, were still caught up in the myth of the fifties and early sixties, perhaps because we'd been raised in provincial Seattle instead of laid-back California. We wanted Joy perfume, not patchouli oil; J&B scotch, not pot; and we still wore straight skirts and angora sweaters instead of bell-bottoms and tie-dyed shirts. Though I harbored a vague hope that Justin and I would one day get back together—we remained in phone contact—the year I had wasted because of him at least taught me to be more practical. I was open to meeting men—especially potential husband material. So was Laurie. As a result, the two of us became pretty good cooks that year.

A friend gave our names to two brothers she knew in San Francisco, one a doctor, one a lawyer (how perfect was *that*?). Instead of waiting for them to call us for a date, I phoned and invited them to dinner, as if throwing dinner parties was something we did every night. We were pros at baking chocolate chip cookies (I have yet to meet a woman my age who wasn't), and I could whip up one of my mother's ground-beef casseroles. For a husband-hunting dinner, however, Laurie and I felt we needed to serve something impressive.

For the first course, we settled on a Canlis salad, the signature dish at the best restaurant in Seattle. Since the early fifties, affluent Seattleites had gone to Canlis for steaks and seafood cooked on an imposing copper-hooded charcoal grill. Laurie celebrated birthdays at Canlis. My parents attended parties there given by hosts who wanted to impress their guests. I had been to Canlis only once, for dinner before the senior prom, but I took home a souvenir brochure with its legendary salad recipe, a variation on a Caesar that calls for lemon juice, crumbled bacon, and a coddled egg. It is still my favorite salad.

Neither of us owned a cookbook, so since I was more passionate about cooking than Laurie, I spent hours researching recipes for entrées and desserts in the cookbook section of the bookstore. For an entrée, I came up with brandied stuffed chicken legs. Trust me, it sounds better than it tasted—and it was a bitch to prepare.

First, Laurie and I spent a couple of hours deboning the chicken legs. If nothing else, the exercise taught us how little meat there is on a chicken leg. Where the bone had been, we stuffed a mixture of bread crumbs and raisins that had been plumped in brandy. Then we sewed the slit shut with thread, a fool's task when attempted with greasy fingers. By the time we were down to the last few legs, we decided to forego the messy stitching process and laid the legs in the pan, slit side down. The stitchless legs lost their stuffing in the baking process. I scooped up the wayward raisins and added them to the rice pilaf I made as a side dish.

For dessert, we came up with a variation on a recipe I had spotted in *Life* magazine: an apple tart that called for apples sautéed in butter and maple syrup, a rich shortbread crust, and crème patissière spiked with Calvados. The tart took two hours to prepare, and in the middle of the process, I had to run out and buy a springform pan to bake it in. While we were making the crème patissière, Laurie and I licked so much from the bowl we got tipsy.

As it turned out, the dinner—with the possible exception of the stuffed chicken legs—was a hit with the doctor and lawyer brothers. But they were not impressed enough to call afterward and ask us out. Laurie and I found solace by polishing off the leftover apple tart.

Canlis Salad
SERVES 4 TO 6

The original 1950s version of the Canlis salad called for a pound of bacon and ½ cup grated Romano cheese, and the herbs were added to the dressing, not the salad. The restaurant's twenty-first-century version calls for less bacon and more cheese, and the herbs are added to the salad instead of the dressing. My version is a combination of the two. I don't always add bacon, though my friends in Seattle consider omitting it a sacrilege.

FOR THE DRESSING

> 1 coddled egg (immerse egg in boiling water for
>   2 minutes)
> ⅓ cup fresh-squeezed lemon juice, or more to taste
> 1 clove garlic, minced (optional)
> 8 to 10 fresh oregano leaves, chopped, or 1 teaspoon
>   dried oregano flakes
> ½ cup fresh mint leaves, chopped, or 2 teaspoons
>   crumbled dry mint
> ½ teaspoon salt
> ½ teaspoon freshly ground pepper, or more to taste
> ½ to ⅔ cup pure olive oil (not extra-virgin)

FOR THE SALAD

  2 tomatoes, cut into eighths

  1½ large heads Romaine lettuce, leaves cut into thin
    strips

  ½ cup chopped green onions

  1½ cups croutons

  1 cup grated Romano cheese

  ½ cup well-cooked bacon, blotted with paper towels
    and crumbled

1. Make the dressing: Place the coddled egg and lemon juice in a bowl and whisk. Add all the other ingredients except the olive oil and mix well, then add the oil in a stream while whisking. Refrigerate until you are ready to use.

2. In a salad bowl, add the tomatoes, then the romaine.

3. Just before serving, add the remaining ingredients and the dressing. Toss well and adjust the seasonings. Add more cheese and lemon juice if desired.

Chapter 5

European Flavors

I emerged from Berkeley in June 1966 with a lifetime secondary teaching credential and a job starting in the fall at what was then one of the best school districts in the country: Los Angeles Unified Schools. My salary would be a whopping six thousand dollars a year. I was relieved that Laurie was moving to L.A. too, to do graduate work at UCLA. My dearest friend would be starting grown-up life by my side.

To celebrate our new adult status, my best friends from high school and I reunited for a trip to Europe for the summer. I borrowed two thousand dollars from Laurie's father so that I could go on what turned out to be a grand tour, sixties-style. With *Europe on Five Dollars a Day* as our bible, we saw all the sights and visited all the museums. Our main focus, however, turned out to be men and food—or, I should say, food and men. We even gave ratings for each: Austria won first place for its tall, strapping, but not too Germanic-looking men. Italy and France tied for best food.

We explored Paris and hung out in student clubs where more

than one "Frenchman" who came on to us turned out to be an Algerian. We also discovered French cuisine. It was exciting to eat croissants so buttery they made my hands greasy, baguettes with crusts so crisp they nicked the roof of my mouth, and Gruyère cheese that with its intense, nutty flavor had no resemblance to the Swiss cheese my mother bought at Safeway, except for the holes. And *jambon*! At my house, my mother never served ham. In Paris, however, our typical lunch was a baguette sandwich containing paper-thin slices of lean, salt-kissed *jambon* and Gruyère. The sandwiches were especially tasty because the vendor placed them in a press so that the cheese melted. If this was a ham-and-cheese sandwich, why had I been eating tuna fish all my life?

The four of us rented a tiny Citroën and spent three hours trying to escape the traffic-jammed Peripherique circling Paris. Once we did, we drove through nine countries in as many weeks.

Everywhere we went, we savored tastes we didn't know existed. I learned the profound difference between real Parmigiano Reggiano cheese and the powdery stuff in the green Kraft container that my mother sprinkled on spaghetti casseroles, and between a *salade Niçoise* and my mother's tuna fish salad. I also learned to recognize Châteauneuf du Pape, Chianti, and retsina, and I had a run-in with slivovitz, the potent pear brandy that my uncle Harry, who had tasted it when he was a soldier in World War II, suggested I try.

On the island of Mykonos, a gauntlet of Greek widows in the black dresses they probably had worn since World War II greeted us when we climbed off a rickety boat in the middle of the night. We followed one who offered us a room for two dollars each. By room, I mean a cement floor in a cramped whitewashed hut with no running water. We blew up the air mattresses we had brought along and used them as beds.

During the day we went to the beach, and at night, before dancing to "Strangers in the Night" with other American college grads in the local disco, we had dinner at a waterfront café. An authentic

Greek salad, I learned, consists of green peppers, cucumbers, tomatoes, Feta cheese, Kalamata olives, and red onions, drizzled with red-wine vinegar and olive oil. After tasting the Platonic ideal of a Greek salad in Mykonos, I have no patience with the bastardized versions containing raisins and orange sections that I've been served in trendy California restaurants.

Dubrovnik was one of the most scenic cities we visited—part of the fifteenth-century walled fortress still remains—but the food made me sick. We checked into a Spartan tourist hotel fronting the Adriatic where dinner consisted of dried-out mystery fish and a skimpy tomato salad. The first night, I came down with a high fever and everything that goes along with a severe case of food poisoning. It was a good thing Branislav, a Yugoslavian student I knew from Berkeley, showed up to visit. He was expecting romance; instead he spent the night on the floor outside of my room, waking me up every few hours to adminis-

ter the medicine that the hotel doctor (or was it a waiter pretending to be a doctor?) had given me. By the time I recovered a couple of days later, Branislav was sharing the bed of a blond coed from Connecticut who looked a lot better in a bikini than I did.

That summer in Europe, my girlfriends and I became closer than ever. Having survived our teenage years together, we knew one another's buttons and how to avoid pushing them, and we appre-

The European tour '66: Robin, me, Shelley, and Laurie in raincoats and sandals.

ciated one another's strengths. But still, just as in high school, each of us still longed for something. Romance? A man? The key, we'd been raised to believe, to happiness?

Robin was preoccupied with thoughts of Jim, the married man she was having an affair with in Seattle, who later became her first husband. Shelley took off several times to join Doug, her college sweetheart and future husband, who was on his own Grand Tour with his buddies. Laurie fell in love with a darling Frenchman in Paris and went off with him several times during our itinerary. And me? I cut my trip short so that I could go to Los Angeles. I was still friends with Ellen, and she'd told me that Justin would be visiting his family. I don't know what I imagined could possibly come of it, but I hoped to see him.

Part II

Playing at Being
Grown-Up

*W*hen we were little girls, the women of my generation dreamed of growing up to be just like our mothers. By the time we reached adulthood, however, we were forced—or chose—to compromise. Many of us married young like they did, but whether or not we had husbands, we had jobs. The term "housewife" was on its way to becoming obsolete.

It's not that we became doctors, lawyers, or CEOs of Fortune 500 companies, like women just five and ten years younger than us did when they grew up. Women's lib didn't arrive until after we'd started on our career paths. We tended to work in traditional women's roles—teacher, social worker, and dental hygienist.

Working meant that we were not dependent on our husbands for money (or at least not as dependent as our mothers had been on our fathers). But whether or not we were married, working also meant we had little time to play. To young women in the late sixties and early seventies, "club" meant health club, not country club. Birth control *pills made it possible for us to put off having children, and it didn't occur to us to worry about the ticking away of our biological time clocks, as young working women do today.*

Having money meant we could travel, and when we came home, cooking wasn't just about putting food on the table. We watched Julia Child on TV, subscribed to Bon Appétit, *and collected cookbooks featuring recipes for dishes we had tasted in France and Italy. We shared our favorites with girlfriends, and we cooked for fun.*

To the music of Elton John, James Taylor—and still, of course, the Beatles—we threw dinner parties that took all day to prepare for, where we served "gourmet" dishes starring Cornish game hens or veal or, only occasionally, fish. Steak was still in—red meat is always in— but we marinated it or draped it with a rich sauce. We still offered scotch on the rocks before dinner, but with the meal we served wine— even if the only wines we knew were Lancers, liebfraumilch, and Chianti that came in a raffia-wrapped bottle.

Chapter 6

Meeting the One

By the time I arrived in L.A. at the end of the summer, Justin was gone. He had left for med school the day before I arrived, perhaps because he had heard I was coming.

His family, however, welcomed me. Ellen, now a senior at UCLA, had mixed feelings about introducing me to her boyfriend Tom's new roommate. It wasn't that she didn't think I would like Paul Boorstin. She anticipated that I *would* like him—and that it would put an end to the fantasy she still harbored about us one day becoming sisters-in-law.

Ellen was right: Paul and I connected on our first date.

The Sunday we met, we went to the beach and it started to rain—unusual for L.A. in early September. Paul and I ran for shelter, our bare feet digging into the wet sand like a couple in a French movie. Paul knew all about French movies. He had majored in French literature at Princeton, he spoke fluent French, and he was now studying film at UCLA. I found him warm, bright, good-looking, and affectionate. Paul made me laugh—and he made me forget all about Justin.

The first time Paul came to my apartment for dinner, I chose a menu that would impress him but that wouldn't require as much effort as brandied stuffed chicken legs. I barbecued a couple of T-bone steaks on a hibachi and made a Canlis salad and baked potatoes. Dessert was chocolate cake à la Duncan Hines. Paul ate everything with relish and showered me with compliments about my cooking. My year of practice at Berkeley had paid off.

Ellen's parents invited us to dinner, and I was happy to see Dorothy, but the tension between Ellen's father and Paul was palpable. We were never invited back. That was the last I saw of Dorothy. Soon Paul moved out of Tom's apartment and into one near mine. I didn't see Ellen again for more than thirty years.

My year rooming with Laurie at Berkeley had strengthened our friendship, but we had decided not to share an apartment in L.A. Laurie and I had marched step-by-step, side by side since we were sixteen, and it was time for each of us to live on our own. There was an unspoken imbalance in our relationship—I tended to be controlling, Laurie tended to be dependent. We needed emotional elbow room.

Laurie and I lived in near-identical stucco apartment buildings a few blocks apart. Both were flanked by palm trees and fronted by gardens snarled with night-blooming jasmine. To this day, I associate the sweet scent of jasmine with the L.A. I moved to after college. It seemed a city, a time, of endless possibilities. After a few months, Laurie and I no longer yearned for romance, for true love, the way we had when we sang along with Ella, Barbra, and Judy at Laurie's pool in Seattle. We thought we had found it. Laurie was in a serious relationship with Steve, the twenty-something man who lived across the hall from her. And I was inseparable from Paul.

When I flew from Seattle to Chicago during Christmas vacation to meet Paul's parents, I was nervous. Paul's father, Daniel, was a renowned historian (he later won a Pulitzer Prize and became the Librarian of Congress). His mother, Ruth, had read just about every book ever published (she later became a published poet). They were far more intellectual than my parents or anyone I knew. Furthermore, I felt ridiculous carrying a gift that my father jokingly called my "salmon dowry"—a whole fresh salmon that my mother had wrapped in newspapers and plastic and secured with electrical tape so that it resembled a jury-rigged violin case.

Dan and Ruth immediately put me at ease—I understood where Paul got his sense of humor and his warmth. Ruth, a cheerful woman with short brown hair, helped me unwrap the

Paul's grandmother Ida was quite the independent woman.

salmon. She took one look at the big silvery fish and asked how I suggested preparing it; she admitted that books and poetry were her thing, not cooking. It's a good thing I knew my mother's recipes for baked salmon and Thousand Island dressing by heart.

Over the course of my visit, often in the kitchen, where I helped her prepare meals, Ruth told me about her upbringing. We bonded over tales of the women who had influenced her—and over chocolate fudge.

Ruth's mother, Ida de Nelsky, grew up in Des Moines, Iowa, in the 1890s. In an era when women were raised to be housewives, Ida was a maverick. She graduated Phi Beta Kappa in German from Drake University and got a job teaching in Colorado, near the Colorado School of Mines, where Ruth's father, Jacob, was a student. Ida began dating Jacob—known as JM—but she was determined to go to Germany with an equally forward-thinking girlfriend, to do graduate work. Ruth showed me a photo of her mother that was taken back then: Ida was wearing a wasp-waisted, ankle-length suit, high boots, and a big, broad-brimmed hat. She looked quite the independent woman.

Ida went to study in Berlin, but by 1913 war was brewing. JM wrote to her, begging her to come home. She returned and they got married and moved to Morensi, Arizona, a Phelps-Dodge company town where JM worked as an engineer at the copper mine. Ruth's mother was not prepared for life as a housewife, let alone in a rough-and-tumble town where drunken fistfights broke out, dogs ran wild, and there were occasional raids from across the Mexican border by Pancho Villa and his men. Ruth was born there in 1917 and she has vague memories of their house: It was small and bare bones, but it had a well-stocked bookcase, a rocking chair, and an upright piano that her father played by ear. Ida taught herself how to cook on the wood-burning stove and, since there was no bakery in town, she baked her own bread.

In 1920, after the war ended, the copper mine closed and JM brought his family to New York. They moved in with his mother, Ilka, a Hungarian immigrant, while he looked for a job. As with my grandmother and me, Ruth found it difficult to communicate with her grandmother; Ilka spoke Hungarian and German but only a smattering of English. Their relationship developed as Ruth spent hours with her in the kitchen, for Ilka did all the cooking for the extended family. "I can still remember the aroma of her apple strudel," Ruth said, describing how Ilka rolled out the dough on the porcelain table in the kitchen until it was so thin you could see the white tabletop right through it.

Ruth described how her grandmother made chicken paprikash: "She started with a whole chicken that still had the entrails in it, including the unborn eggs if it was a hen. She burned off the feathers and threw the feet and insides into a pot for soup; the rest she used for the paprikash. The chicken was so moist, the meat fell off the bone." Ruth and her grandmother grew close during their afternoons in the kitchen. The first sadness in Ruth's life was when she died.

In 1928, Ruth's family moved to the house in the Long Island suburbs. Ruth said that her mother did not enjoy cooking but that she did a good job with standard items like leg of lamb and roast beef. "I kept a diary, and in it I'd write: 'Stew—bad day; roast chicken—good day.' " Ruth shared her mother's blasé attitude toward cooking and had no desire to learn how. Instead, she spent hours walking in the woods, picking flowers, and writing poetry. "I lived in my imagination."

Ruth went to Wellesley College and after she graduated—Phi Beta Kappa—like most unmarried girls in the late thirties, she moved back in with her parents. She got a job in public relations in New York that paid fifteen dollars a week. On Christmas Day in 1940, when her brother was on vacation from Harvard Law School, he asked Ruth if she'd like to meet his professor. "I don't want to meet some stuffy old professor!" she told him. But she and Dan met. Ruth was twenty-three, Dan was twenty-six. They were married three months later.

On their wedding day, Ruth's mother gave her a notebook of her pet recipes—Hungarian goulash, Swiss steak, and fudge. "The notebook even had a recipe for Jell-O," recalled Ruth. "My mother knew my limitations." Her brother, Bennett, gave her a cookbook entitled *Meals for Two*, in which he inscribed, "To Ruth: To remind you of the recipes you may have forgotten." He was kidding, of course. "My brother knew I didn't have the slightest idea how to cook!"

The first meal Ruth cooked for Dan was a boiled frankfurter—just about the only thing she knew how to prepare. During their first year of marriage, however, she expanded her menu repertoire. Ruth often phoned her new friend, also named Ruth, the wife of an English professor, for culinary advice. "She was older and she was a good cook, so whatever she told me, I did," recalled Ruth. "I would take out all the ingredients for a recipe, and then I'd call her. My friend would walk me through each step over the phone. I wanted so much to get it right."

One thing Ruth's friend taught her was how to dress up the dinner table with candles. "I always put a candle in an empty wine bottle and lit it," said Ruth. "My dinners weren't gourmet, but at least they were romantic."

The last weekend I stayed with Paul's family in Chicago, we drove out to their country house in the sand dunes near Lake Michigan. There was so much snow and ice on the ground, I couldn't see where the shore stopped and the water began. We spent most of the time inside by the fire, dancing to "Ella Fitzgerald Sings Gershwin," playing poker for pennies, and talking, reading, and eating. I realized that I would be happy having Ruth and Dan as in-laws someday. Paul admitted his parents liked me so much that they had advised him to propose—even though we'd only been dating for three months. At the time, we both treated their eagerness as a joke.

In that cozy house in the dunes, Ruth taught me how to make chocolate fudge from the recipe her mother gave her on her wedding day. She said her mother never made fudge on a rainy day—the moisture in the air worked against you—and that she always held the bowl tightly on her lap for the final stage, when she beat the batter with a wooden spoon until it was just about to stiffen. The trick was pouring it into the pan before it hardened.

Ruth's Chocolate Fudge

MAKES 12 TO 16 PIECES

This old-fashioned recipe requires patience—and a strong arm—but the results are worth the effort.

> 1 scant cup milk
> 2 cups sugar
> ⅛ teaspoon salt
> 2 ounces unsweetened chocolate, broken into
>   pieces
> 2 tablespoons butter
> 1 teaspoon vanilla extract
> ½ cup chopped walnuts (optional)

1. Butter an 8 by 8-inch square pan. In a heavy pot, bring the milk to a boil. Remove the pot from the heat and add the sugar, salt, and chocolate. Stir until the chocolate is dissolved.

2. Over medium-high heat, bring the mixture to a boil and cook, covered, for 3 minutes. Lower the heat to medium-low, uncover the pot, and continue cooking without stirring for another 20 to 30 minutes, or until the fudge reaches the "soft ball" stage. To judge this, fill a bowl with ice water. When the fudge is bubbling evenly on the surface, scoop up a bit on a spoon and drip it into the ice water. If it forms a soft ball that holds its shape when you touch it, it's ready.

3. Remove the pot from the heat, and place it in a larger pan full of ice water, to cool down the fudge. Do not stir. When the bottom of the pan is cool, remove the pot from the water, add the butter to the fudge, and blend well. Add the vanilla, then rapidly stir the fudge constantly until it looses its glossy sheen. This may take another 20 to 30 minutes. The fudge is almost ready when, if you drip it from a spoon and turn the spoon over, it holds its shape against the bottom of the spoon. At that point, stir it another 5 minutes.

4. Add the chopped nuts, then pour the fudge into the buttered pan. Score it for squares before it hardens completely, then cut.

Chapter 7

New Friends

Brad was a classmate of Paul's at UCLA's film school, and his wife, Mary Ann, was an artist and interior decorator. The two had been sweethearts since junior high school and got married at twenty. They were our first "couples" friends in Los Angeles. Mary Ann decorated their rented house with her artsy good taste, and their shaggy English sheepdog, Humphrey, was not just a pet but also a conversation piece. I was in awe—okay, a little jealous—that Mary Ann and Brad lived and entertained as if they were much more established in their careers than we were.

Mary Ann was less than five feet all, yet she exuded the self-confidence of an Amazon. She found the humor in the gravest of events, the absurdity in the most tragic, and she was boldly outspoken. Since both of our mates were angling for careers in Hollywood, where the saying goes, "It's not enough that you succeed, your friends also must fail," there was an underlying competition between us. That never stopped Mary Ann from being a considerate and loyal friend.

Like me, Mary Ann learned to cook the basics from her mother, but though she enjoyed cooking, she didn't spend hours in the kitchen. She preferred painting at her easel, decorating a house, or shopping for one of the clever little metal wind-up toys that she collected. She specialized in dishes that were fashionable yet easy, usually variations on chicken or steak. Once in a while she served gourmet dishes like escargots Bourguignonne. Yes, there was an "ick" factor involved, but if you enjoyed snails (or at least acted like you did), it was a sign of sophistication. Mary Ann actually liked the taste of the shriveled gray critters. I preferred the garlicky melted butter that they swam in, and swabbing it up with French bread.

What I most remember from Mary Ann's cooking repertoire is one of the recipes I rediscovered in my recipe notebook. Grapes brûlée has about as much in common with crème brûlée as chopped liver has with pâté. Mary Ann found the recipe in a magazine article about the movie producer Bob Evans, whose butler served it at Evans's Hollywood soirées. In 1967 Mary Ann served the dessert at a dinner party that was a near disaster.

It was on a Saturday night when Mary Ann and Brad were entertaining a group of UCLA student friends, including Paul, and their dates. During the cocktail hour, conversation focused on the war in Vietnam—we were unanimously against it—and the Stones blasted over the sound system. Paul and I believed that Stones fans had a dark side, whereas Beatles fans like us were more cheerfully straightforward. Looking back, perhaps we should have thought twice about the fact that Brad was a Stones fan. It wasn't until thirty years later that it made sense to us.

The main course was beef fondue, a trendy dish in the late sixties, like its cousin, cheese fondue. Eating beef fondue was a fun, communal endeavor, for it required guests to skewer pieces of raw steak and then cook them together in a pot of near-boiling oil. I tossed the salad while Mary Ann laid out bowls of sauces for the fondue—spicy ketchup, honey mustard, blue cheese—on the long teak table in the dining room. The guests sat down, and Mary Ann stepped into the kitchen to retrieve the Dansk fondue pot of oil that was heating on the stove. As she was carrying the pot to the table, the handle loosened and the pot overturned—spilling scalding hot oil all over her arm. She screamed out in pain, then quickly got hold of herself and urged everyone to finish dinner. She retreated to the bedroom and phoned her father, who was a doctor. He showed up, treated the burn, and doped her up with painkillers. As an example of the inner strength that would serve her well in later life, in her matter-of-fact, life-goes-on manner, Mary Ann rejoined us at the table for dessert.

My best new unmarried friend was Irma (the woman I mentioned in the introduction), an exuberant Berkeley grad with a short Afro, a broad smile, and a perfect figure no matter how much she ate. And since she suffered from hypoglycemia, she was always eating to keep up her blood-sugar level. Irma was one of my fellow English teachers, and we carpooled to work, usually in my new stick-shift Volvo whose red paint job quickly faded in the harsh Southern California sunshine. Inching down the 405 freeway in heavy traffic, I would try not to notice the layer of smog hanging over the city. It wasn't easy: Smog has a distinctive smell, one that sticks in your nostrils and blocks out such sweet smells as jasmine.

The commute was long, but Irma and I always had more than enough to talk about—work, men, books, and food. Like me, Irma was an avid cook and had been raised to believe that being a good cook helps you get a husband. She often invited Paul and me to dinner at her apartment, along with a date. One of our favorites of

Irma's boyfriends was Ahmed, a charming Indian who fostered an aura of mystery about him. Ahmed lived in a furnished apartment that was devoid of personal touches, as if it were just a temporary base, and he threw money around as if he had tons of it; he insisted on paying for the four of us whenever we went out to dinner. Ahmed claimed he was in the United States working with computers—this was long before computers became mainstream—on a project that concerned Southeast Asia. That's all he said he could tell us about his job; the rest was classified. We suspected that Ahmed was in the CIA or was some sort of spy. Either that or he was a pathological liar.

One night when we went to Irma's for dinner with Ahmed, she cooked Indian tandoori-style chicken accompanied by a basmati-rice biryani (pilaf) chock-a-block with plump white raisins and nuts. I say tandoori-*style* because a few years later, I was to learn what *real* tandoori chicken is, at the source. Still, with Ravi Shankar sitar music playing in the background and Ahmed's exotic tales of growing up on the subcontinent, the evening was my first taste of Indian food and culture. I didn't know that it foreshadowed one of the greatest adventures of my life.

Mary Ann's Fresh Fruit Brûlée

SERVES 4

Perhaps in the late sixties this recipe tasted better with grapes than it did when I made it in 2001. I came up with a variation using raspberries and blueberries, however, that is a winner. This dessert is easy to make, and the crème fraîche lends a somewhat sweeter taste than sour cream. Just be sure to watch the brown-sugar crust when it is under the broiler. If you blink, it can turn from a bubbling gold to black.

Three 6-ounce containers of fresh blueberries or
raspberries, or a combination
¾ cup crème fraîche or sour cream
1½ cups firmly packed golden brown sugar

1. Rinse the berries well in a colander and let dry. Pour them into a bowl, and gently fold in the crème fraîche or sour cream, until the berries are evenly coated.

2. Spoon the mixture into an ovenproof 8- or 9-inch soufflé dish. The berry mixture should come no higher than one inch below the rim. Spoon on the brown sugar and spread evenly, so that all the berries are covered, then gently pat it down. Refrigerate until 30 minutes before serving.

3. Position a rack in the middle of the oven, and preheat the top broiler to medium. Slide in the dish and check frequently as the brown sugar melts, about 8 to 10 minutes. Remove the dish from the oven when the sugar is solid and bubbling slightly. Don't let it burn!

4. Serve with a big spoon, digging down so that you get berries and crust in each serving. Garnish with more crème fraîche or sour cream, if desired.

Irma's Tandoori Chicken

SERVES 6 TO 8

One shelf of a cabinet in my kitchen is a hodgepodge of tins and jars containing spices and herbs. Though the labels say ginger, cumin, and chili powder, many have been there for so long that they all smell alike—like, well, nothing. Before you make this dish, be sure that your spices are fresh and spicy.

2½ cups yogurt
¼ cup lemon juice
2½ teaspoons salt
2 teaspoons ground chili powder
1 tablespoon ground coriander
1 teaspoon grated fresh ginger
1 teaspoon ground nutmeg
1 teaspoon ground anise
2 cloves garlic, minced
1 teaspoon ground pepper
1 teaspoon cumin
1 teaspoon ground cardamom
2 chickens, quartered

1. In a large bowl, mix all the ingredients except the chicken. Add the chicken and turn each piece a few times to coat it evenly.

2. Cover and refrigerate the marinating chicken for 24 to 48 hours, turning occasionally.

3. Place an oven rack in the upper third of the oven and preheat the oven to 400°F. Remove the chicken from the marinade, and place, skin side up, in a shallow roasting pan. Roast for 55 minutes to 1 hour, turning once and basting the chicken several times with the pan drippings.

4. When serving, spoon the pan drippings over the chicken.

LOW-CAL VARIATION
Use skinless chicken breasts and nonfat yogurt, and reduce the baking time to 30 to 35 minutes. Baste often.

Chapter 8

Getting Down to It

The summer after my first year of teaching, Laurie married Steve, the man who lived across the hall from her, at an elaborate wedding in Seattle. I was her maid of honor, and Paul was my date. My parents had met Paul and adored him. In fact, my father admitted that he was relieved I hadn't married Justin—that he had never liked or trusted him. (*Now* he tells me.) Paul was honest and dependable, my father concluded, the kind of man he could trust to treat his daughter well. Plus, Paul had a new job at Wolper Productions, the leading documentary-film-production company in Hollywood. Though he continued taking film classes at UCLA at night, now he had a future. My father hoped I'd marry Paul. My mother did too. Sooner rather than later.

After Laurie and her groom left the wedding reception in a hail of rice, my mother got that furrowed-brow look of hers and took me aside: Robin had just gotten married, and now Laurie, she said, and Shelley was engaged. How come I was still just *dating* Paul? She knew that though Paul and I had separate apartments a block away

from each other—twenty-somethings did that in those days to keep
up appearances—we were virtually living together at mine.

Like most men in their early twenties, Paul was perfectly content
with the status quo: I cooked for him, he loved everything I served,
and we spent every free waking—and sleeping—moment together.
My mother, who lived by a strict moral code, convinced me that this
"just wasn't right." At her goading, when Paul and I returned to
L.A. after Laurie's wedding, I announced that I was going to date
other men—Paul could sleep at his own apartment and cook his
own food. Paul didn't quite know how to take this, but at my insistence, he stuffed his clothes into a laundry bag, grabbed his tooth-
brush, and moved to his own apartment a block away.

The next afternoon a good-looking guy visiting my neighbor
was sunning himself by our apartment pool. I flirted with him and
learned that he was a psychiatrist. Hmm, I thought, a *doctor*. He
asked me to go to a Dodgers game, and the next thing I knew we
were driving downtown in his red Mercedes sports car with SHRINK
emblazoned on the license plate. I loathed sports events—one reason I liked Paul was that he hated them too and took me to movies
instead—but I suffered through all nine innings, Dodger dogs,
warm beer, and all.

The following night Paul walked into my apartment, dropped
his briefcase, got down on one knee, and proposed.

Chapter 9

The Princess Grace
of Beverly Hills

After we announced the news of our engagement to our parents, the first couple Paul and I told were his uncle Bob and aunt Hannah, whom I had met shortly after we started dating.

I was nervous the first time Paul took me to Hannah and Bob's house in the "flats" of Beverly Hills. It was on one of those impeccable palm-tree-lined streets where mansions—American Colonial, Spanish Colonial, English Tudor—stand shoulder to shoulder, each fronted by a garden filled with blossoming flowers all year round. Hannah and Bob's house was of the Spanish Colonial variety—my favorite because it best suits L.A.'s Mediterranean climate—with Mexican-tile floors, a sweeping staircase with wrought-iron banisters, and thick stucco walls. Two olive trees shaded the front yard, and in the back a hedgerow hid the swimming pool so that when looking out a window from the house, all you saw was lawn and garden. As wealthy as they were, Hannah and Bob weren't showy with their money. In other words, they were not your typical Beverly Hills couple.

My ideal Beverly Hills family:
Robert and Hannah Boorstin, with
Anna, Robert, and Louis.

Hannah had decorated the house with burnished antiques and overstuffed sofas and chairs in stylish European fabrics, so that despite their imposing size, the rooms felt welcoming, even cozy. Often, when she entertained, she placed Rigaud candles in their green frosted-glass containers on each step of the staircase in the foyer. To this day, the heavenly scent of those candles makes me think of Hannah and Bob's house.

I'd been in one or two of what were considered "mansions" in Seattle, but they were not half as grand as Hannah and Bob's. For my first visit, I wore my most fashionable outfit—a black-and-white checked miniskirt and matching jacket, and black fishnet stockings (what was I *thinking*?). The result was that as I sat politely on the sofa making chitchat, Miss Fathergill's face kept flashing through my mind. "Don't let your panties show" had been rule number one in charm school. I kept my knees together, pressed so tight that I had red marks on the insides of them by the time I left.

Clive, the cultivated English butler, served cocktails in cut-crystal tumblers on a silver tray, and Hannah and Bob's children were summoned downstairs to meet me before bedtime. Anna was a darling eight-year-old with long brown hair and greenish gray eyes like her mother's; the six-year-old twins, Robert and Louis, looked precious in their matching blue bathrobes. I was enchanted by the way these picture-perfect children firmly shook my hand when they were introduced. Miss Fathergill would have been impressed.

After Paul and I got engaged, I turned to Hannah for advice on choosing silver and china patterns. It wasn't that I thought of her as a stand-in mother figure—she was only ten years older than me. A true daughter of the fifties, she had married Bob even before finishing college. Hannah was my ideal of a housewife and mother, a woman I could only dream of emulating someday. A thin, long-necked beauty with light brown hair that was sometimes streaked with blond, she carried herself like a model and exuded elegance even when she was wearing jeans and driving her three kids to their tennis lessons in her Buick station wagon.

When it came to choosing a wedding dress, Hannah took me to I. Magnin, at the time a department-store landmark in Los Angeles. She had many of her own clothes made there by Stella, the resident designer, and all the saleswomen greeted Hannah as if she were royalty. Perhaps that's one reason I thought of her as the Princess Grace of Beverly Hills.

Before and after our marriage, Hannah often invited Paul and me to dinner. The guests ranged from family to movie producers to famous Russian émigrés like violinist Jascha Heifetz and cellist Gregor Piatigorsky. Hannah was a talented pianist in her own right, and she studied Russian so that she could converse with them.

Hannah was close to her mother, Gertrude, a small woman with perfectly coiffed white hair and the self-confident bearing of a matriarch—which she was—who always dressed as if she were going to a ladies' tea. Hannah was also close to her older sister, Myra, who was as self-assured and elegant as she was. It was clear that Gertrude had raised Myra to be the intellectual daughter, Hannah to be the social one. Myra garnered quite a reputation as a children's poet and expert on children's literature. Hannah's reputation was as the consummate Beverly Hills hostess. Who would have guessed that one day she would have a distinguished literary career?

For large dinner parties, Hannah often arranged a series of round-top tables, each adorned with flowers from her garden. In spring, they might be Iceland poppies with luminescent orange and yellow petals so delicate that you could see light through them. Hannah proudly arranged the flowers herself. It was a skill that her mother had taught her, along with choosing antiques.

Unlike most Beverly Hills hostesses, Hannah did her own cooking when she entertained. And she was quite a cook, the master of vitello tonnato in summer and cassoulet in winter, dishes that in the late sixties were usually only found on the menus of Italian or French restaurants. Whenever Hannah served a dish that I admired, she was happy to give me the recipe.

In my old recipe notebook from that time, I still have a yellow carbon copy of her typed-out recipe for a rich chocolate cheesecake. At the top of the page, you can just make out Hannah's delicate handwriting: "*Sherry, dear, this time I think it turned out much better. There's some in the fridge if you'd like to drop by and try a piece.*"

Hannah's Chocolate Cheesecake

SERVES 12

The original recipe called for a stick of butter and more sour cream but one less package of cream cheese. When I featured this recipe in the article about my recipe notebook that appeared in More, *the recipe testers in the* More/Ladies' Home Journal *kitchen created this luscious, more modern version.*

FOR THE CRUST

   1½ cups graham-cracker crumbs
   5 tablespoons butter, melted
   One 1-ounce square semisweet chocolate, melted

FOR THE FILLING

> 2 large eggs
> 1 cup granulated sugar
> Three 8-ounce packages cream cheese, softened
> 8 ounces semisweet chocolate
> ½ cup sour cream
> 1 teaspoon vanilla extract

FOR THE GARNISH

> Powdered sugar
> ½ cup fresh blueberries or raspberries

1. Preheat the oven to 350°F. In a large bowl, blend the crust ingredients well. Press the mixture into the bottom of a 9-inch springform cake pan.

2. Beat the eggs and sugar with an electric mixer on medium-high speed for about 5 minutes, or by hand, until the mixture falls in thick ribbons from the beaters when they are lifted from the bowl. Beat in the cream cheese thoroughly.

3. Melt the chocolate in the top of a double boiler. Cool to room temperature, add it to the cream cheese mixture, and blend well. Beat in the sour cream and vanilla until the mixture is thick and smooth. Pour the mixture into the prepared pan.

4. Bake 55 to 60 minutes, or until the cake puffs in the center. Remove from the oven, let it cool, and refrigerate overnight.

5. Before serving, remove from the pan. Sprinkle the cheesecake with powdered sugar and garnish with a few fresh berries. Cut with a hot knife.

Chapter 10

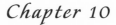

Finally . . .

My first wedding—the one I planned but never went through with, thanks to Justin and his psychiatrist—was to have been an elaborate affair. I had lined up five bridesmaids—my sister Sheila, Justin's sister, Ellen, plus Robin, Laurie, and Shelley—and my parents had invited a couple of hundred guests. When I got engaged to Paul two and a half years later, I couldn't bring myself to plan a wedding extravaganza; I felt like I'd already had one. My parents were more than happy to keep the wedding small and save money.

Paul and I tied the knot in my parents' house in Seattle two days before Christmas in 1967. Sheila performed a Brahms intermezzo on the piano that brought tears to everyone's eyes. While I waited with my father in the stairwell for the processional, I was seized with separation anxiety, as I had been when I was a little girl and my parents were leaving for New Year's Eve. Only now my mother and father weren't the ones who were leaving me; I was leaving them. My father put his hand on my arm, looked me in the eye and steadied me, then walked me down the world's shortest aisle.

Because the venerated senior rabbi from our temple was already booked that night, Paul and I were married by a rabbi whose dream in life was to play Tevye, the bigger-than-life lead character in *Fiddler on the Roof*. I don't remember what he said to us in his long-winded speech; he could have been belting out "If I Were a Rich Man." All I remember was that my fingers were too swollen for Paul to slip on the ring, and that by the time he stomped his foot on the wineglass (actually, it was a napkin-wrapped lightbulb standing in for the wineglass), my tears—of nervousness, joy, separation anxiety—were rolling down. Mascara streaked my face, and my false eyelash hung like a broken flag off my left eyelid.

If you ask my mother, she'll tell you that the best part of my wedding came next. She laid out platter after platter of fresh Dungeness crab legs and jumbo shrimp on the dining room table, and the guests descended. "They would have been happy to stay at our house all evening!" my mother says to this day.

Instead, after all the seafood was eaten, guests piled into cars—it was raining, and one of the cars got stuck in the mud in our front yard—and drove through the wet, cold winter night to Canlis. My mother had wanted to have a buffet dinner at home—more crab and shrimp, plus fresh salmon and blintzes—but I got my wish to hold the wedding dinner in the best restaurant in town. We took over the upstairs private room for a sit-down meal consisting of Canlis salad, roasted Cornish game hens stuffed with wild rice, and a five-tiered wedding cake that Paul and I fed to each other with our fingers for the camera.

My only girlfriends who attended the wedding were Laurie and Robin; Shelley had married Doug a few days before and was on her honeymoon in Hawaii. For budgetary reasons, my mother limited the guests to around sixty, which meant that Mary and Edith and their husbands were invited, but not their daughters, Gloria and Laurie, my best childhood friends. Nor was there room for my other high school, college, or new L.A. friends. If I had my wedding to

Let us eat wedding cake.

plan over again, I would invite more of my friends, even if it meant trading an expensive dinner at Canlis for a casual buffet at home.

Not that I had many girlfriends—just Irma and a few other teachers, and Mary Ann. After I started dating Paul, I devoted little effort to nurturing female friendships. It wasn't Paul's fault, but my own.

Paul's parents, his great-aunt Frances, and his youngest brother, David, were his only guests. Everyone else was a friend or relative of my parents. Paul particularly remembers several very short, very old men who all seemed to be named Uncle Dave, tearfully embracing him around his knees and welcoming him to our family.

My sister Sheila and Paul's brother David—Paul's other brother, Jon, was in England, and my sister Susan was in a mental institution—were our attendants. Sheila was so happy that I was now out of the running when it came to men that she dropped her resentment toward me. From that point on, we were friends. We both wept when she and David dropped us off at the airport.

After a brief honeymoon in Palm Springs at the exclusive Racquet Club—Aunt Hannah got us in—I started married life. It was exactly what I'd been raised to do, and I planned to do it right. One advantage of being happily married, I soon found, was that I stopped eating out of depression, anxiety, and boredom, as I had done in high school and college. As a result, I got down to an acceptable weight and held it.

Paul and I were fortunate to find an idyllic apartment in West L.A. on a quiet street poetically named Pandora. One of eight units, ours was in the back of the building and faced a lawn bordered by birds of paradise and electric-pink bougainvillea. The other tenants never used the backyard, and I was just about the only one who swam in the pool. Paul and I felt as if we had a slice of the California dream for a remarkably low four hundred dollars a month.

We bought a black leather couch with rosewood sides and back that was fashionable but slippery. Hannah's old teak table worked in our dining room. In a Venice junk store we found an antique Federal desk with little cubbyholes and a top drawer that hinged down to make a writing table. Since Paul turned the second bedroom into his office, we moved the desk into an alcove near the kitchen, and that became my workspace.

I wrote all the thank-you notes for our wedding gifts on the Federal desk. In Berkeley and other cities where women's lib was catching on at the time, young women were starting to call themselves Ms. Not me. My proper, off-white Crane thank-you notes had my new name engraved on them: MRS. PAUL TERRY BOORSTIN.

I can picture myself the first day I came home from teaching after my honeymoon: I was wearing a black tweed wool dress that came just below the knee (thirty-three years ago, before global warming, it was cold enough in January in L.A. to wear wool), nude nylon panty hose, and low-heeled black pumps. My long, straight hair was pulled back conservatively in a faux tortoise clip. A couple of packages were waiting for me on the doorstep, and I opened them to find a place setting of the Tiffany silverware I registered for, a few dinner plates in our Wedgwood Florentine Black pattern, and two delicate Baccarat crystal wineglasses. It was wishful thinking when I picked out such expensive crystal. Those goblets that weren't broken in the course of regular wear and tear went flying out of the kitchen cabinet during the big earthquake of 1972 and were smashed to bits.

After writing the requisite thank-you notes, I started dinner. I never entertained on school nights—never even had a sip of wine because I had to grade papers and rise-and-shine time was six the next morning. But I always set a nice table with candles, and I whipped up something simple but tasty in our tiny dishwasher-deprived kitchen. Unlike my mother, I enjoyed the process.

My everyday meals bordered on the mundane—broiled steak, roast chicken, broiled steak. Paul was content as long as I served rice on the side; he'd developed a taste for rice when he was twelve and his family lived in Kyoto for six months while his father was teaching there.

When it came to cooking for guests, I went all out. If I was having a dinner party on Saturday night, I started planning the Monday before. I combed through recipes in the newspaper and *Bon Appétit* and leafed through those in the black loose-leaf notebook where I kept the recipes given me by friends and relatives. My specialties included the Canlis salad, of course, stuffed Cornish game hen patterned after the entrée served at my wedding, beef Stroganoff, and flank steak marinated in a honey-lemon-soy sauce. As a side dish, I invariably served a rice pilaf loaded with two or three of the following: raisins, currants, walnuts, almonds, peas, shallots, and parsley.

If I was really trying to impress someone, I served escargots Bourguignonne as an appetizer. Mary Ann had taught me how to prepare them. ("It's simple," she'd said. "You open the can, pour the little guys into a pan, and drench them in garlic butter.") Mary Ann was impressed when Ruth, my mother-in-law, sent me a set of dimpled escargot-serving plates and pincers for the shells. I also had Ruth to thank for a set of individual porcelain soufflé dishes, and delicate *pots-de-crème* dishes with tiny lids. Ruth figured a young bride should have such special-occasion tableware, and I occasionally made chocolate soufflés or chocolate *pots de crème* for dessert so that I could use them.

Looking back, I find it puzzling that I didn't serve fish in those days—maybe it was a revolt against all the tuna fish sandwiches, salmon, and crab I ate growing up in Seattle. I also never served pasta. The Italian thing didn't kick in until the eighties.

Regardless of what I was making, I never precisely followed the measurements called for in the recipe, and I usually added a few ingredients of my own. My mother would have dubbed me a *shiter-ein* cook, like her. I was like my mother in another way: I became so uptight about making everything perfect for my guests, I often was worn out by the time we sat down for dinner. Many of my friends admit to feeling the same way when they entertained as young brides. It wasn't until I was older—postkids—that I learned to plan less complicated meals, to slow down, and to not take it all so seriously. In other words, to be relaxed enough to enjoy my own party.

I spent weeks planning the first Thanksgiving dinner after our marriage. Since Irma was one of the guests, we discussed the menu on our way to and from school. Thanksgiving had been a big deal when I was growing up, a feast at our house for at least a dozen relatives. The one dish from my mother's Thanksgiving dinner that I wanted for mine was her moist egg-bread stuffing. She dictated the recipe to me over the phone but suggested that instead of stuffing it in the turkey, I bake it in a casserole dish; she prepared it this way now because it required less effort. I insisted, however, that stuffing should be stuffing, and I jammed as much of it as I could into the bird's cavity and sewed it up with thread. Just as when I had stuffed and sewed up brandied chicken legs with Laurie in Berkeley, it was a difficult—and painful—task with greasy fingers.

Irma arrived early to help with the side dishes: sweet potatoes with fresh pineapple instead of the traditional marshmallows;

mashed potatoes with sour cream and chives instead of milk; and a brussels sprouts recipe that called for maple syrup and chopped walnuts. Everyone hates brussels sprouts, Paul argued—at least he did—but I felt we needed a green vegetable to round out the rich, starchy meal, and to Irma and me, the notion of using sweet maple syrup with a vegetable was intriguing. The cabbage stink wafted through the house while the sprouts were cooking.

Our first Thanksgiving.

The first course was a Canlis salad. No, that's not true. The first course was what I served during the predinner entertainment.

In the late sixties, VCRs and videotapes had not been invented yet, so Jeff, one of Paul's film-school classmates, rented a sixteen-millimeter projector and an old black-and-white Hitchcock movie, *The Lady Vanishes,* to watch while the turkey was roasting. He also brought several experimental computer-graphic films that in those days consisted of changing designs and patterns and weird music that added up to, well, a psychedelic experience.

Unlike some of our friends, Paul and I did not smoke marijuana—Paul was afraid of losing precious brain cells; I was afraid of getting the munchies and eating everything in sight. But since it was Thanksgiving, a holiday of indulgence, without Paul's permission—or knowledge—I decided to heighten the sensory experience by making marijuana-stuffed mushrooms.

Earlier that week at school my friend, Sue, a flamboyant English teacher, had procured a Baggie full of marijuana from one of her students (don't ask). When Sue arrived for Thanksgiving dinner, she brought it along. While the men settled down with their movie, Sue, Irma, and I mixed the grass with leftover egg-bread stuffing and pressed it into giant mushroom caps. The smell was acrid when they were baking—worse than brussels sprouts. Still, though Paul abstained, everyone else managed to get several down—even me. A cook has to taste her own cooking, right? Instead of giving me the munchies, the rubbery mushrooms with the strawlike stuffing made me sick.

Mom's Egg-Bread Stuffing

ENOUGH FOR A 20-POUND TURKEY WITH SOME LEFTOVER
TO BAKE IN A CASSEROLE

This is a recipe that cries out for improvisation, for you can toss in just about anything that adds crunch and perhaps a bit of sweetness, and it will taste good. Just be sure you use egg bread as your base. It is also a recipe for which it is difficult to give precise measurements. Taste and adjust the ingredients and seasonings for flavor and texture.

4 to 5 loaves sliced egg bread, crusts removed (you can
    substitute multigrain bread for 2 of the egg-bread
    loaves if desired)
3 to 4 big onions, chopped
1 stick butter
1 bunch celery, chopped
2 cups chopped mushrooms
1 each turkey giblet, heart, and liver, chopped
1 to 2 tablespoons poultry seasoning
1 to 2 tablespoons salt
Pepper to taste
1 to 1½ cups sliced water chestnuts, well drained
2 to 3 pippin or Granny Smith apples, chopped

1 to 1½ cups dried cranberries or chopped dried apricots

2 carrots, chopped (optional)

1 cup sunflower seeds, or chopped walnuts or almonds (optional)

4 eggs, beaten

3 to 4 cups chicken broth, at room temperature

1. Cut the bread into cubes about 1½ inches square. Set aside for a day or two so that they dry out, tossing occasionally, or toast them lightly in a 350°F oven, until they are crisp but not brown.

2. In a large heavy pan over medium heat, sauté the onions in the butter until they are soft, about 10 to 15 minutes. Stir frequently and be sure the onions do not burn. Add the celery, mushrooms, giblet, heart, liver, and seasonings, and cook over medium-high heat for 15 to 20 minutes, stirring often, until the turkey parts are cooked. Remove from the heat and let cool completely.

3. In a large pot, in batches, add the cooled onion-giblet mixture and about three quarters of the bread cubes. Toss gently. (You may need to do this with two wooden spoons or with your hands.) In batches, add the water chestnuts, apples, dried fruit, and any optional ingredients, tossing gently after each addition.

4. In a separate dish, whisk the eggs with 3 cups of the broth, and gradually add the liquid to the stuffing mixture, blending gently. Add more broth-egg mixture and the remaining bread cubes if needed. You do not want the stuffing to be soggy, but it shouldn't be dry, either. Adjust the poultry seasoning, salt, and pepper to taste.

5. Just before roasting the turkey, stuff it loosely—do not pack it in. Bake the remaining stuffing in a buttered casserole, covered lightly with foil, at 350°F for approximately an hour, until brown on top.

Chapter 11

Wild Horses, Wild Pheasants

In the early seventies Paul and I spent one Christmas vacation in London. I had been there during my summer tour of Europe, when London stayed light until ten o'clock at night and it was warm enough for tourists to gather in Trafalgar Square and watch buskers and Beatles impersonators. In December London was dark until nearly ten o'clock in the morning and then again after three. And was it *cold*! I bought a mod sheepskin coat with purple and yellow embroidery and long-hair-sheep-wool fringe—like one John Lennon wore—to keep me warm. We settled in at the Cadogan, a staid hotel whose claim to fame was that in 1895 Oscar Wilde was arrested in the lobby.

We went to London principally to visit Paul's brother David, who was spending the year after college exploring a career in theater. David lived in a trendy section of the city, in a communal house with a bathroom wallpapered entirely with *New Yorker* covers. It inspired me to save *New Yorker* covers for years for that purpose, until a housepainter convinced me that they would peel right off the wall because of steam from the shower. (The bathroom in London had just a toilet and sink.) The owner of the house, David's land-lady, had become his girlfriend and would later become his first wife.

A voluptuous redhead with ivory skin, green eyes, and a jolly laugh, Molly was from an aristocratic family—her grandfather had been the British ambassador to Ethiopia—and had grown up in what she described as a "nursery life": When she and her siblings were children, they dressed up for tea, and tea was the only time of day they saw their parents. When I grew up in Seattle, tea was some-thing my grandparents drank after a heavy meal, and the children weren't allowed to have any.

I admired Molly's zest for life and I shared her tendency to, well, in the words of Paul and David, "give in to impulse." She was also artistic—a sculptor—and a very good cook. On Christmas Day I helped Molly prepare a roast-turkey dinner, and the four of us spent the afternoon drinking Bordeaux—claret, as the English call it—and nibbling on Stilton cheese. I never had tasted Stilton, and it took several glasses of claret before I appreciated its pungent flavor. After dinner and a brandy-soaked Christmas pudding, we played a rowdy game of charades.

A few days later the four of us bundled into Molly's tiny car and set off for her family's stately Georgian country house in Wiltshire, about an hour's drive from London. It was even colder there than it had been in London, but Molly's parents had given her permission to heat only the drafty, old-fashioned kitchen. The dreary, icy weather did not stop Molly and me from going horseback riding. David and Paul pronounced us impulsive and stayed behind to sip sherry by the fire.

Molly learned to ride not long after she learned to walk, and she had owned a horse since she was a little girl. I, on the other hand, had taken riding lessons only for a few years in my youth. Every Wednesday my mother picked up my sisters and me after school, and we changed from skirts and saddle shoes into jeans and cowboy

Molly, a spirited horse, and a terrified me.

boots in the backseat of our red-and-white '53 Olds while she drove us to Jimmy Rainwater's. Jimmy Rainwater, a half Native American who looked like Roy Rogers but lacked Roy's beatific smile, taught the rudiments of horseback riding by yelling, "Trot!" and "Lope!" to a class of prepubescent girls as they nudged their horses around the ring in a drafty barn. My childhood friends Laurie Warshal and Gloria Brown took riding lessons with us. To this day, whenever we see each other, Laurie reminds me that "the Silver sisters insisted on only riding *spirited* horses." It's true—I preferred them to the usual riding-lesson nags that had to be kicked until your heels hurt just to get them to move. But when I rode spirited horses, I always felt a stab of terror.

That cold day in Wiltshire, frost slicked the ground, and although I bundled up in several sweaters and one of Molly's heavy jackets, Molly was toasty wearing only jodhpurs and a turtleneck. I assured her that I was an experienced rider, so she put me on Forge

Medlar, her sleek white Arabian. She made do with a former cart horse named Huckleberry that she had rescued from the glue factory.

I felt a lot less secure on Forge Medlar's flat English saddle than on the western saddles with big "hang-on-if-necessary" horns at Jimmy Rainwater's. Yet off we went. Forge Medlar must have sensed my insecurity, for he broke into a gallop. "He's just happy to be out of the stable!" Molly's voice echoed from far behind as the Arabian flew into a forest that dated back to the Middle Ages. The last time I looked back, Molly was trying to goad the cart horse into a trot.

Despite my efforts to rein in the Arabian, he continued at a breakneck clip. Since the forest had been preserved for centuries, it was thick with trees and undergrowth. I hung on to the horse's mane, running a gauntlet of tree branches that cracked against my arms and legs like whips. Each time I ducked to avoid getting beheaded by one, my mind swirled with images from Disney's *Headless Horseman*, which was shown on TV every Halloween when I was a kid.

By the time Forge Medlar tired of his romp, my heart was racing—I was amazed I'd survived. Still, I let out a whoop of joy. Forge Medlar was the very model of a spirited horse.

For dinner that night, Molly and I roasted a brace of wild pheasants that a neighbor had shot. (That's when I learned that a "brace" means a pair—the way fresh-shot wild pheasants come in England.) While the birds were in the oven, Molly and I joined Paul and David for claret and Stilton cheese in front of the fire, and I relayed a somewhat embellished tale of our horseback-riding adventure. If Molly had recognized my near panic out there in the icy woods that day, she didn't mention it. Now, *that* was a good friend.

Chapter 12

Sharing My Sister's
Best Friend

A few days after Judy moved to Los Angeles, I took her out to lunch, delighted that one of my childhood friends—or at least Sheila's childhood friend—was living close by. Judy had recently graduated from Stanford with a major in Spanish, and she was dressed for her new job as a Spanish-speaking social worker: a conservative stitched-down pleated-wool skirt, two-inch heels, panty hose, and a white blouse whose Peter Pan collar was emblazoned with a gold circle pin.

Judy was petite—five-one, maybe—and tiny from the hips up. *Below?* Judy had been a champion ice skater and high diver in high school and was a near-pro tennis player as an adult; she had legs of steel. As Judy described her figure: "My thighs were so big, you could hear me coming down the hall by the sound of my nylons rubbing together—*wssshhh, wssshhh, wssshhh!*"

Over the next year or so, Judy's figure transformed from near clunky to sleek—such things happen in Southern California—and she gave up conservative wool skirts for minis. She changed careers

from social work to journalism via a short stint doing PR for the city
bus company. We met often in the sauna of our mutual health club
for conversation and gossip about work, family, and recipes. Judy's
family, after all, had been nearly as obsessed with food as mine.

Judy and I grew to be as close as sisters. We had such similar
backgrounds and so much common history: her father and my
mother had played tennis together in high school; her family had
lived across the street from mine when we were little kids. Judy and
I understood each other without any explanation required; it was
comforting for both of us.

I often fixed Judy up with Paul's friends because I knew they
wouldn't be disappointed. Judy was one of those women who men
fall in love with on the first date. She was cute, funny, smart, and
ebullient, and perhaps because she was so tiny, men wanted to pro-
tect her. She didn't fall in love until several years later. In the meantime, she got pleasure from cooking for friends. She said she had
Leida, her older sister, to thank for her best recipes.

Leida, who was my sister Susan's best friend when we were
growing up, got married at the age of twenty. Judy once told me how
angry she was that the rehearsal dinner for Leida's wedding fell on
her sixteenth birthday, and that her parents all but forgot about her.
Here's how she got back at Leida: After the wedding, their mother
carefully stored the top tier of the wedding cake in their basement
freezer, to save it for Leida's first anniversary. Over the course of the
next year Judy snuck into the freezer and chipped off bites, little by
little. When Leida went to retrieve the cake on her anniversary, all
she found was what Judy described as a "teensy little unidentifiable
mound." Judy never confessed, but she knew Leida realized who
had demolished her cake. "That's when I began to appreciate what
a loving sister Leida was," said Judy. "She never said a word about
it to me or anyone."

On many a Saturday night, Paul and I went to Judy's apartment
near the Veterans Administration for dinner. Judy's dates changed,

but certain things did not: Cat Stevens singing "Moonshadow" on the stereo; a big salad that was a match for Canlis's, tossed with Judy's secret-recipe dressing; a rice pilaf loaded with goodies like raisins, nuts, and peas; and entrées like chicken breasts stuffed with mushrooms and green onions, one of the recipes that Leida had given to Judy. Judy liked serving the dish because she could prepare it in advance and pop it into the oven just before dinner—and it came with a wine sauce, another Leida thing. Judy cooked with wine long before I figured out the difference between sherry, port, and Marsala, all of which were staples in her cabinet.

At Judy's there was always plenty of wine to drink with dinner too, but there was rarely dessert. Judy wasn't partial to sweets. Perhaps that's how she kept her slim figure. She also didn't like to stay up late. At eleven, almost like clockwork, a drunken vet stumbled past her window shouting to passing motorists—or perhaps just to the voices in his head. It took us a while to figure out the mantra he repeated ad nauseam—"*Motherfuckingshitassturds!*" We considered it a signal that Judy's dinner party was over and it was time to go home.

Judy's "Moonshadow" Chicken
SERVES 4

You can prepare this a few hours in advance and refrigerate it until 15 minutes before you're ready to bake it. I use shiitake and/or brown Italian (crimini) mushrooms because they are more flavorful than white mushrooms. Bake the breasts in a pan that is just big enough to hold them, so that they don't have room to fall apart during baking. Chicken breasts overcook—and get tough—easily, so keep an eye on them when they're in the oven.

4 big skinless, boneless chicken breasts
4 green onions, white and green parts, minced
2 tablespoons extra-virgin olive oil
2 cups mushrooms, minced
½ teaspoon salt, or to taste
½ teaspoon pepper, or to taste
1 teaspoon fresh minced marjoram, or ½ teaspoon
  dried
¾ cup dry white wine
¾ cup chicken stock
1 tablespoon Wondra flour (optional)
2 teaspoons lemon juice

1. Wash and dry the chicken breasts. Gently flatten them with a mallet or by placing them between two pieces of waxed paper and rolling them with a rolling pin. Set aside.

2. In a heavy pan over medium-high heat, sauté the green onions in the olive oil until soft. Add the mushrooms and sauté for 2 more minutes. Season with salt, pepper, and marjoram. Let the mixture cool to room temperature.

3. To stuff the chicken breasts, place 1 to 1½ tablespoons of the filling on a flattened breast and spread it evenly, then roll the breast up so that the seam is at the bottom. Carefully transfer the chicken roll to a small greased baking pan and secure with two toothpicks. Continue stuffing the chicken breasts and adding them to the baking pan.

4. Make the sauce: In the frying pan, add the white wine and the chicken stock to the remaining mushroom-onion mixture, and bring to a boil. Cook over medium-high heat, stirring often, until it thickens, 5 to 10 minutes. If it is too watery, sprinkle in the flour and mix well. Remove from the heat, add the lemon juice, and stir. Set aside until you're ready to bake the chicken.

5. Preheat the oven to 350°F. Pour the sauce over the chicken breasts, and bake them uncovered for 30 to 35 minutes, basting them with the sauce a few times. Make sure they are not over-cooked; cut slightly to see if the meat is tender. Spoon the pan juices over each portion and serve with rice.

Chapter 13

Hippie School

I enjoyed teaching high school students because I understood their teenage angst, and perhaps because I saw my former self in them. Though I quit the public school system—the bureaucracy had started to get to me—I continued to teach. Not just because I loved it—I had no idea of what else I could do for a living.

The early seventies were what people today look back on as the sixties, a time when many teens thought it was cool to be artsy hippies doing their own thing. "Alternative school" was the buzzword in education, and I helped establish one where they could.

At Horizons, the students took academic courses in the morning and spent the afternoon immersed in their choice of music, dance, drama, or art. They lived in worn Birkenstocks and ragged jeans (even though many were the children of wealthy Hollywood producers and movie stars), didn't brush their long hair, and doused themselves in patchouli oil to mask the smell of pot. The boys were Jim Morrison wannabes; the girls emulated Joni Mitchell. When they hung out in the parking lot smoking cigarettes, their music of choice ranged from the Stones to the Doors, with Aerosmith and the Who somewhere in between.

I was the assistant director and English/you-name-it teacher at Horizons for four years. The art teacher, a former nun, led women's consciousness-raising groups for the girls, and I sometimes sat in. I tried to act blasé when she instructed them how to use a mirror to "get to know" their vaginas—a lesson that Miss Fathergill never taught us in charm school. The aura of women's lib in the air at Horizons rubbed off on me. I abandoned my wool dress, panty hose, and two-inch-heel public-school persona and took to wearing hip-hugging bell-bottoms, my long hair down instead of pulled back in a prim faux-tortoiseshell clip. Many a parent who came to visit said to me, "Boy, they sure didn't have teachers like you when *I* was in school."

As part of the effort to create a school community that felt like a family, the staff and students cooked and ate together often. The spread involved a wide variety of dishes, for many kids and teachers were either vegetarians, vegans, or macrobiotically inclined. At Horizons the term "brown rice and good vibes" was taken literally. You never saw so many dishes garnished with alfalfa sprouts.

I was often in charge of the cooking, and I found that my student helpers—mostly girls—were genuinely motivated to nurture others with food. They believed that food equaled love, perhaps because these were the days of free love. I had a mutual-admiration thing going with "my girls," as I called them, and it nurtured my soul. Up to our elbows in salad greens, pasta, and, yes, brown rice, we bonded. There was only one teenager who resisted my attempt to reach out to her.

The first time I met Nell she was fifteen years old, and her eyes—as piercingly blue as her famous father's—flashed with anger. Paul Newman and Joanne Woodward, her parents, brought her to enroll at Horizons, and this sullen adolescent didn't make it easy for us. Nell resented the fact that because her family moved back and forth between their homes in Connecticut and Los Angeles she was for-ever switching schools. Horizons was just one more in a list of about a dozen that she had attended since kindergarten. After she plod-ded through a year at Horizons, she dropped out. She was one stu-dent of mine that I never would have pegged for success, or that I ever expected to see again. I was wrong on both counts.

P aul's uncle Bob had been only forty when he died of a heart attack while he and Hannah were on a Mediterranean cruise. Gregor Piatigorsky played a mournful piece on his cello at Bob's memorial service.

Bob's death was a tragedy for Hannah and her young children, and Paul deeply missed him too. We made it a point to stay in close touch with his family. A few years later, Hannah began seeing Alan Pakula, the director of *Klute* and later *All the President's Men*. Alan was every bit as elegant and sophisticated as she was. In fact, if Hannah was the Princess Grace of Beverly Hills, tall, handsome Alan was Prince Rainier.

One summer while I was teaching at Horizons, Hannah planned a trip to Spain to visit Alan on the set of *The Prime of Miss Jean Brodie*. She asked Paul and me to stay with her kids. When the time came, she handed me the keys to her Buick station wagon and gave me permission to use her account at Gelson's, the best supermarket on the west side of town.

Nearly every day that we stayed at Hannah's house, I cooked for Anna, Robert, and Louis, Hannah's children, and for friends who joined us for dinner. Somehow, my dishes tasted better when they were prepared in Hannah's kitchen and served on Hannah's china at the glossy antique table in her dining room. Living in a Beverly Hills mansion with three perfect children was a fantasy come true.

During our stay, I grew to know Anna, who at fifteen was the same age as my students. Unlike the laid-back kids I taught at

Horizons, Anna was a nose-to-the-grindstone A+ student at a girls' school where gray skirts and white blouses, not torn Levi's and T-shirts, were the uniform. Anna showed more interest in books than in boys, and she spent her spare time caring for and showing her thoroughbred horse or reading in her bedroom. I sought her out for quiet conversations and learned how much she missed her father. She was a brilliant, complex girl who was easy to love, and we were both bolstered emotionally by the connection we made.

Anna wasn't the least bit interested in cooking—an admitted rebellion against her mother's passion for it—but she liked to bake cookies. That week we baked several batches of chocolate chip cookies that we ate half of ourselves. Just as when I was a teenager baking them with Robin, chocolate chip cookies were the comfort-food glue that connected us.

Chapter 14

Real Tandoori Chicken

While I was teaching at Horizons, Paul was asked to produce, write, and direct a Wolper TV special for the National Geographic Society called *The Big Cats*. Paul had worked on Wolper documentaries about everything from blondes to dung beetles, but this one was a plum, and it would require him to spend three months filming Asiatic lions in India. I wasn't about to let Paul go off on this adventure without me. I found a substitute teacher to take my place at school, endured yellow-fever and hepatitis shots, and went with him.

Up until now, my only experience with anything Indian had been Irma's mysterious friend Ahmed and her tandoori-style chicken. My three months in India opened my eyes to a culture that challenged every belief system I knew, from the Judeo-Christian basis of Western civilization to Freudian psychology. It was a difficult but enlightening experience for me, a coming of age. As usual in my life, food played a memorable role.

My first impression of Bombay (now called Mumbai) was bound up with the sight of thousands of people asleep on the streets. The jeep that drove us from the airport into the city in the middle of the night caught row after row of bodies in its headlights. For a few days, while Paul obtained the necessary permits to film, we found refuge in the Taj Mahal Hotel, a grand Victorian building that dated back to 1903 and had sumptuous rooms, marble floors and hallways that were constantly being scrubbed, a gilded, high-ceilinged lobby, and a mosaic-tiled swimming pool. After my first swim, I floated on my back and watched ravens— Bombay was full of the aggressive black birds—chase sparrows from the bougainvillea to the tops of the palm trees. Once, I swear I saw one of the big birds catch and eat one of the little ones.

Of the hotel's many dining rooms, I preferred Tanjore, which served Northern Indian cuisine in an opulent setting complete with tasseled pillows, sitar music, and exotic Indian dancers. Here I had my first taste of *real* tandoori chicken; it was quite a different animal from what I'd eaten at Irma's. Not that Irma had messed up the recipe. It's just that tandoori chicken (or tandoori lamb, shrimp, or fish, for that matter) must be cooked in a tandoor, a searingly hot brick-and-clay oven fueled by wood, to achieve its authentic combination of succulence, smokiness, and spiciness. At Tanjore, I was so impressed with the tandoori chicken and the accompanying naan—puffy rounds of flat bread filled sometimes with onions, garlic, or even cherries—that I talked my way into the kitchen. I watched the chef skewer skinless pieces of chicken dyed startlingly reddish orange in a yogurt-based marinade and lower them into the barrel-shaped clay oven. While the chicken was roasting, he patted rounds of bread dough between his palms, slapped them onto the interior walls of the tandoor, then peeled them off when they puffed up moments later. For dessert we were served a delicate custard scented with rosewater and topped with slivers of gold leaf.

The first time I ventured out of the hotel, I was assaulted by Bombay's mixture of steamy heat and fetid human odors, and accosted by beggars. On top of that, I felt nauseated and dizzy from the food poisoning I must have picked up from the mangoes that had seduced me in my hotel room's fruit basket. I was overwhelmed with a fear that I would faint among the hundreds of people surrounding me and never be seen again. I had had panic attacks before, but none as scary as this.

I calmed down once we left the humid, crowded city and took up residence in the hot, dry, sparsely populated Gir Forest. Besides, I discovered two little pills that alleviated my stomach problems and my panic attacks, both of which were sold over the counter: Valium and Lomotil, an antidiarrhea drug that contained opium. I kept a supply of each in a fanny pack I removed only at bedtime.

The Gir Forest is the last sanctuary of the Asiatic lions, the lion of Judah mentioned in the Bible. The animals look similar to African lions except for a few differences—the Asiatic males, for example, have shorter and scruffier manes than those of African lions. Because of a severe drought, "forest" was pretty much a euphemism for the Gir. The dirt roads were rivers of dust; the undergrowth had thinned to a labyrinth of twigs; and whatever leaves on the teak trees that had not died in the heat were being eaten by cattle that herders illegally brought in to graze.

"Guest house" was definitely a euphemism for the cinder-block building where Paul and I stayed with the four-man Dutch film crew. Our rooms faced a garden that was snarled with dead flowers and had a dried-up fountain. Occasionally, a peacock wandered through, its piercing wail like the cry of a baby in a nightmare. Every morning before dawn, a racket on the porch awakened us—the rattle of china plates and teacups as a pair of ravens swooped down on the tea and toast that were set there for our breakfast.

After breakfast and again before sunset, the crew plus a couple of armed forest rangers and one goat (if a lion attacked, the hope

Paul's film crew in India, plus one woman (me!) and one goat.

was that it would go for the goat, not a person), piled into a van. We journeyed out into the forest sometimes for an hour or more to where the rangers had spotted the lions earlier. Filming the big cats was tedious work and involved much sitting around, waiting for them to *do* something. Still, I found it fascinating to observe the majestic wild animals in their natural habitat. It struck me that a pride consisted of mature female lions and young males and females—the adult males lived off on their own and only paired up with females during mating season. The rest of the year, the females taught the young lions hunting and survival techniques, much like mothers and grandmothers teach young girls to cook.

During the day the weather was so hot—sometimes 110 degrees—that the lions slept on and off in the bushes. We slept on and off in our stifling rooms. The only interruption was lunch. Sangha, the guest-house cook, was a wizened, toothless man who was friendly but had dirt under his fingernails, and he served the same menu daily: rancid goat curry; limp *papadum* crackers; greasy pea-

and-potato samosas, and steamed basmati rice, the only dish we considered safe to eat. For dessert we picked mangos from a tree in the garden. Andre, the head cameraman, taught me how to slice a mango in two, discard the seed, score the flesh with a pocketknife, and then flip the skin inside out so that you could eat the little squares of flesh without your lips touching the possibly contaminated skin.

Since the water was undrinkable and the temperature was over 100 degrees, each crew member drank over ten bottles a day of Limca, a lemony Indian soft drink similar in taste to Squirt. In one month we went through all the bottles of Limca at the guest house and in the nearby village. I commandeered a jeep and a driver and over a three-day period visited every village within a hundred miles of the Gir, buying every case of Limca available.

On the third day, as we were driving back to the forest, I asked the driver to take a detour to the Arabian Sea, for I longed to glimpse water after a month in the dusty, dried-out forest. On a windswept beach we happened upon a fish market—by which I mean a canvas-shaded series of tables where barefoot fishmongers gutted fish and the sand was slick with fish entrails and blood.

Silence fell when I ducked under the canvas canopy. The fish vendors and their customers clearly had never seen a westerner before—certainly not a twenty-something female in jeans, sunglasses, hiking boots, and a bulging fanny pack. All eyes were on me as I walked across the slimy sand, trying not to slip. My audience was gravely solemn; I wondered if they would burst into laughter if I fell in the muck.

Finally, beyond the octopus tentacles, the shark fillets, and the pale pink fish the size of my fist, I found lobster. They weren't as big as lobsters from Maine or even from California, but they'd do. I bought a gunnysack full and brought them back to the guest house, triumphant. That night, instead of Sangha's rancid goat stew, the film crew feasted on lobster I cooked on the wood-fired stove in the guest-house kitchen.

Chapter 15

Mississippi White Bread

relayed the fish-guts-and-lobster story to Kay Clapp a few nights after we returned from India, when Paul and I were sitting around the table in her cozy canyon house in Hollywood. She had prepared a sumptuous dinner, anticipating that we would appreciate it after our ordeal.

Kay's husband, Nick, was Paul's executive producer on *The Big Cats,* and Nick and Kay were our friends and mentors. A slim, attractive woman with short, blond-tipped brown hair and bangs that reached her eyebrows, Kay had been raised to be a Southern belle in Jackson, Mississippi, but she defied the cliché. She worked as a federal probation officer and dealt with hardened criminals on a daily basis.

I always enjoyed dinner at Kay and Nick's house. They had an open kitchen, which meant that Kay cooked while the guests watched from the adjoining dining area or helped her, and conversation flowed easily. She never put a tablecloth on her long, antique farmhouse table. The wood was too pretty to cover up, she said. On one side of the table guests sat on chairs, but those on the other side shared a long antique rocking bench. The "mammy bench" was a Southern thing, derived from the benches on plantation porches where a mother or a nanny rocked a half dozen children at once. At Kay's table, it took mutual cooperation for a group of adults to sit on the rocking bench and keep it still; that added to the camaraderie at her dinner parties.

Kay said the first thing she ever cooked was starch—but not cornstarch. When she was a teenager growing up in Mississippi in the fifties, she cooked laundry starch until it was the consistency of pudding. Then she dipped crinolines in it, a few square inches at a time, wrung them out, and hung them on the back clothesline to dry. Stiff, starched crinolines—sometimes three or four—were essential to provide fullness under the cotton shirt-waist dresses that she and her girlfriends wore. She wore soft Capezio flats with them. One of her favorite pairs were pink-and-white checked gingham with little roses; the other were black velvet with teardrop rhinestones across the top.

When there was nothing to do on Saturday night, Kay and her girlfriends rode around in her dad's Pontiac. They all chipped in twenty-five cents for gas and drove out to Natchez Trace, a nature preserve where the teenage boys raced their cars. Afterward they followed the aroma of baking bread to the wholesale bakery. Kay was convinced that it was called the Holsum Bakery because the owners didn't know how to spell *wholesome*. She and her girlfriends would walk up to the loading dock and flirt with the clerk until he brought out a loaf of bread fresh from the oven. "We called it white cotton bread," she said. "We paid him a quarter, pulled the loaf in half, and slapped a stick of butter in the middle. Then we tore the bread apart and ate the pieces while they were still warm."

Kay's mother was an excellent cook and made everything from

scratch, from bread to chocolate pudding. "There were no mixes in those days except Jell-O," Kay recalled. For every dinner, she made three or four side dishes to serve with the entrée and arranged everything neatly on the plate. "Mother cared about 'presentation' long before that word was used."

Kay's mother rarely let her help in the kitchen. She claimed her job was to cook and Kay's job was to eat. The only dish Kay made with her was fried okra. "I had to dip each little piece of okra in batter and then cornmeal—my fingers got all sticky—and then Mother would fry them in a hot pan," she recalled. Fried okra was often served with fried chicken and mashed potatoes for Sunday supper, the only meal of the week served family-style. Kay's mother fried chicken in leftover bacon fat that she kept in a big can by the stove. "Can you imagine eating chicken fried in bacon fat today?!" Kay is convinced that it was the bacon fat that made her mother's fried chicken so delicious.

Kay's mother was the proud member of a women's gourmet club—twenty ladies who took turns giving luncheons once a month. "The day after the gourmet club met," said Kay, "we'd read in the Jackson *Clarion Ledger* who attended and what they ate." In those days, the women in Kay's mother's social circle were all housewives, and they gained status from being considered good cooks. The women were friends, but there was unspoken competition over who made the best dish or set the most beautiful table. "Once, when it was my mother's turn to host the luncheon," Kay recalled, "she dyed five white tablecloths and twenty napkins a soft pink called 'raspberry' so that her linens would match the centerpieces she made with roses from our garden."

The women got all dressed up for the gourmet-club luncheons, completing their outfits with white gloves and hats. Kay's mother had white kid gloves that she washed carefully with a brush while they were still on her hands. Then she'd dry them for two or three days on little plastic hand frames. "Mind you, this was in

Mississippi, and there was no air conditioning in those days," said Kay. "You can imagine what it was like having to cook for twenty women, let alone to get all dressed up in hats and gloves and go to a luncheon, on a hot summer day!"

Kay didn't become interested in cooking until she moved to Los Angeles after college. She recalled the first time Nick took her to dinner at his boss's house, and his boss's wife made a dish with "toast points" that was fashionable at the time: "You took slices of bread, cut off the crusts, and pressed the slices into muffin tins," explained Kay. "You baked them until they were brown and stiff, then removed them from the tins and filled them with creamed chicken or creamed tuna made with Campbell's cream of mushroom soup."

After Kay got married, she taught herself to cook the basics. Her mainstay was hamburger Stroganoff, made with ground beef, sour cream, and noodles. "In those days, you didn't drain off the fat from the meat after it cooked," she said. "We didn't know beef fat was bad for you; we thought it added flavor."

The night Paul and I had dinner at Nick and Kay's house after our return from India, she served an upscale version of Stroganoff in our honor. Instead of making do with hamburger in the recipe, she used juicy strips of sirloin steak. The salad contained tomatoes from Kay's garden, and dessert was a chocolate icebox cake—one that Kay served often when guests came. I remembered the cake as being delicious, so I recently tried to duplicate the recipe: You mix gelatin with melted chocolate, beaten egg whites, and egg yolks, and fold in cubes of angel food cake. Then you chill it in a gelatin mold until it is set. My version turned out lopsided, wet, and bland. Either my memory had played tricks on me or my taste had changed—or the dessert simply needed Kay's magic touch.

Chapter 16

Taming the Wild Escargot

My sister Sheila, who had practiced piano for hours on end when she was a little girl, grew up to be a composer. Though she was only two years younger than me, while she was in college, women's lib "raised the consciousness" of open-minded, forward-looking girls like her. Sheila wasn't daunted by the fact that musical composition was a field in which it was hard to earn a living, let alone that it was dominated by men. Composing is what she decided she wanted to do with her life, so she went and did it. Like my mother (and me), Sheila had a steely determination. Also like my mother, she had musical talent.

Sheila's studies took her from the University of Washington to the University of California, Berkeley, and then, with the help of various fellowships and prizes, to Europe. She had just completed a year of composing in Stuttgart, Germany, when she visited Paul and me for a few weeks at the chalet in the French Alps where we spent the summer of 1974. Sheila had not had as much cooking experience as I had—I was the married sister, after all. As with everything else she loved, however, she cooked with a passion, and France was *the* place to do it.

Paul's parents had bought La Cassine when his father taught for a few months in Geneva, and the mountains of the French Haute Savoie were an hour's drive away. Dan and Ruth imagined retreating to the cozy chalet for summers after they returned to Washington, where they had moved a few years earlier from Chicago. As it turned out, they always were too busy traveling to return to La Cassine, and eventually they sold it. For that one summer, however, Paul and I had it all to ourselves.

The chalet was perched on a steep Alpine slope overlooking a valley. Built of native stone and timber, it felt solid and cozy. The living room featured a big fireplace, the kitchen was small but functional, and a broad porch ran the length of the house. Cassis-berry bushes had taken over the garden, and the earth was so fertile that when I put baby lettuce plants into the ground, they were mature enough to eat in seven days. Across the road, cows grazed in a pasture dotted with plum trees. The animals had no fear of me when I climbed over the fence and picked plums. I turned them into jam that was runny and had chunks of juicy plum in it, just like my mother's.

After Sheila arrived, while Paul worked at home writing, the two of us ventured off on long Alpine hikes. Often they led up through pastures where we dodged cow patties and listened to the tinkle of the bells tied around the necks of the dairy cows. With their varying rhythms and timbres, the bells gave Sheila inspiration for a string quartet, the first composition, she said later, in which she discovered her true musical voice. Above the pastures, the trails climbed through thick woods. We scavenged in the underbrush for *frais du bois*, intending to take the tiny wild strawberries home for dinner; instead, we ate most on the spot. Above the tree line we discovered *Sound of Music* territory—grassy fields polka-dotted with wildflowers and sweeping vistas of the surrounding mountains. Our favorite trail ended at an Alpine lake. The water was ice cold, but we, after all, were two sisters who grew up on the shores of Lake Washington; we stripped and jumped in.

One day on a hike through the woods, Sheila and I met a French family who were scouring the underbrush for wild mushrooms. I asked how they knew the difference between those that were edible and those that would kill you. The monsieur smiled and explained in French that it was knowledge that Savoyards pass down from one generation to the next. He advised us against mushroom hunting but encouraged us to hunt for escargots. I said no thanks: I had already tried cooking some snails I'd found in the garden, and it was a disaster. I had shuddered when the critters squeaked as they hit the boiling water. Furthermore, they were gritty and tasted bitter— and they were as tough as chewing gum that's been left on the bedpost all night. Like a typical Frenchman, the monsieur insisted that I'd done it all wrong, and went on to explain the *proper* way to prepare escargots.

After the next rain, Sheila and I were ready. Once the sun broke through the clouds, the road past our chalet, just as Monsieur predicted, became a highway for snails—big guys that had grown fat feasting on the sweet Alpine grass. Families of Savoyards appeared out of nowhere, competing for snails that they snatched off the pavement and stuffed into gunnysacks. Sheila reminded me that when we were growing up, after it rained our yard was full of slugs—it was a Seattle thing. Only our family didn't collect them for food. We walked around with saltshakers and watched as they shriveled and died in a hail of sodium.

Sheila and I collected a batch of snails and, per the monsieur's instructions, dumped them into a shoe box dusted with *farine* (flour). Then we poked little holes in the lid of the box, like we did when we collected grasshoppers as kids, and put the box in a shady spot on the porch. Monsieur had said that we should allow the snails to gorge on the *farine* for *huit jours* (more or less a week). This would clean out their systems and get rid of any grit, pebbles, and insects they had eaten—and tenderize them. Afterward, they would be ready to boil (I would just have to get used to their squeaking) and drench in garlic butter for *escargots Bourguignonne*. I planned to describe our triumph in my next letter to Mary Ann.

The next morning, when Sheila and I went outside to check on our snail herd, we found the lid of the box ajar. A dozen floury white trails zigzagged across the porch and disappeared into the garden. Only one snail was left, slowly making its way up the side of the box. We took pity on the puny thing and, singing "Born Free," released it in the pasture across the road.

The Silver sisters take Mont Blanc.

The last day of Sheila's visit, we took an extralong hike, then shopped for her farewell dinner. We picked out a plump hen that, as usual in small towns in France, came with its head and feet intact as well as with a few feathers. At the open-air market we bought tomatoes that were still warm from the sun and exuded that musty but appealing toma-to aroma that you rarely find in American grocery-store tomatoes, along with two dozen small, firm potatoes, and golden onions with bits of earth still clinging to their roots. At the pâtisserie, we chose the six most seductive French pastries, and then returned to the chalet to cook.

I had been perfecting a chicken recipe all summer, one that com-bined pungent Dijon mustard with the tart-sweet jam I'd made using the plums from the orchard across the road. While the chicken was in the oven, we baked potatoes that we had cut into quarters and sprinkled with coarse-grained salt and olive oil. Sheila tossed a salad of butter lettuce from the garden with an olive-oil vinaigrette scented with fresh tarragon. To round out the dinner was a crusty baguette and a couple of bottles of Côtes du Rhone, a wine we settled on because it was inexpensive yet robust enough to go with the chicken.

Dessert deserved a fanfare: the six French pastries that Sheila and I had carefully chosen. Among them were a lemon tart as yellow as egg yolk, a caramel-frosted éclair, a tart crowned with glistening *frais du bois*, and three chocolate delights, each more decadently rich than the next. Sheila did the honors. With a sharp knife, she care-fully cut each pastry into three precise pieces and passed them out. Paul, Sheila, and I savored every bite.

That night, as we dined outside on the porch, we could glimpse the top of Mont Blanc above the distant mountains. For a few moments during dessert, the sunset turned the peak a vibrant shade of fuchsia. It reminded Sheila and me of the view of Mount Rainier from the house where we grew up in Seattle. Back then, we re-sented each other; now we savored our friendship. Paul and I toasted Sheila, wishing her good luck in her composing career. She toasted me for creating such a succulent chicken dish, which we dubbed Chicken La Cassine.

Chicken La Cassine

SERVES 4

This juicy, sweet-and-salty chicken goes well with rice. Baste the chicken pieces often, and if the skin starts to burn, tent the pan with foil.

½ cup Dijon mustard
½ cup plum jam
5 to 6 cloves garlic, finely chopped
1½ tablespoons fresh rosemary or tarragon leaves
1 whole fryer, washed and patted dry, cut into quarters
Dash of salt and pepper, or to taste

1. Preheat the oven to 375°F. In a bowl, put the mustard, jam, garlic, and rosemary or tarragon, and mix well.

2. Dip the chicken pieces into the marinade and coat them evenly. Lay them in a roasting pan, skin side down, and sprinkle with salt and pepper.

3. Bake for 45 minutes, basting with pan juices every 15 minutes. Raise the oven heat to 400°F and turn the chicken pieces skin side up. Baste them with the pan juices and bake for 15 minutes more, until the skin is lightly browned.

4. Spoon the pan juices over the chicken pieces. Serve with rice.

Part III

Getting Serious About Life
and Turkeys

*T*he women of my generation entered our thirties at a time when psychotherapy—or at least psychobabble—was the rage. Many of us saw shrinks to help us better understand who we were, to come to terms with our pasts, and to contemplate changes in our futures. In therapy we realized that our lives were not the same as our mothers', but we were okay with that. Talking to our therapists taught us to communicate on a deeper level with our girlfriends— about our relationships, our work, and about having children. Women no longer saw themselves as either mothers or wage earners. We felt strong enough to be both and so much more.

Having children was no longer just something that wives did, as in our mothers' generation. Perhaps as a result, those of us who made a conscious decision to do so gave their kids more freedom and allowed them more self-expression than our parents allowed us. We indulged them with the electronic games and computers that didn't exist in our day, and we pushed them to be smarter faster than we had been.

Working and raising children left us little time for ourselves. We gave up aerobics for Mommy-and-Me class, and time we once spent jogging we now spent helping our toddlers dig in the sandbox at the park. We made friends with the women we met there and in our kids' schools, and we socialized as families. Each mom brought a dish—usually on the theme of pasta, salad, and brownies—and shared tips on potty training while the kids played underfoot.

When our children grew older, we went out more often; who had the time or energy to entertain? Besides, a restaurant revolution had started at Chez Panisse in Berkeley and was spreading to parts north, south, and east. In Los Angeles, new restaurants, not recipes, became the hot topic.

The late seventies and eighties were exciting times for people who loved food, and the term "foodie" was born. First, nouvelle cuisine arrived from France, stressing the use of fresh ingredients and simple preparations. Nouvelle cuisine evolved into California cuisine, where "fresh" ingredients meant "from California." A gourmet restaurant was no longer one that served classic French food. Soon, if they didn't serve California cuisine, hip restaurants served Italian. And wherever we ate, we now had hundreds of wines to choose from.

In the nineties tastes broadened. The passion for Italian extended to one for the cuisines of Asia and Latin America—or a fusion of them. Just as film buffs get excited talking about movie directors, foodies began discussing their favorite chefs. Celebrity chefs put their names on as many eateries as they wanted—never mind that they couldn't be in every kitchen at the same time. And a growing number of chefs and other influential forces in the food world were women.

Chapter 17

Shrinking onto a New Path

My mother blossomed after I, and then Sheila, went away to college. Instead of investing more time in golf and bridge, as some of her friends did after their children grew up and left home, she dusted off the violin that had sat in her closet for decades (except for the few years I reluctantly played it in junior high school) and practiced until she was once more its master. She joined an orchestra, formed a string quartet, and rediscovered a talent that had lain dormant since she was twenty. For years afterward, playing the violin was a major source of satisfaction for her and the focus of her social life.

I know I inherited my mother's determination and perseverance. Okay, and her tendency to be controlling. I'd like to think I inherited at least half of her empathy and kindness, and a third of her looks. (The small nose, the long eyelashes, the skinny legs—those I got. The big boobs went to my sisters.)

Like many mothers, mine was critical, but she never criticized me about big things, just small ones. She might say she didn't like a certain lipstick color on me or that I could stand to lose a few pounds. (After I got married, that changed to "You could stand to *gain* a few.") She never criticized me, however, for foolishly compressing two years of college into one and relinquishing a social life because I was determined to hang on to Justin. Okay, later she told me I was crazy to live with Paul without being married to him, but that was not as much a criticism as it was her taking a moral stand. My mother had a strict sense of what was and what wasn't "right."

Most important, though all of her friends' children ended up living in Seattle, close to their mothers, she never once criticized me because I didn't. (I feel guilty about it nonetheless.)

When I was around thirty, my mother had what at first the doctors thought was a mild heart attack. Typical of her, it turned out to be nothing more than a minor gastrointestinal problem. During the week she was forced to stay in bed, however, I flew up to Seattle to take care of her. It was the first time our roles had been reversed, and it made me anxious. I wasn't ready to have my mother dependent on me.

The days I spent with her gave us time for long conversations. In one, I mentioned that when I was growing up, I sometimes wished that she had done something more important with her life than just play golf and bridge. My mother reacted with hurt and anger: Yes, she had been a "mere housewife," not a career woman, but that's what most women did in her day. And besides, what she had accomplished all those years *was* important—she had raised my sisters and me.

I apologized profusely. Still, I was plagued with guilt. By the time I got home, I realized that I had issues with my mother I had never dealt with. Among them: my inability to show anger toward her—or to deal with hers.

Many of my friends were doing it, so I took a bold step: I went into therapy. I was fortunate that I found a psychologist who not only was wise and understanding but also needed a training case to qualify him as a full-fledged psychoanalyst. I was the sister of a schizophrenic and mildly neurotic but not psychotic, so my case qualified. For the next several years I spent an hour a day, four days a week, lying on his couch and free-associating about my past. I only had to pay a pittance for the privilege. As my mother would have said, it wasn't just that I got psychoanalyzed. I got psychoanalyzed *wholesale.*

Therapy gave me the self-confidence to make changes in my life, starting with my career. Teaching was considered an appropriate job for a girl raised to be a housewife, and I had found it safe to deal with teenagers who looked up to me. Furthermore, the fact that I got summers and vacations off had made me feel a bit like I was still a kid in school myself, protected from the real world. Now I was ready to move on.

Therapy also gave me the courage to become a parent. For a girl raised to believe that "mother" went hand in hand with "house-wife," it took me an unusually long time to accept that role.

Though I liked teenagers, I didn't get a warm, fuzzy feeling inside when I saw babies—I never had. I also had unspecific fears about my body. I was the kid who had nearly fainted (and sometimes did) when I went to the doctor's office. Could I put up with monthly medical exams during a pregnancy? Could I accept a new life grow-ing inside my body? I learned that I might not get the chance. After I stopped taking birth control pills so that I could let nature work its ways, I didn't menstruate. The doctor at the fertility clinic con-cluded that I wasn't ovulating.

The news made me want what I might not be able to have. They started me on fertility drugs and told me not to obsess about it, to just carry on with my life. I decided to look for a new job. I figured that since I had spent eleven years editing kids' term papers and Paul's writing, I would make a good editor. But editing *what*?

Our stay in India had whetted our appetites for adventure, and in the years afterward, I accompanied Paul to exotic destinations for documentary films he produced and travel stories he wrote for various magazines. We visited the Dogon tribe in West Africa, where men in masks evocative of faces in a Cubist painting danced on stilts. From there we traveled to Timbuktu, where the food—even the French bread—was shot through with the smooth, round sand grains of the Sahara Desert.

In Casablanca we searched for a café similar to Rick's in the famous movie; we discovered one, along with a taste for Moroccan food. In Liberia, where the food was lamentable, we discovered architectural remnants of the American slaves who had found refuge there before the Civil War. We ate jungle rat in the Amazon Basin, and in Communist Poland, after a dinner of roast duck and sweet-and-sour cabbage, Paul was nearly arrested on the trumped-up charge of changing money on the black market.

In our journeys Paul had realized that when it came to describing the food—a big part of travel writing—I knew and cared much more about the subject than he did. His favorite example was how on a trip to Spain, I kept notes about every variation of gazpacho that we tasted, in search of the best. (I found it at a small café in Seville, James Michener's favorite in his book *Iberia*; the recipe follows.) Paul suggested that I approach *New West,* one of the magazines he wrote for, and propose some ideas for food articles that I might edit.

A spin-off of *New York* magazine, *New West* had in 1976 opened offices in Los Angeles and San Francisco. It was a New Yorker's delusion to think that one magazine could cover the two cities as if they were really one and the same, just in different locations. Anyone who lived in either knew that people in San Francisco care about aesthetics, culture, food, and wine, while those in Los Angeles care mostly about the entertainment industry. Still, *New West* was provocative, entertaining, and trendy—and we were friends with the managing editor and his wife, who was the food editor and restaurant critic.

Frank and Carole Lalli had been brought out to Los Angeles by

Clay Felker, the founder of *New York*, to start *New West*, and we had met them through common friends. Carole knew everything about food and wine, yet she wasn't a food snob. A petite woman with straight brown hair, she wore little makeup and had a nice figure without worrying about what she ate. Furthermore, she was one of those rare women who are so comfortable with themselves, they don't feel jealous or competitive with other women. It was easy to be Carole's friend, and her story of how she became a food writer intrigued me. Like me, Carole fell into the specialty by chance.

Carole grew up in New Jersey in a close-knit Italian-American family. After her father died when she was four years old, her grandparents moved in with them and her grandmother did most of the cooking. Carole described her as a simple woman with dignity and very high standards. She woke up early in the morning and wore a housedress while she did her chores. At 9 A.M., she changed into what she called "clothes for the street"—even though she wasn't going anywhere. "When my grandmother put on clothes for the street," said Carole, "it meant that her house was clean and neat enough for guests to see it."

Carole's grandmother cooked fresh, simple Italian fare, not the heavy, red-sauce-laden dishes served in most Italian-American restaurants in the fifties. Carole remembered that she was especially good with vegetables, particularly what she called an "asparagus raft," three or four fresh asparagus side by side, dipped in egg batter and then lightly fried, almost like tempura. When she was growing up, Carole watched and sometimes helped her grandmother cook. What intrigued her was how she got tastes into a dish, or how adding one ingredient could completely change the flavor.

Carole married Frank soon after she graduated from college, and they moved to New York. Like a lot of women who got married in the late sixties, Carole got what she described as a "vague" job. "I didn't really know what I wanted to do other than that it should have something to do with editing," she recalled. Her first editing jobs were with trade magazines for the rubber and electronic-engineering industries, subjects that didn't exactly fascinate her. She found a creative outlet in cooking. Every time she entertained, she tried something new, dishes that she had never tasted before. She found it intellectually stimulating as well as pleasurable to cook.

A friend who liked Carole's cooking asked if she would cater a dinner party for her. On a whim, Carole did it. The party was so successful that she attracted more catering jobs. Finally, her business became so large that she took in a partner. Carole's catering repertoire included quiche, rare duck breast, Italian *cassata*—all the dishes that were fashionable in the early seventies.

Carole voraciously read cookbooks and restaurant reviews—Gael Greene in *New York* magazine, Craig Claiborne in *The New York Times*. "I remember reading an article where Claiborne described *genoise* as 'surely the king of cakes,'" said Carole. I didn't know what a *genoise* was, but I had to make one."

After Carole and Frank moved to L.A. to launch *New West* for Clay Felker, Felker asked Carole what she would like to do for the magazine. Carole told him she wanted to write about restaurants and food. "Clay laughed and said that every restaurant writer in L.A. was after that job," recalled Carole, "but that he didn't trust any of them. He knew I was honest and that I could write—and that I was a good cook—so he gave me the chance."

Perhaps it was Felker's blind faith in Carole that led her to take a chance on me. I proposed several food-story ideas with the intention of editing them. Carole misinterpreted and thought that I was asking to *write* them, so she gave me an assignment. Paul encouraged me to tackle it. I took a deep breath and plunged in. Carole was pleased with the results.

Over the next few months, I wrote articles about the fish of

California, the difference between Mandarin and Cantonese dim sum, and Egg City, the largest egg ranch in the United States. I particularly enjoyed writing behind-the-scenes stories, for it harked back to when I wrote reports on the life cycle of the salmon in elementary school and I quoted my father, the salmon maven.

My favorite article from that period was entitled "The Life and Death of Your Thanksgiving Turkey." For research, I visited a turkey ranch in Apple Valley, a barren spot in the high desert whose only claim to fame is the Roy Rogers Museum. Paul came along to take the photographs.

The Stoddard Jess Ranch was a small, family-owned facility. Stoddard Jess, a self-described old geezer with loose skin on his neck that made him look a bit like a turkey himself, was our guide. The most memorable fact I learned was that the neck and gizzards you find stuffed inside a turkey come from the turkey two steps ahead of it on the killing line.

With fond memories of the taste tests our animals did on my father's pet-food products when I was growing up, I decided to complement the article with a blind turkey tasting. For that I needed an oven big enough to roast five turkeys at the same time, so I turned to the Café Four Oaks, about as "Thanksgivingy" a restaurant as there was in Los Angeles. A white clapboard building in rustic Beverly Glen Canyon, the Café Four Oaks had a big stone fireplace, a homey kitchen, and a patio shaded by gnarled sycamores, one of the few kinds of trees in L.A. whose leaves turn color and drop in autumn. (They only become a sort of washed-out yellow, but at least they fall.)

I also needed my mother. What was a Thanksgiving turkey without my mother's egg bread stuffing? Besides, I didn't want to undertake this task alone. I wanted my *mommy*. One phone call, and a few days later she was on a plane to L.A., eager for the challenge.

To make the test legitimate, it was important to stuff and roast the turkeys identically. My mother and I bought five turkeys: a

Taste-testing turkeys. Yum.

Stoddard Jess; a kosher; an organic free-range; a fresh Gelson's; and a frozen Butterball with a pop-up thermometer. I helped her make a vat of stuffing—we went through twenty-five loaves of egg bread—then we stuffed each turkey. Unlike me, Mom was a champ at sewing up turkeys, even with greasy fingers. We spent hours getting the turkeys right, and it was perhaps the first time that my mother cooked not to feed her family or friends. Because we did it for my magazine article, it qualified as "work," but we also had fun. Several times my mother shook her head, laughed, and said, "I can't believe I'm stuffing five turkeys!"

Four hours later, having basted them with currant jelly, we brought the five golden brown birds to the table. Among the official "tasters" were foodies and friends—Mary Ann, Irma, and Carole included. I sliced white meat and dark meat from each bird and placed the pieces on numbered plates. Only my mother and I knew which turkey went with which number.

The tasters tasted, made notes, and tasted again. Finally, the ballots were in. First place went to the organic, free-range turkey; the kosher turkey came in second; while the Stoddard Jess bird took the bronze. Not surprisingly, the frozen Butterball with the pop-up thermometer came in last place. I opened several bottles of Cabernet Sauvignon, and we sat down to dinner. The tasters complimented my mother on her egg-bread stuffing, and she beamed. We donated the leftover turkey to a food bank, and the next day my mother flew back to Seattle with a proud story to tell.

A few months later, Frank Lalli left *New West* to become managing editor of the *Los Angeles Herald-Examiner*, the city's second-largest newspaper. Carole went with him to become the *Herald* restaurant critic. I succeeded her as *New West*'s Southern California restaurant critic. (Ruth Reichl was the magazine's restaurant critic in Northern California.)

One of my friends warned me that I'd get fat going out to dinner several times a week for work, but I wasn't worried. Since I'd been married, overeating was no longer the issue for me that it had been on and off in my teens. Besides, I had gone out to dinner with Carole when she was reviewing, and I saw how she did it: she tasted food—*really* tasted it—rather than gulped it down. I could do that, I told myself. I soon discovered that the better food tastes, the less of it you need to satisfy you. That might sound odd, but it's true.

I took my new job seriously: I studied cookbooks and took courses in wine appreciation. I made reservations under fake names and never revealed to restaurateurs who I was or what I was doing. Each time I dined out, I surreptitiously scribbled notes on a pad under the napkin on my lap.

Only one restaurateur figured out who I was and what I was up to: Patrick Terrail, the proprietor of Ma Maison, the Hollywood hot spot where Orson Welles lunched daily at a corner table and Wolfgang Puck became *the* chef to watch. Patrick had a reputation as a haughty Frenchman who parked his Rolls out front and judged women by their handbags. I didn't own a Chanel purse or even a knockoff, so I felt awkward the first few times I dined at Ma Maison. Still, I discovered Patrick's warm and humorous side, and we became friends. Patrick did more than anyone at the time to promote the Los Angeles restaurant scene, starting with the annual waiters' race. Waiters from competing restaurants ran (or I should say speed-walked) while carrying a glass full of wine on a tray. The object was to reach the finish line without losing the glass or half of the wine—not an easy accomplishment, but the endeavor inspired lots of laughs.

For *New West* I wrote reviews of all sorts of restaurants: California, French, Indian, Mexican. One Italian restaurateur was so happy about my review that he sent me enough roses for a Mafia funeral. Another Italian restaurateur was so *un*happy that he threatened to send the Mafia after me. One night, however, when I was reviewing a new Greek restaurant in Venice with Mary Ann and Brad (Arnold Schwarzenegger was seated two tables away, with a blond-bimbo date who didn't take her hand off his thigh the whole evening), I suddenly lost my appetite. Moussaka that minutes before had tasted scrumptious to me now made me sick. Mary Ann guessed what my OB-GYN confirmed the next morning: I was pregnant.

James Michener's Favorite Gazpacho

SERVES 6

The Spanish have about as many variations for this cold summer soup as the Italians do for tiramisù. This one is delicious and a cinch to make in a food processor. In fact, I can't imagine how the Spanish made gazpacho before the food processor was invented. The soup should be thick and almost gritty in texture, and orangy pink in color. Serve it ice cold. It tastes better if you refrigerate it overnight. The condiments add color and taste, and it's fun to choose from them.

FOR THE SOUP

> 8 large ripe tomatoes, coarsely chopped
> 5 large cucumbers, peeled and sliced
> 2 green peppers, seeded and coarsely chopped
> 1 large red onion, peeled and coarsely chopped
> 2 to 3 slices stale French or Italian bread, soaked
>   briefly in water
> ¼ cup olive oil
> ¼ cup red-wine vinegar
> Pinch of sugar
> Salt and pepper to taste

FOR THE CONDIMENTS

> 1 tomato, seeded and finely chopped
> ½ cucumber, peeled and finely chopped
> ½ red onion, finely chopped
> 1 small can sliced black olives
> 4 hard-boiled eggs, chopped

1. Put the soup ingredients into a food processor in batches, so that when you blend it, the liquid doesn't spill over. Transfer the blended soup to a big pot while you process more ingredients.

2. When all the ingredients have been blended, stir the soup in the pot and transfer it back, in batches, to the food processor and blend well again. The soup is finished when everything is puréed and there are no vegetable chunks present. Taste for seasonings—you may need more oil or vinegar, salt or pepper.

3. Refrigerate for several hours or overnight before serving. Put the condiments in separate little dishes, and pass them around so that guests can serve themselves.

Chapter 18

Roller Baby

I regretted having to put my career as a restaurant critic on hold, but until my baby was born, I knew I couldn't assess restaurant food fairly. My taste buds were off-kilter, I couldn't drink wine, and the odor of sautéing garlic or onions—aromas I'd enjoyed as much as Joy perfume in the past—now made my stomach turn. I didn't care that I had to turn the job over to others on the *New West* staff. My fears about a life growing inside me transformed into warm, maternal feelings, and I was excited about the prospect of motherhood. In the meantime, instead of writing about food, I accepted an offer to write a book about roller-skating. I had no passion for the subject, but the experience led to a new friendship that included a mutual interest in cooking and food.

When I was growing up, roller skates were heavy, metal contraptions that you strapped onto your shoes and tightened with a key. (For years I felt guilty about the time I bashed Sheila in the shins with a broom because she wouldn't give me the key when we were roller-skating around our oil-slicked carport.) In the late seventies, thanks to the invention of polyurethane wheels, roller skates were transformed into what looked like Nikes with wheels, and the roller-skate key became obsolete.

In the course of my research for the book *Keep on Rollin': The Complete Guide to Rollerskating in America*, I met several skating fanatics who were trying to invent in-line skates. They couldn't get it right; that would take another fifteen years and start another roller-skating trend. At Venice Beach in the late seventies, however, girls in bikini tops and guys in cutoffs were grooving on roller skates to "Stayin' Alive" by the Bee Gees, and roller rinks became roller discos. And there I was with a yellow pad and Paul's Nikon, taking notes and pictures. I learned more than I ever wanted to know about the fad. When the book was finished, *People* magazine sent a reporter to interview me for a story.

At 5 feet 10 inches, Suzy Kalter Gershman was attractive and slim enough to be a model; in fact, she had done a little modeling when she was younger. She was much too hyper, however, to stand still for a photo shoot, and as Suzy joked, without her superthick glasses she couldn't make it down a fashion runway without falling on her face.

Suzy was bright and funny, and she turned what could have been a boring article—girl who doesn't roller-skate writes roller-skating book—into a quirky, amusing one. Even though I wasn't supposed to roller-skate because I was pregnant, Suzy persuaded me to pose on skates with Darwin, our droopy-eared basset hound (we named him Darwin because he was no Einstein) so that it looked like the dog was pulling me up the street by his leash.

Suzy and I knew many of the same journalists, including Sheila's and my childhood friend, Judy Kessler, who had moved to New York to work at *People*. When Suzy was having trouble getting pregnant, I sent her to my fertility specialist. Sharing the trying-to-get-pregnant ordeal brought us closer. Her son was born a year after my daughter.

In the cozy, dark-wooded Greene and Greene bungalow that she and Mike rented in the Hollywood Hills, Suzy entertained seemingly effortlessly, and her parties always had a theme. One was a black-tie "Tupperware dinner," where guests brought their favorite dish in a Tupperware container. Another was a "barter brunch" where guests wrote down what they were bartering on a slip of paper and gift-wrapped it, then took turns choosing; sometimes a man ended up with a mammogram. Suzy's theory was that theme parties united guests, added to the fun, and gave people something to talk about the next day around the water cooler. "We're all eager for a little pizzazz in our lives," she used to say.

The food at Suzy's parties was simple but always had pizzazz. At brunch, in a time when croissants were as trendy as bagels are today but they only came plain, Suzy served platters of sliced croissants along with myriad fillings, from cream cheese and lox to shrimp and dill to scrambled eggs. At another brunch the featured item was oversized baked potatoes that guests split and heaped with a choice of toppings, from cheese and bacon to Wick Fowler's 2-Alarm Chili made with a mix that Suzy's mother sent her from San Antonio, her hometown.

Suzy admitted that when she was growing up, she wasn't particularly interested in food. She was tall and skinny and was such a picky eater, her mother worried that she'd be stuck with what she called "the Dachau look" for the rest of her life. "I was worried too," she said. "When I was in junior high school, I would have *killed* for breasts."

What Suzy referred to as her "ugly duckling phase" ended when she turned eighteen and got a nose job to go with her newly curvaceous, long-legged body. After she went off to the University of Texas, she returned to San Antonio one vacation craving a Tex-Mex fix. Her mother didn't know how to make Tex-Mex dishes or very many others. She had come from a family in which, according to Suzy, "the women didn't cook because it would ruin their manicures." As a surprise, her mother invited Maggie, a family friend who was ten years older than Suzy, to come over and teach Suzy how to make enchiladas.

Suzy described Maggie as a classic Texas beauty—big and blond, with big hair. "Maggie came from a wealthy Texas oil family and lived in a house full of Dufys and Renoirs," said Suzy, "but when it came to cooking, she wasn't afraid to get her hands dirty—even though she was wearing a ten-karat diamond ring!"

There were no packaged flour tortillas in those days, so Maggie taught Suzy to use corn tortillas fried in a little oil just to soften them. It was also before packaged shredded cheese was sold, so they grated the sharp Cheddar themselves. Next, they added ground beef and chopped onions to a package of Wick Fowler's 2-Alarm Chili mix—a San Antonio favorite. They put the chili along with a strip of cheese and onions down the middle of each tortilla, rolled them up, laid them seam side down in the pan, and poured more chili and cheese on top. Enchiladas were another dish that Suzy served at parties in the late seventies.

Though Suzy and I were not best *best* friends, I admired her and we enjoyed each other. We lost touch after she and Mike moved back east. I wouldn't have imagined that Suzy and I would become much closer several decades later.

Chapter 19

Life After Birth

Going through psychotherapy gave me the courage to change careers and to become a mother. As my daughter's birth drew near, therapy made me reluctant to let my own mother near her.

Today, with the hindsight that comes from age—and having brought up two children—I realize that my anger toward my mother at the time was unwarranted. She had done a better job of raising her kids than most mothers. Perhaps it was just that the more I explored my fears and anxieties about impending motherhood, the more I laid blame for them on her. As a result, though my mother assumed that she would help out when I brought her new grandchild home from the hospital, as her own mother had done when my sisters and I were born, I asked her not to come to L.A. until the baby was a few weeks old.

My mother was hurt—she had waited a long time for her first grandchild—and she didn't understand why I wanted to hire a professional baby nurse when I could have her help for free. I argued that it was important for me to begin my journey as a mother on my own. She didn't push it.

A week before the baby was due and minutes after we returned home from dinner at Canter's Deli, I went into labor; Paul said it must have been the three kosher dill pickles. Julia's birth was painful but exhilarating—surely the most exciting experience that Paul and I had ever had. But when it was time for us to take the baby home, we learned that Olga, the stalwart baby nurse that we had lined up, was stuck caring for a baby that had been born a week late. The baby-nurse agency scrambled around to find a replacement.

Mrs. Johnson turned out to be a skeletal old crone with one forearm so swollen that she looked like a victim of elephantiasis. She didn't smile and she spoke very little. We expected her to ooh and ahh over our magnificent infant. All she did was lie down and rest.

The first night, Julia woke up crying at 4 A.M. Mrs. Johnson had been instructed to bring the baby to our bedroom when she cried so that I could nurse her. Paul and I lay in our bed, listening to Julia wail and waiting for Mrs. Johnson's grand entrance with her. The wail grew to a scream. Finally, Paul hustled to Julia's room and scooped her out of the bassinette. Mrs. Johnson was sprawled in the cot beside it, snoring.

I knew what I had to do. Even though it was the middle of the night, I phoned my mother. "Mommy, I *need* you!" is all I had to say, and she was on the next plane. Mrs. Johnson was gone by 4:30 A.M. At 10 A.M., my mother appeared on our doorstep. She opened her arms and I deposited the bundle known as Julia into them. Mom cried, I cried, Julia cried. Darwin the basset hound wailed.

Over the next ten days, my mother ran our household with a deft hand, most of the time while wearing her nightgown and bathrobe because she was too busy to change. She handled the diapering, the bathing, and the endless laundry. She also did the shopping and the cooking. While Julia napped, my mother made ground-beef casseroles, spaghetti casseroles, tuna casseroles, and several variations of baked chicken. I even agreed to let her make liver—she argued that since I was nursing, I needed the iron. It wasn't half bad, in fact, when doused with ketchup. Whatever food we didn't eat, she stowed in the freezer.

Who has more hair?
Grandma or Julia?

My mother also handled our basset hound problem. Darwin was cute and lovable, but his personality combined stubbornness and stupidity with a bit of the clown tossed in. We had treated him like our baby, showered him with love and attention—until the day we brought Julia home from the hospital. Darwin quickly figured out that he'd been reduced to the status of a dog. All basset hounds look depressed; now Darwin really *was* depressed. He refused to eat, and we worried that he would starve himself to death.

It was my mother who came up with a solution. She got down on the kitchen floor where Darwin lay, his tongue lolling out of his slobbery mouth, his eyes reduced to slits, and offered him food out of her hand. Not dog food, but the ground beef from one of her casseroles. Darwin took a tentative bite, then another. He was cured—as long as he could eat out of my mother's hand. Now we worried that she'd never be able to leave him and go home. Darwin, however, soon proved the theory that hound dogs live through their noses. He discovered the olfactory pleasures of Julia's diaper pail and quickly returned to his sloppy, stubborn, but lovable self.

Throughout the weeklong blur of night and day that my mother helped with the baby, I began to understand and appreciate her in a new way. It wasn't just that she knew by instinct the right way to diaper, bathe, and rock the baby, and that she kept everyone in the house well fed. She beamed with joy every time she laid eyes on Julia—she couldn't get enough of her little granddaughter. I wondered if she had showered me with love like that when I was a baby. The one thing I knew for sure was that it thrilled me to share the pleasures of motherhood with my own mother. The angry feelings I had toward her dissipated like steam from the humidifier in the baby's room.

Shortly after Julia was born, I resumed writing restaurant reviews and food articles for *New West*. In addition, I was working with Paul on various screenplays. My roller-skating book had inspired us to write one about a roller disco. When we sold it, it led to other screenwriting assignments and even a novel based on a movie script we were writing for MGM. I needed help taking care of the baby. The truth? Even if I had not been working, I couldn't run a household, write, be a mom, walk a basset hound, and still have some semblance of a life without someone in addition to my husband lending a hand.

Thus, through a friend, I found Oralia, a quiet, middle-aged Guatemalan woman. While I worked in my home office, Oralia held Julia, played with her, fed her. The minute Julia lay down to nap, Oralia cleaned the house, did the laundry, made the beds. She even did windows. The only task she wouldn't do was walk Darwin.

When Oralia announced that she was returning to Guatemala, I panicked. She assured me that she had a replacement—her younger sister, Lily, who was arriving in the States the following week. *Illegally*. Oralia had saved up two hundred dollars for a down payment to the "coyotes" who were smuggling Lily into the country, but she didn't have enough cash for the final payment upon delivery. I chipped in the three hundred dollars myself.

I found it hard to sleep the night that Lily was due. The hot, dry Santa Ana winds blowing in from the desert burned my throat and rattled the leaves of the eucalyptus trees that tower over our house. I was awake when a truck rumbled up our street and stopped at our door. Fears I had had that the coyotes were dangerous men vanished when in the predawn twilight, I saw that they were humble and frightened. I handed them the cash and thanked them for delivering Lily safely. A woman who looked like a younger version of Oralia jumped out of the truck and broke into a grin that revealed a gold front tooth. When Lily embraced her sister, my eyes filled with tears, as did Paul's. We welcomed Lily to our country—and to our home.

Oralia had been a loving caregiver to Julia, but she was shy and a little quiet. In contrast, Lily had an easy laugh and never tired of playing with the baby. When Oralia left, I knew that Julia was in good hands.

Lily lived with us from Mondays through Fridays until Julia started kindergarten. During that time, she learned to speak English and traveled with us to New York, Boston, and Washington, D.C. Lily was devoted to Julia and easy to live with, and we became friends. Working in our house five days a week, she knew everything about how our family interacted. When she helped me in the kitchen, she revealed bits and pieces about her own family back in Guatemala—especially about her mother-in-law, Amalia, who had taught her how to cook. Lily regularly made one of Amalia's specialties, a spaghetti sauce that got its zest from tomatillos.

L ily was seventeen when she got married, and her husband, Guillermo, was afraid to leave her at home alone while he was at work, so every day, he dropped her off at his mother's. "Amalia

Veronica was thirty-seven and very beautiful, with fair skin and light brown hair," Lily recalled. "She had nine children, and they were all as good-looking as she was—especially Guillermo." Amalia loved Lily like she was one of her own. "When Guillermo tried to boss me around, she'd shake her finger at him and tell him she wouldn't allow it."

Amalia showed Lily how to make soup from beef bones, chayote squash, corn, and yucca; and chicken *jocon* with cilantro, green onions, and green peppers—"You just throw in everything green," explained Lily. On Christmas they

Julia loves Lily.

made chicken and pork tamales. Every day they made tortillas from scratch. "There were always at least ten people at the table for dinner. It was very important to Amalia that the whole family sit down and eat together."

Lily revealed some of the tricks that Amalia had taught her for making the spaghetti sauce: Use little tomatillos instead of big ones—they have more flavor—and brown the ground beef over high heat, not low, so that it won't be watery. She always spooned some of the mixture onto the heel of her palm and tasted it before adding salt and sprinkling on fresh oregano leaves. Lily used a lot more salt than I would have. "The salt cuts the sourness of the tomatillos," she explained. "The fresh oregano makes the flavors sing." Indeed, when I tasted Lily's sauce, it had a tang almost like lemon, and it was not at all salty. It was *deliciosa*.

Amalia taught Lily to use the salsa part of the recipe (tomatoes, tomatillos, garlic, and onions) on *carne asada* and on top of meat-balls as well as on spaghetti. "Amalia was such a great woman." Lily said. "I was very sad when she died from cancer; she was only forty-two. She gave me the attention my own mother never gave me. I loved her more than I loved my mom."

Twenty-one years after Lily showed up on our doorstep in the dead of night, she is still essential to the smooth running of our household. She comes twice a week for a couple of hours—our house is one of several that she tends each week. Lily is in her fifties now. Her gold tooth has long been capped, and she needs to wear glasses when she chops onions, but she has the same trim figure as when she was twenty-eight. If anything, she's in better shape because she is a dedicated runner. She even ran in the Los Angeles Marathon.

Lily has become a U.S. citizen, and she has brought three sons, one daughter, three nieces, and four nephews to live in Los Angeles with her; all have jobs and are prospering. "When I told my night-school class how I came to the U.S. and what I've done since I've been here, they applauded," she proudly told me. "The teacher said to me, 'Lily, this country needs more people like you!' "

Lily's Spaghetti Sauce

SERVES 4 TO 6

Lily says that small tomatillos deliver more flavor than large ones, and that adding salt cuts their sourness. Fresh oregano is far more flavor-ful than dried. My son, Adam, loves this dish and calls it Guatemalan spaghetti sauce.

1 large onion, finely chopped
3 cloves garlic, finely chopped
2 teaspoons corn or olive oil

1 pound lean ground beef
4 to 5 medium tomatoes, finely chopped
6 small tomatillos, finely chopped
1 teaspoon salt, or more to taste
10 fresh oregano leaves, or 1 teaspoon dried
Pepper to taste
1 pound spaghetti

1. In a large heavy frying pan over medium heat, sauté the onion and garlic in the oil until soft, about 10 minutes, stirring frequently.

2. Turn the heat up to high, add the meat, and sauté, stirring constantly, for another 10 minutes, until the meat is cooked. Add the chopped tomatoes, the tomatillos, and the salt. Mix well and cook for 5 more minutes, stirring often.

3. Reduce the heat to low, add the oregano leaves, and simmer, uncovered, for 20 to 30 minutes, stirring occasionally. Adjust the seasonings.

4. Cook the spaghetti according to package directions. Drain but do not rinse. Mix the pasta with the sauce, or serve it in individual bowls, with the sauce on top.

Chapter 20

Pheasant Follies

In the early eighties, I became the restaurant critic for the *Los Angeles Herald-Examiner*. Once again I had Carole Lalli to thank. She and Frank moved back to New York, and Carole recommended that I succeed her in the job. Until the *Herald*'s unfortunate demise near the end of the decade, I wrote a weekly review based on one or two anonymous restaurant visits, plus a gossipy "what's new" restaurant column. Among my favorite coconspirators on the restaurant-reviewing circuit were Susan and Al.

Al was a bright and witty UCLA English professor and a psychoanalyst. His wife, Susan, was . . . well, Susan was a knockout. What you noticed first about her was her Jane Russell figure and classic, high-cheekboned beauty. She had flawless ivory skin that bespoke her Irish heritage, and straight, dark brown hair that came just below her chin. Her hair often fell across one eye and she'd brush it away, like a sultry woman of mystery in a forties film noir.

Because Susan and I both had young daughters, we had more in common than just our love of food. When the two girls were toddlers, they played together often—Julia the darling blond, Katy the cute brunette. Almost every sunny weekend for several years, Susan and I met at the UCLA pool and took turns swimming laps and looking after the girls. Every few weeks our families got together for dinner, so Susan and I cooked together often.

I have always been the type of cook who prefers preparing dishes in advance. Susan, on the other hand, was notoriously late for just about everything and always ended up cooking after the guests arrived. I didn't mind, though, as it gave us time alone in the kitchen while I helped her. Besides, she always tried new, sophisticated recipes that intrigued me.

Susan was one of the few women I knew who became a good cook not because she took after her mother. According to Susan, she became interested in cooking precisely because her mother was such a *bad* cook.

"By the time I was six, I realized that my mother's cooking was blah," Susan recalled. "I remember coming home from summer camp—where the food actually had more flavor than the food at home—and deciding that from now on, I wanted to do the cooking in our family. Since my mother was working, she was happy to have me help her in the kitchen."

Susan cooked throughout high school, but in college, at the University of California–Santa Cruz, her confidence was undermined by a boyfriend. He insisted that she use only organic ingredients, which were not readily accessible at the time, and it severely limited her menu options. Soon he began criticizing her cooking and did most of it himself. "I had always attached a certain significance to making a good dinner," said Susan. "Now, when I cooked, I felt rattled that I'd ruin everything. One night the swordfish turned out like leather."

Susan soon left the guy for Al; they moved to Provence for a year, where Al worked on a novel. In France she bought an armful of French cookbooks and spent hours mastering classics like cassoulet, coq au vin, and beef Bourguignonne. The highlight of Susan's week was going to the open-air market, where she bought fruits, vegetables, and buttery Bries and pungent chèvres. "Once the mushroom vendor sold me some wild mushrooms and told me not to wash or wipe them, but just to throw them in a pan with butter for a few seconds," she recalled. "I did what he said—and a bunch of worms crawled out of the mushrooms! I didn't know if it was a mistake, whether the worms were part of the dish, or if the mushroom vendor was just trying to put one over on an American!"

By the time Susan and Al returned to Los Angeles, Susan was an excellent—and self-confident—cook. A few years later, when Al was up for tenure at UCLA, he invited some influential members of his department over for dinner, along with Paul and me. Susan planned an ambitious menu, and I volunteered to help her prepare it.

The starter was a mushroom salad—no worms—and the entrée was pheasant. Susan had bought a brace from the painter who was working on their house at the time and raised pheasants for restaurants as a sideline. A few days before the dinner party, she read in an English cookbook that to tenderize pheasants for cooking, you hang them by the necks in a cool room until the skin is soft. But these were not wild pheasants, like those sold in England, and Susan's house, like most in Los Angeles, did not have a cool room. She hung the pheasants by ropes from the lattice railing of her out-'door deck. That night the hot, dry Santa Ana winds came whipping in off the desert and sped up the tenderizing process. The next morning Susan discovered the ropes dangling in the breeze, the headless pheasants slumped on the hillside below the deck; the ropes had cut right through their quickly softened necks. Susan stashed the birds in the fridge until the evening of the party.

The pheasant recipe called for browning the birds in a pan

before roasting them in the oven. That night, when Susan began the process—the party had already started, but as I mentioned, she was always late—she couldn't get them browned. "They just sat there in the pan, pink and naked," she recalled. Susan and I didn't know what to do, and the guests were getting hungry—and drunk. The tipsy wife of a senior professor joined us in the kitchen and came up with a plan: She doused the pheasants in Jack Daniel's and lit a match. Flames exploded—browning the birds to a point just short of burnt—and we were able to go on with dinner. The mushroom salad was delectable—the shiitakes and chanterelles were complemented by an earthy walnut-oil vinaigrette—but the pheasants tasted like Jack Daniel's. The guests didn't seem to mind. A few months later, Al got tenure.

Chapter 21

The Junior Cook
and Critic

From the time my daughter, Julia, was old enough to walk, she enjoyed helping me cook, and she developed a talent for baking. She sculpted little animals with leftover piecrust dough on Thanksgiving, and beginning on her second birthday, she decorated her own birthday cakes. After Adam was born, when Julia was five, she decorated his birthday cakes too. Adam was her sous chef, content to lick the bowl. Each year on their birthdays, I baked a cake-mix sheet cake and Julia slathered it with canned frosting. On top, she created designs and figures—a bear for her, a G.I. Joe for Adam—using tubes of colored frosting made of artery-clogging hydrogenated oil, along with Jelly Bellies, candy corn, gumdrops, and M&Ms (one for the cake, one for her mouth). One shelf of my kitchen cabinet is still sticky from the cake-decorating supplies and candy that I stored there.

Because she was a budding cook, I took Julia to a cooking demonstration given by Julia Child at Ma Cuisine, the culinary school attached to Ma Maison. She sat on my lap, mesmerized, and watched as the icon of American cooking whipped up a soufflé with her famous whisk, while at the same time tossing out cooking tips and down-to-earth chatter. When she cracked an egg on the side of the mixing bowl and it spilled onto the floor, the great master just chuckled. "Just like you do, Mommy," Julia whispered to me.

Julia not only liked to cook with me; she enjoyed getting dressed up and going on restaurant-reviewing expeditions. Having a child at the table proved to be a good cover for my secretive mission. Julia drew

Adam was Julia's sous chef.

pictures in a notebook while we waited to be served and in between courses. When I wanted to note something for my review, I jotted it down in her notebook. If a restaurateur saw me scribbling away, no doubt he thought, "Thank God—that mom is keeping the kid from making a scene."

Sometimes Julia's insights about the food were helpful. She became a connoisseur of capellini with fresh tomatoes and basil— she liked the idea of eating *angel hair*—and she would try just about any food. In fact, she said that she wished someone would go to Mars and come back with something delicious that didn't exist on Earth so she could taste it. The only dishes that Julia would not touch were what she called "cute food." These included rabbit, duck, vension, and veal, along with small birds such as quail. Chickens, turkeys, fish, and cows, in Julia's estimation, were not cute.

At the end of 1983, the L.A. restaurant with the best vibe in town was Spago. Wolfgang Puck had left Ma Maison a few years before to open the eatery to great fanfare, and with its movie-star-filled dining room overlooking Sunset Strip and Puck's ground-breaking food, the place lived up to the hype. Dining at Spago, you felt as if you were at the center of the Hollywood universe.

Puck and his chefs worked in full view of the diners in an open kitchen that lent the restaurant a homey, informal feel and gave Wolfgang the chance to meet and greet his customers. His genuinely warm, cheerful, easygoing personality contributed to Spago's sky-rocketing success. So did the hospitality, design sense, and flair of Barbara Lazaroff, his glamorous girlfriend, partner, and future wife.

A former actress who was on her way to medical school when she met Wolfgang, Barbara had dramatically long jet-black hair and wore eye-catching, avant-garde gowns. She designed Spago and just about every restaurant they opened together afterward. The look she created for Spago was the epitome of California casual-chic: white walls, blond wood, and exposed-beam ceilings. It was the little touches of Barbara's that created the pizzazz: sumptuous floral arrangements, provocative modern art, and colorful tile work swirling around the wood-burning oven.

Paul and I had spent the previous New Year's Eve at Spago with friends and stayed well past midnight. But this year I knew I'd be ready for bed by ten. I was eight months pregnant with Adam, and I felt like an elephant. During this pregnancy I didn't suffer from morning sickness and the aversion to food that had prevented me from reviewing restaurants when I was carrying Julia. This time, for nine months, I was ravenous. Thanks to such quirky cravings as munching on a whole mozzarella cheese as if it were an apple and devouring just the insides of entire loaves of sourdough bread, I gained fifty pounds, twenty more than I had gained when I was pregnant with Julia.

I made reservations for an early New Year's Eve dinner at Spago with Beth and John, whose daughter, Brooke, was Julia's best friend. Neither child had been to Spago, and we hoped they would behave well—because neither Beth nor I could get a baby-sitter. Julia wore a rose taffeta dress with a white lace collar, and I combed her long blond hair and made two little topknots on the sides with barrettes.

She looked like a demure little princess, and she acted like one.

That night at Spago Julia and Brooke created a secret hideout under our table, and after they finished eating their pizza, they played there while the adults enjoyed dinner. It was also the night that Julia became enchanted with Barbara Lazaroff. The feeling was mutual, and their friendship has lasted to this day. From then on until Julia graduated from high school, we took her to Spago every year on her birthday. Barbara always decorated the table, arranged for a cake, and came by to congratulate Julia. If she was out of town, she called while we

Julia gets the star treatment at Spago.

were at the restaurant to send Julia her best wishes. Paul and I joked that if we wanted good service at Spago, we had to go with Julia.

What's the obvious question for the wife of one of the country's most famous chefs? *"So, Barbara, have you ever cooked for Wolfgang?"*

"Once," she said. "The morning after the first night Wolf slept over. I whipped up omelets—I loved cooking eggs—and he looked at his and wrinkled his nose. 'It stinks,' he said. It turns out Wolf hates the smell of frying eggs." Barbara is not easily intimidated, and she wasn't that morning. "I told him if he didn't like his omelet, he could flush it, but I was eating mine. So I ate and Wolfgang flushed!"

In fact, Barbara was an accomplished amateur cook. Just six months earlier, she'd thrown a bash for two hundred people on her twenty-fifth birthday. She made all the food herself, from lasagna to sushi. Barbara had learned to cook various ethnic foods from friends when she was a theater-arts student at NYU. On Friday nights they gathered at one apartment and everyone took turns bringing food and cooking. "In one semester, we went all around the world with those dishes," she said.

Barbara credits her mother, Ellie, for the pleasure she takes in nurturing her family and friends with food. The family lived in the Bronx, and her mother worked as a bookkeeper at night, but every morning when Barbara and her brothers woke up, Ellie had break-fast on the table, and before she left for her job in the evening, she prepared dinner. Some nights the main dish was skirt steak; other nights it was salmon croquettes or meat loaf. Barbara said that the food was nothing exciting because her mother was always on a bud-get but that she arranged everything to look nice on the plate. And when she made chocolate pudding, Barbara and her brothers fought over who got to lick the pot and the spoon. Ellie still remem-bers those occasions: "I always left a little extra in the pot for them," she said. "They'd get covered in chocolate pudding from their chins to the tips of their noses."

Barbara's most pungent memories of childhood relate to food. Every Sunday the family went to dinner at her grandmother's house. Her grandmother didn't use much seasoning in her food, but Barbara loved it anyway. "I can still taste her vegetable barley soup, and I can still smell the distinctive smell of her kitchen," recalled Barbara. "It's the delicious shared memories of food that become ingrained in us."

Barbara so enjoyed sharing holiday meals with family and friends when she was growing up that she introduced a tradition of holding a seder at Spago on the second night of Passover. Good customers were invited, the proceeds went to charity, and everyone joked that even though Wolfgang wasn't Jewish, he made the best matzoh balls in town. Paul and I took Julia to the Spago seder when she was six. She so loved Wolfgang's crisp homemade matzoh, she got the recipe and has been making it for our family Passovers ever since.

Among Barbara and Wolfgang's Spago "family" at the seder were Mark Peel and Nancy Silverton, the restaurant's first chef and pastry chef. "Nancy made such great chocolate cake," recalled Barbara, "that I'd take the discarded edges and roll them into little balls and pop them into my mouth."

Barbara convinced Nancy to put cheesecake on the Spago dessert menu. "Nancy didn't think cheesecake was sophisticated enough, so for months she resisted. I followed her around the restaurant, begging. *'Fuzzy head,'* I called her. *'Pleeese* make cheesecake.' Finally she did, only Nancy would never make anything plain. She added a layer of apple filling to her cheesecake. It was delicious."

Nancy and Mark eventually got married and moved on to open their own restaurant, Campanile; in 2001, it won the coveted James Beard "Outstanding Restaurant" award. Their adjoining La Brea Bakery expanded into a multimillion-dollar business. Today, you find crusty La Brea Bakery baguettes and dense walnut-raisin loaves in upscale restaurants and grocery stores throughout the country. The bakery was the idea of a woman who had no interest in cooking until she was in college.

"When I was in high school, my specialties were fried bologna and sautéed canned potatoes with paprika," Nancy recalled, "and I resented my mother for making experimental dishes like stuffed grape leaves and beef Bourguignonne. 'Why can't you make normal food like other mothers?' I used to complain."

At Sonoma State University, Nancy took one look at a cute guy who was cooking for the vegetarians in her dorm and volunteered to help him. "I lied and said I was a vegetarian and a great cook, so he hired me," she said. "I ran out and bought *Cooking Creatively with Natural Foods* and read it from cover to cover. Pretty soon I was making breakfast, lunch, and dinner at the dorms." Nancy admitted that she didn't last long as a vegetarian but that she "got the guy." (Not Mark; she didn't meet him until later.)

After college, Nancy apprenticed in restaurants in Northern California and then went to the Cordon Bleu cooking school in London. Eventually she ended up at Michael's in Santa Monica, at the time the most influential California-cuisine restaurant south of Chez Panisse. The only job open was as the computer operator, a job she not only hated but, in her words, was "lousy" at. When an assistant pastry-chef position opened up, she took it. "At Cordon Bleu, they had taught us that in pastry making, every step and every ingredient must be exact," she explained. "I wasn't very good at

Barbara and Nancy make chocolate bags—and a mess—on a TV show.

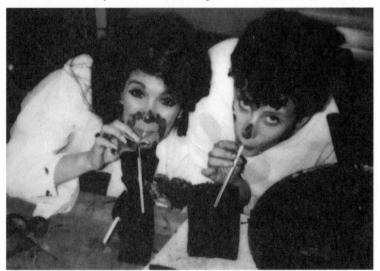

'exact,' so I didn't find pastrymaking fun. But Jimmy Brinkley, the head pastry chef at Michael's, was a kooky genius; he taught me that there is plenty of room for creativity in desserts."

Michael McCarty, the owner of Michael's, spotted Nancy's talent and sent her to study at Lenotre, the leading pastry maker in France. When she returned six months later, she got a call from Mark, who had been a chef at Michael's earlier. Mark wanted her to join him at the new restaurant Wolfgang Puck was about to open. "I was afraid to leave Michael's—it was the hottest place in town," admitted Nancy, "and Wolfgang . . . well, this is before Wolfgang was *Wolfgang*. My mom talked me into taking a chance."

After she made her mark at Spago, Nancy found that one of the benefits of becoming a "celebrity" chef was that she was invited to participate in culinary fund-raising events around the country. That's where she made friends with other female chefs. "We would all go out for drinks and get a little rowdy, but we caught up, exchanged ideas about cooking—and gossiped," said Nancy. "Plus it felt good when we were all working together to support an important cause, like SOS (Share Our Strength) or Meals on Wheels."

In the course of getting together at charity events, Nancy and her female-chef pals had an opportunity to philosophize about cooking. They concluded that there is an essential difference between what they call "girl food" and "guy food." "Men cook to impress, while women cook to please," Nancy explained. "In other words, guys put lots of ingredients in their dishes—they complicate things—while women tend to keep it simple." Sometimes the male chefs teased Nancy and the other female chefs that their food was too touchy-feely. "I think it's just more natural for women to cook simply—it's a girl thing."

Nancy found that the male and female chefs differed in their work ethic at the fund-raisers, too. "When the guys were finished with what they had to prepare for the meal, they were outta there," she said. "When one of the women was finished, she'd go around to the other chefs and ask if she could help out."

One time Nancy flew to Miami for a charity food event, and Barbara Lazaroff tagged along to surprise their friend Maida Heatter, the famous dessert-cookbook writer who is now more than eighty years old. Nancy and Barbara had to share a bed, and Barbara recalled that the experience was like a kids' sleepover: "We stayed up practically all night eating and talking. Maida was big on snacks; she kept bringing out cookies and ice cream. At five A.M. she walked in and said, 'You've got to try this new cake I made!' For breakfast, she whipped up a chocolate soufflé."

Over the years since Spago opened, Barbara has found that the greatest satisfaction of being in the restaurant business is sharing important moments in the lives of the customers: "I've come to know families who celebrate birthdays and anniversaries at Spago. I have a slew of goddaughters, like Julia, who grew up in the restaurant. They will always remember the events they celebrated at Spago and what they ate. I've been thrilled to be a part of that."

Wolfgang's Matzoh

MAKES 4 LARGE MATZOH

The secret to making the matzoh crackers crisp is to roll them out as thin as possible. You will need to add more flour while you're kneading the dough. Brush it off once you've transferred the dough to the baking sheet. Seasoned with salt or bits of garlic or onion, they become crackers good for every day, not just Passover. They don't keep their crispness long, however, so eat them while they're fresh.

2 cups flour
¼ cup water
Kosher or sea-salt crystals (optional)
Chopped onions or chopped garlic (optional)

1. Preheat the oven to 450°F. In a bowl, mix the flour and water. If it is too sticky to work with, add more flour.

2. Turn the dough out onto a floured board, and knead for 5 minutes or so. You may need to add more flour to make kneading easier. Divide the dough into four balls. Roll out each ball, one at a time, until the matzoh is as thin as you can get it. Sprinkle the matzoh with any optional ingredients.

3. Transfer to ungreased or parchment-covered baking sheets, punch all over with a fork, and bake for 10 minutes, or until the matzoh are crisp but barely brown.

Chapter 22

The Ultimate Foodie

I bonded with Willette Klausner over truffles. Not chocolate truffles, but fresh, white truffles from Italy that exude a musky aroma and cost up to sixteen hundred dollars a pound for the few months they are available each fall. A stunning black ex-model turned high-powered marketing executive at Universal Studios and today a theatrical producer, Willette was seated next to me during an annual truffle dinner in the eighties at La Toque, a charming California-French restaurant on Sunset Strip. Ken Frank, the young chef-owner, a tall, lanky guy with piercing blue eyes and a formidable culinary talent, was crazy about truffles. He served an appetizer napoleon with truffles, fettuccine with truffles, a veal chop with truffles—and even truffle ice cream, which tasted a hundred times better than it sounds. I was invited to the dinner as a member of the press, but guests like Willette and her husband, Manny, a brilliant and lively white lawyer who is a leader in Libertarian politics, paid over two hundred dollars each for the privilege.

To this day, Willette and Manny think nothing of dropping hundreds of dollars on dinner if the food is stellar. Dining in great restaurants is not just their hobby but also their passion. They eat out twice a day, count the most important chefs in the world among their dearest friends, and are investors in La Toque and a half-dozen other restaurants including Campanile. At least once a year Willette and Manny make a pilgrimage to the great restaurants of France and sometimes of Italy, Hong Kong, and Bangkok.

When I was reviewing restaurants for the *Los Angeles Herald-Examiner,* I'd often walk into a new restaurant that I thought I was the first to discover and find Willette and Manny sitting there. The term "foodie" was invented for people like them. Ardison Phillips, the owner of the now-defunct Studio Grill in Hollywood and a pioneer in eclectic cooking, even named a salad after them: The Klausner Salad contained lettuce, foie gras, and a vinaigrette made with Sauternes.

Recently I met Willette for lunch at Campanile. Even though she's well into middle age, Willette still turned heads when she walked into the sunlit room. Statuesque, she wears her hair in a short Afro and has a smile that takes over her whole face. She was wearing a fashionable Thai-print pants outfit that looked vaguely African. Her wooden necklace and earrings looked African too, but she explained they were from her "Danish phase"—the year she accompanied Manny to Denmark when he was on a Fulbright fellowship and she ended up becoming one of the country's leading fashion models.

I complimented Willette on how chic she looked, and she laughed. "I was skinny when I was younger, but I put on weight after I hit my fifties. I don't care; I always hated being skinny! Besides, with all the money I've spent on dining in great restaurants and drinking great wine over the past thirty-something years, I have the most expensive body in the world!"

Willette stays fit by walking for an hour every morning and skipping dessert—"except for Campanile's strawberry-rhubarb cobbler." She asked the waiter if it was on the menu today. When he said no, she breathed a sigh of relief: "Good. I won't be tempted." Willette starts every day with the same breakfast: a smoothie made with coffee yogurt, a banana, a few coffee beans, and a touch of prune juice. "Yes, prune juice," she said. "I bet you didn't know that prune juice is one of the ingredients in Dr Pepper."

Willette traces her passion for food back to her childhood. Her father, Bill Murphy, was the busiest caterer in Santa Barbara, and he always served his family whatever he was serving his clients, whether it was lobster Newburg, filet mignon, or rack of lamb. Willette's father did the cooking, and she and her sisters did the dishes. "But we inherited his genes for loving food," she said. "You either inherit that love or you don't."

When Willette moved to Los Angeles to attend UCLA, she started cooking on her own. "At first, all I wanted to eat was junk food—whatever my dad had *not* fed me when I was growing up," she explained. She shared an apartment with three other women, and they took turns cooking dinner. Willette's specialty was frozen tacos with grated orange cheese and chopped tomatoes. "My roommates got sick of them!"

Willette met Manny at UCLA, where they were active in student government, but they didn't hook up on a permanent basis until later, when they both lived in New York. They got married and saved up their money so that they could go to Europe. Once they got there, they went to one two- or three-star restaurant a day. "In the early seventies, tourists wore jeans into the old classic restaurants, but I always tried to look chic," recalled Willette, who wore a designer suit and a big hat to Lasserre, one of the most famous restaurants in Paris. "After we had a fabulous lunch with many courses and many wines, we were told the owner wished to speak to us. I was worried he was going to kick us out! Instead, an elegant elderly gentleman came over and apologized for not speaking English. Can you imagine a *Frenchman* apologizing for not speaking English?!"

Through an interpreter, the restaurateur thanked Willette for "gracing his restaurant" and invited her and Manny to return anytime; he promised to give them the best table in the house. "That was a pivotal moment for me," said Willette. "I realized that it doesn't matter who you are. If you look fashionable and you come prepared to eat, even the snobbiest French restaurant will welcome you."

Willette's best girlfriends are women who love to eat as much as she does. One is Gay, who does theatrical public relations and some producing. "Gay and I never just go eat; we always *dine*," said Willette. "But the thing I like about Gay is that she's just as happy going to In-n-Out Burger with me as she is going to Patina."

Another of Willette's friends is one of her producing partners. "When I first met Brenda, I didn't realize she could eat," said Willette. (To Willette the word *eat* means not just to partake of food, but to savor it with passion.) Brenda didn't know a lot about good food and wine, but she was open to trying new restaurants and she wanted to taste everything. "Not just in gourmet restaurants. We love junk food as long as it's *good* junk food. And when it comes to dieting, Brenda doesn't even go there!"

Willette's pet peeve is women who don't like to eat. One time she was asked to arrange a dinner for a businesswomen's group, so she planned an elaborate meal—several courses and wines—at Citrus, a glamorous (but now defunct) Los Angeles restaurant. She was annoyed when her colleagues worried that it would cost too much, take too much time—and make everyone fat. She convinced them that if they were going to celebrate, they should dine leisurely and on the best food and wine. "Of course, once the dinner was over," she said, "the women had such a good time, they all thanked me."

Willette revealed that she believes she could never be good friends with a woman who didn't like to eat as much as she does. "Besides," she added, "I've found that people who love to eat are more open to other people and to new experiences. They are less uptight and have better senses of humor. Those are *my* kind of people!"

Willette's Breakfast Smoothie

SERVES 1

This perky pick-me-up can be made with a frozen banana, for a consistency more like ice cream.

> 1 cup coffee yogurt
> 1 banana
> 1 teaspoon prune juice
> 5 to 6 coffee beans

Put all the ingredients in a blender or food processor, and mix until all the beans are pulverized and the liquid is smooth and creamy.

Chapter 23

Blood and Tomatoes

During the eighties and early nineties, in addition to writing about food, I worked with Paul writing screenplays. Some of the scripts that we wrote together were made into movies, but we were always worrying about what our next job would be, and there was lots of competition. As we got older, it didn't help that in Hollywood, youth is valued over experience.

Mary Ann had become Brad's screenwriting partner too, and their career was as much of a roller-coaster ride as ours. On the one hand, our similar career paths meant that Mary Ann and I had more in common than before; we compared notes on how working with one's husband was sometimes satisfying and often stressful. On the other hand, though we never discussed it, there was a greater edge of competition between Mary Ann and me than when it had just been our spouses—not us—who were in the film biz.

To our credit, Mary Ann and I managed to prevent a rivalry from destroying our friendship. We didn't see each other socially as often as we had when we were young marrieds—we were both busy and

I had two little kids—but she and Brad came along on restaurant-reviewing dinners, and every summer our family spent several Sunday afternoons at Mary Ann and Brad's, enjoying the pool. I envied Mary Ann because her house had a big-enough backyard for a swimming pool; they had built one on the site of the bomb shelter left by the previous owners. After a day in the sun, Brad would throw steaks and chicken on the barbecue, and Mary Ann and I would head into the kitchen to prepare the salad and baked potatoes that went with them. It was a time to catch up and gossip, and to complain about work. I got to know Mary Ann's kitchen as well as my own.

One day in July I invited Mary Ann and Brad to dinner along with Barbara, a film-development executive—in Hollywood parlance, a "D girl." Paul and I were either writing a screenplay for Barbara or hoping to—the distinction blurs after so many years. Since I was never very good at barbecuing—my steaks and chicken always tasted more like lighter fluid than smoke—I decided to make a summery pasta: penne with chopped fresh tomatoes, fresh basil, and plenty of garlic, plus capers, chopped olives, a touch of olive oil, and chunks of fresh mozzarella cheese. The dish should be served at room temperature, not piping hot, but the previous time I'd made it, because I worried that the heady raw garlic would overwhelm the other flavors, I heated the dish on the stove at the last minute. As a result, the mozzarella cheese melted and turned the pasta into a gummy mess. I was determined not to make the same mistake this time.

Julia was around ten years old at the time, and whenever I invited guests to dinner she helped me cook. Her specialties were bread and dessert. A relatively easy bread for her to make—and for me to clean up after—was Italian focaccia; she topped it with everything from fresh rosemary and kosher salt to caramelized onions.

I put on a CD—*La Bohème* was a favorite—and while I chopped garlic and tomatoes for the pasta, Julia set the focaccia dough aside to rise and began beating egg whites for a lemon meringue pie. She was fascinated by the transformation of gooey, clear egg whites into stiff, snowy peaks. While we worked, she filled me in on the ups and downs of her friendships, what was going on at school, and her dreams of being a doctor or a lawyer or a reporter someday. Today, Julia says she treasured our times in the kitchen because she could have me all to herself, without her little brother underfoot. On this particular afternoon, however, Paul was too busy to look after five-year-old Adam, so I insisted that he play in the kitchen where I could keep an eye on him. I had turned a bottom drawer into a "toy chest" for such situations, replacing dishtowels with plastic G.I. Joe figures.

As I chopped tomatoes, with a barrage of "*Yeeeeoooo, Kabooms!*" Adam advanced his G.I. Joe army to a position under the cutting board. One glance down to ask him to be quiet and my knife slipped. Cutting myself while cooking wasn't unusual; I inherited my grandmother's tendency to be careless in the kitchen. But this time a nasty little chunk of my left index finger ended up on the cutting board.

Julia took one look at the gushing blood and screamed for her father. Paul dashed in, and as proof of what a good, solid husband he is, instead of chiding me for taking my eye off the knife, he wrapped my finger in a towel and put the sliver of detached flesh on ice. We all piled into the car and rushed to the Cedars-Sinai E.R.

We went to the emergency room at Cedars so often for Adam's accidents—a split lip when he fell while trying to climb onto the table at Fat Burger, a gashed head when a girl in his toddler class beaned him with a sand pail—Paul joked that they held our mail. This was the first time, however, that the Boorstin patient was Sharon, not Adam. The admitting nurse trundled me off to a room where patients waited to get stitches. Before me in line was a sous chef from L'Orangerie, the best French restaurant in town. He laughed when I showed him the piece of fingertip I hoped the doc-

tors could reattach. His cut was a lot worse than mine, one of the
dangers of the job, he said.

When it was my turn, the doctor took one look at the scrap of
flesh and trashed it. He applied some newfangled bandage that was
guaranteed to heal the wound (though I would forever have a dent
in my fingertip) and sent me home with Percodan in case of pain.
Pain? *What* pain? I was determined to go through with my dinner
party.

Paul urged me to call the guests and cancel dinner, but I reminded him of the time when Mary Ann burned herself with hot oil
from an overturned fondue pot. She didn't send guests home but
bravely went on, right through her grapes brûlée. Besides, I argued,
our other guest, Barbara, was an important Hollywood contact.

With Julia's help, I managed to get the table set and the
pasta ready, and I resisted the urge to heat it on the stove before
serving it, so that the fresh mozzarella remained plump instead of
sticky. There were compliments to the chef, who sat at the table with
a bandaged finger pointing upward, like Uncle Sam saying, "I want
God."

Paul did the dishes after everyone went home. I crawled into bed
and fell asleep—until 1 A.M., when my finger began to throb with
pain. Since I had imbibed two glasses of wine during dinner, Paul
insisted that I phone the E.R. before taking the Percodan they had
given me. The doctor on call said, sure, no problem, take *two*
Percodan—the wine was probably already out of my system by now.
He obviously didn't know my system.

One Percodan later, I slumped to the floor faster than Paul could
dial 911. Within a few minutes an ambulance pulled up and the
medic took my blood pressure. *What* blood pressure? He shoved a
syringe full of epinephrine into my arm, then he and his partner carried me out of the house on a stretcher. "I'm so embarrassed," I said
to them.

"They'll call you about when to pick her up," the medic told

Paul as they slid the stretcher into the back of the ambulance. Off we went to Cedars-Sinai, sirens screaming.

In the E.R. I was given more epinephrine and hooked up to a heart monitor until my blood pressure normalized. Just to make sure there would be no complications, instead of sending me home, a nurse rolled my gurney into a corner for the night. Just before I drifted off, I remember thinking, "At least the pasta turned out right."

No-Blood Summer Pasta

SERVES 4 TO 6

I came up with a foolproof way to make this pasta without the danger of slicing fingers along with tomatoes: Use cherry tomatoes instead of big tomatoes. You can make the sauce in the morning and let it sit, covered, at room temperature, until you add the pasta. Using yellow along with red cherry tomatoes makes the dish even more colorful.

2 cartons cherry tomatoes
¾ cup chopped fresh basil leaves
½ cup chopped fresh Italian parsley
4 cloves garlic, minced, or more to taste
1 or 2 tablespoons capers
1 small can sliced black olives
1 large fresh mozzarella cheese ball, or 4 small, cut into
    small chunks
3 tablespoons good balsamic vinegar
½ cup extra-virgin olive oil
Salt and freshly ground pepper to taste
1 pound penne or bow-tie pasta
½ cup grated fresh Parmigiano-Reggiano cheese, plus
    more for passing

1. Wash the cherry tomatoes in a colander, then place the colander in the sink. Using a big spoon or a potato masher, gently press them until they pop and the juice and seeds drain off. Do not overmash them.

2. Transfer the tomatoes to a pasta serving bowl and add ½ cup of the basil and ¼ cup of the parsley, plus all other ingredients except the pasta and grated cheese. Mix well, cover, and let sit, mixing occasionally, at room temperature, for 6 to 8 hours.

3. Make the pasta according to the package directions. Drain well in a colander, but do not rinse.

4. Gradually add the hot pasta to the serving bowl, continually mixing. Add the grated cheese and mix again. Sprinkle the remaining basil and parsley on top and serve immediately. Pass the grated cheese along with a pepper grinder.

Chapter 24

A Bright Shining Light

Luz Montez blew into our family's life one day in the late eighties, the new love of Bill, Paul's best friend since childhood. Fifteen years younger than Bill, Luz had an entry-level job at the TV network where he was an on-camera correspondent. With dark eyes, shiny black hair, and a confidence about her body that I could only dream of, she radiated sensuality as well as intelligence. The name Luz (pronounced "loose") was an apt one for this exuberant young woman, for *luz* means "light" in Spanish.

Julia, who was around twelve when Bill introduced Luz to us, aspired to be just like her when she grew up. To Adam, who was around seven, Luz was the embodiment of the ideal woman—you could see it from the way he lit up when she showered him with attention. I pity the poor girl who will one day have to live up to Luz's perfection in Adam's mind.

On Labor Day weekend we took the kids to New York and camped out in Bill and Luz's small apartment. Paul and I shared the pullout sofa in the living room, while Adam slept on two chairs put together and Julia nestled on a cot in Bill's study. The six of us got along so well that we didn't mind the close quarters.

One of the high points for Julia was when Luz took us to Zabar's. Julia marveled at the balls of fresh buffalo mozzarella cheese floating in milky water, the pungent dried porcini mushrooms, and the big wheels of Parmigiano Reggiano. Luz scooped sun-dried tomatoes from a barrel and handed one to Julia to taste, surprising her that anything so dry and wrinkled could explode with such flavor—an intense saltiness overlaid with a hint of sugar and the essence of tomato.

Luz had taught herself to cook, and, not surprising given her outgoing personality, favored rustic, big-flavored Italian dishes. One of her favorites was pasta puttanesca from a recipe she created after ordering the lusty Neapolitan "whore's pasta" in every Italian restaurant she went to for months and poring over Italian cookbooks. Luz's version called for green as well as black olives, tons of garlic and capers, and an entire can of anchovies. She still remembers what I said when I first tasted it: "I could *swim* in this sauce."

After our Zabar's run, Julia and I helped Luz turn handfuls of sun-dried tomatoes into a creamy pasta sauce that she learned to make from her high-school friend Susan. As we cooked, the aromas of garlic and basil—homey Italian smells—filled the apartment, and Luz told us about her friendship with Susan.

S usan and I stole horses together!" said Luz. She recounted how they tooled around in Luz's secondhand Triumph Spitfire, singing at the top of their lungs, the summer they were sixteen and ushering at the Melody Top Theater in Milwaukee, their hometown. "We permed each other's hair—Susan had this great head of curly red hair—and we partied with the out-of-town actors who played the Melody Top."

Luz and Susan came from different backgrounds: Susan was one of eight children in a family where each person had a robust taste

Luz and Susan working hard at the Melody Top Theater in Milwaukee.

for food as well as life. Her father was the fire chief and main cook at the firehouse; his favorite kitchen line, Luz recalls, was "Guess the secret ingredient." Susan's mother did the cooking for the brood at home. Susan learned to cook from her parents, and she was a natural. "Susan could throw ingredients into the Cuisinart without measuring, pour the batter into a pan and bake it, and out would come perfect zucchini bread," said Luz. "The Cuisinart had been used so often at her house, the plastic container was cloudy—you couldn't see what was inside!"

Unlike Susan's family, Luz's family of six was not focused on food and cooking. "Mom's idea of dinner was pork chops, mashed potatoes, and canned asparagus, or some stew with doughy dumplings that were never cooked all the way through, and no way was there a bottle of olive oil or fresh garlic in the house!" Luz recalled. "Some nights, she'd say, 'Okay, kids, tonight we're gonna have tongue!' We'd all go, 'Gross!' "

Luz's mother was German, her father Mexican. When Luz was growing up, the only time she got excited about the food in her house was when her Mexican grandmother, Elvira, came from Texas to spend the summer. Elvira only spoke Spanish and Luz only spoke

English, so Luz could not communicate with her. Like my Yiddish-speaking grandmother and me, they connected by cooking together.

Luz's grandmother spent all afternoon making tortillas from scratch. "I watched her measuring and pounding and kneading," said Luz. "She had muscular hands with long, bony fingers; I think I inherited my grandmother's hands. Her tortillas had so much lard in them, she never had to grease the griddle. I slathered them with butter and ate them while they were still warm."

Luz and Susan learned how to entertain from Guy Little, the producer at the Melody Top summer-stock theater, whom Luz considered an important mentor. When Debbie Reynolds came to town to do *The Unsinkable Molly Brown*, or George Chakiris to do *Funny Girl,* he used it as an excuse to throw a party. "Guy would take Susan and me to Sendik's, the Balducci's of Milwaukee in those days, and we would fill the basket with whatever he told us—chickens, fresh bread, pasta, flowers," she recalled. They brought everything back to Guy's apartment overlooking Lake Michigan. "Guy threw the flowers into vases so that they looked like they'd been arranged by a pro. Then Susan and I helped him cook enough food to feed the guest stars and all the starving actors in town."

After Luz moved to New York and eventually into Bill's apartment, she started entertaining with what she calls "a vengeance." She threw cocktail parties, dinners for twelve, and she insisted on doing all the cooking herself. She often called Susan for advice on how to do a variation on a recipe in a cookbook, or for one of Susan's own recipes. "Susan's recipes were always foolproof," claimed Luz. "The only dish of hers I've never made is one she pitches me every time she calls: 'Now I know this may sound too *Wisconsin,*' she always says, 'but it's really good: baked gouda with Dijonnaise sauce.' Susan, I say, let's not even *go* there!"

Luz admitted that she and Susan lived in different worlds now: Susan was married, taught kindergarten, and had two daughters in Milwaukee, while Luz was speeding along on a career path in New

York. "We're still of the same mentality, though," insisted Luz. "We're both happy when we're surrounded by people, and we like to keep them well fed." Whenever Luz goes home to Milwaukee, Susan cooks a special dinner for her. "The last time I was home, I walked into her house and she was cooking sun-dried tomato sauce for pasta. It smelled so wonderful, I had to take the recipe back to New York with me."

Luz and Susan's Pasta with Sun-Dried Tomato Cream Sauce

SERVES 4 TO 6

This simple but rich sauce smells so good when it's cooking that everyone who gets a whiff will feel homey—and hungry. You can do step 1 of the sauce a few hours in advance, then add the cream and thicken it just before serving. For a heartier dish, Luz tops the pasta with boneless chicken breasts that have been quickly sautéed with chopped garlic (1 to 2 cloves per breast) in a little extra-virgin olive oil.

2 tablespoons butter
3 to 4 cloves garlic, minced
1 cup chicken stock or bouillon
**1 cup minced dry-pack sun-dried tomatoes (cut with a
   sharp scissors)**
1 pound penne or farfalle
1 cup whipping cream
Salt and pepper to taste
3 to 4 tablespoons chopped fresh basil

1. In a heavy pan, melt the butter over medium heat and cook the garlic for 30 seconds. Add the stock and sun-dried tomatoes. Bring the mixture to a boil, then simmer over low heat for 10 minutes, until the tomatoes are tender.

2. While the sauce is simmering, make the pasta according to package directions.

3. Add the cream to the sauce and bring to a boil, stirring constantly. Lower the heat and simmer until the sauce is thick enough to coat a spoon, approximately 5 minutes.

4. Drain the pasta and gradually add it to the sauce, off the heat, and mix well. Add salt and pepper to taste.

5. Transfer the pasta to a serving dish, garnish with the chopped basil, and serve immediately.

Chapter 25

The Too Hots

The makeup room was wall-to-wall mirrors at Sony Studios where the *Donny & Marie* talk show was being taped, but the next guest didn't even watch as the stylist took a hot curler to her hair. Susan Feniger, a girlish-looking forty-something despite the gray streaking her black hair, had more important concerns than her appearance. Wearing a pale-blue chef's jacket over baggy black-and-white checked chef's pants, she was talking intently on her cell phone about square footage, parking-lot size, and other issues facing a restaurateur in search of a new space.

Mary Sue Milliken, in a bright coral chef's jacket, walked in and plopped into the makeup chair beside Susan's. At five feet seven inches, with short, blondish hair, Mary Sue is Annie Hall compared with Susan, who is barely five feet two and wears a dozen tiny hoop earrings and a nose stud. Mary Sue sized up Susan in the mirror: "What's the deal, Feniger? You're just doing hair today? No makeup?"

"*I . . . already . . . had . . . my . . . makeup . . . done!*" Susan retorted. She turned to the makeup artist who was powdering

Mary Sue's face. "Forget trying to put lipstick on her. She never shuts her mouth!"

The makeup artist paused—were these two kidding? Susan and Mary Sue burst out laughing. No wonder the two women are often described as the Abbott and Costello of the food world. Their back-and-forth shtick has helped make them the best-known female chef team in the country. If ever there were two women whose friendship was based on food and cooking, it's Susan and Mary Sue, aka the Too Hot Tamales. They own five successful restaurants in Southern California and Las Vegas; they have written five cookbooks. They hosted two popular cooking shows on the Food Network, and today they have one in the works for PBS.

I have known Susan and Mary Sue since they opened their first restaurant in Los Angeles in the eighties, when I was the restaurant critic for the *Herald*. I tagged along with them to *Donny & Marie* for an article I was writing about them for *More* magazine. I could see why these two women with a passion for food have struck a chord with the American public. Like an old married couple, they finished each other's sentences, contradicted each other, and punctuated anecdotes with that not-afraid-to-show-your-teeth laughter that comes easily to both of them.

We moved from the makeup room to the backstage buffet set out for the cast and crew. It was obvious that the food—Chinese chicken salad, wings, taco chips, and bottled salsa—had been sitting out on the table all day. That didn't stop Susan and Mary Sue from picking. "One thing Susan and I have in common," said Mary Sue, trying a wedge of cheese quesadilla: "We both love to eat."

Susan settled for an apple that she was soon sharing with Mary Sue, bite for bite. Neither of them has ever had a weight problem or gone on a diet. "Working around food all the time, you learn to eat what's healthy," explained Mary Sue.

Susan turned to her: "Yeah, right. When we first opened Border

Grill, you used to skim the fat off the *carnitas* pot and eat it with your fingers!"

"Mmmm, it was so delicious!"

The two women first met at Chicago's Le Perroquet in 1978, when Mary Sue was twenty and just out of chef's school. "I applied for a job as a cook, but they only would give me a job as the hat-check girl! I bugged the chef until he finally allowed me to work on the prep line."

"It was because Mary Sue was so good that they hired me," added Susan. The then twenty-four-year-old came to Chicago after graduating from the Culinary Institute of America in New York and a short stint at a French restaurant in Kansas City. The only women in Le Perroquet's kitchen, Mary Sue and Susan became fast friends. "I'd never met anyone who cared as much as I did about food and cooking as a career," recalled Susan. "In our spare time, we read cookbooks, not novels. We'd go out for a beer after work and discuss them."

It wasn't until several years later that they decided to join forces. Susan moved to Los Angeles to work at Ma Maison, and with owner Patrick Terrail's encouragement, she went to train at the three-star L'Oasis on the French Riviera. When the restaurant closed for the season, Susan visited Mary Sue, who was apprenticing at a restaurant in Paris.

"My apartment in Paris was about the size of a dining room table," recalled Mary Sue. "Susan slept on the floor."

"We'd walk the markets, get wine and food, and go back and cook, drink, cook, drink, and eat."

"We cooked things like veal kidneys and horsemeat—"

"The thought of horsemeat makes me sick now, but in those days we ate anything and everything—"

"One night, after a couple of bottles of wine, we decided to go back to L.A. and open our own restaurant."

Their first "restaurant" was a hole-in-the-wall on trendy Melrose

The Too Hots: Susan and Mary Sue in the early years.

Avenue, with thirty-eight seats, one hot plate in the tiny kitchen, and a hibachi for grilling in the parking lot. Once they installed a stove with four burners and an oven, the City Café was born. "The guy who washed the dishes was also our busboy," recalled Susan. "And we had two waitresses—one a heroin addict, the other a punk rocker. But we had a blast."

Susan introduced Mary Sue to her husband-to-be, architect Josh Schweitzer, her best friend since fifth grade. Mary Sue and Schweitzer have been together since their first date. It was Schweitzer who designed all the women's restaurants.

Though they trained in French cuisine, Susan and Mary Sue were drawn to the flavors of Mexico. "We worked in French restaurant kitchens where Latino guys did all the prep," explained Susan. "For staff meals, they made home-cooked dishes from Oaxaca and the Yucatán, and terrific, fresh salsas. We liked it better than the fancy food we were serving to the guests!"

Mary Sue and Susan went on several road trips through Mexico and picked up recipes and techniques from market vendors and home cooks. They returned to L.A. and transformed their City Café into the Border Grill, where according to *Los Angeles* magazine, "they applied the same intelligence to green-corn tamales that other chefs might to *foie gras*."

In 1990 Schweitzer designed a spacious, colorful new home in Santa Monica for the Border Grill. It's a fun, raucous restaurant, where guests sip margaritas and share dishes like roasted lamb tacos and beer-marinated chicken with *pasilla*-tequila sauce. Today their restaurant empire includes Border Grills in Pasadena and Las Vegas, and Ciudad, which serves food from throughout Latin America in downtown L.A.

As their business grew, the women's friendship changed. "We have learned to give each other plenty of room for evolving in whatever direction we each need," said Mary Sue.

"We trust each other more and respect our individual abilities," added Susan.

"Our friendship is so solid, it's almost like we're family."

"Like sisters. I think we adored each other from the day we met and that we augmented our 'real' siblings with this deep friendship. Maybe it filled a need in each of us that hadn't been filled before. That's not to say that our families were inadequate, but we just got a lot out of each other."

With minutes to go before their cooking demonstration on *Donny & Marie,* Mary Sue and Susan moved to the demo kitchen backstage. Mary Sue arranged the spices for the turkey escabeche they were preparing to make. "You're gonna do the turkey," she told Susan.

"I don't want to do the turkey; I'll do the onions."

"Fine. I do better turkey anyway."

As they prepped, they talked about their differing cooking styles: Mary Sue doesn't like too much garlic or spice, while Susan likes plenty of each. Mary Sue is also more precise in her cooking than Susan. "I am definitely *not* into measuring!" admitted Susan.

"Susan always wants more components and bigger helpings while I'm more of a minimalist," explained Mary Sue. "But we are surprisingly in sync when we're cooking. After we taste something, we both reach for the same ingredient to add seasoning to it."

To some extent, the two women play different roles in their business. "I spend days working on new projects so I can spend evenings with my husband and our kids," said Mary Sue. "I like to cook for my family, and give parties."

"You never invite *me*!"

"You'd never come! You'd rather be in the restaurant!"

"It's true," admitted Susan, who spends six nights out of seven in at least one of their restaurants. "I love the pressure, the intensity, the food, dealing with the staff and customers. When I'm *not* working, all I want to do is stay home with my girlfriend and our dogs."

Finally, it was showtime. The audience cheered as Mary Sue and Susan hustled onstage. Donny and Marie greeted them like long-lost friends. The clock was ticking—Susan and Mary Sue knew they had only seven minutes—so they got down to business: Mary Sue showed Donny how to pound turkey breasts while Susan taught Marie the safest way to chop onions. The four were laughing and joking and talking all at once, but somehow the turkey cutlets and the onions got thrown into a pan, and Donny figured out how to shake the pan over the heat without losing a morsel. Marie ground on the pepper. Susan and Mary Sue whipped out spiced yams and sautéed brussels sprouts to go with the entrée. Donny wrinkled his nose at the vegetables, but after one taste, he was eating them with his fingers (the secret ingredient—a squeeze of fresh lime juice).

Time's up! Donny and Marie hugged Susan and Mary Sue; the audience applauded; the tape stopped rolling; and the crew descended on what was left of the food.

Backstage, Susan and Mary Sue pulled off their aprons. "Did I tell you about this great space I found for a restaurant?" Susan asked.

"Not *another* new restaurant!" But Mary Sue couldn't resist. As the Too Hot Tamales sauntered off the Sony soundstage, they bickered about whether it was possible to expand their restaurant empire while maintaining their private lives. Every chef-restaurateur should face such a dilemma.

Grilled Turkey Escabeche

From *Mexican Cooking for Dummies*
by Mary Sue Milliken and Susan Feniger
SERVES 4

This dish takes no time to make and it has a spicy kick. Instead of grilling the turkey separately, I toss the turkey slices right onto the onion mixture in the pan and stir for a minute or two over high heat until they are cooked.

>   Pinch of ground allspice
>   Pinch of ground cloves
>   ½ teaspoon ground cumin
>   ½ teaspoon dried oregano
>   1½ pounds skinless, boneless turkey breast, cut into
>   thin slices
>   Salt and pepper to taste
>   4 to 6 tablespoons cold butter
>   1 large red onion, diced
>   1½ teaspoons salt
>   ⅔ cup white vinegar
>   1½ cups turkey or chicken stock, or canned broth
>   1 tablespoon cracked black pepper
>   Chopped fresh parsley and chopped fresh cilantro for
>   garnish

1. To prepare the seasoning mixture, mix together the allspice, cloves, cumin, and oregano in a bowl.

2. Cover the turkey slices with plastic wrap and pound to flatten. Sprinkle all over with the salt, pepper, and the seasoning mixture, and reserve.

3. Preheat the grill or broiler to hot.

4. Melt 3 tablespoons of the butter in a medium skillet over low heat. Cook the onion with the salt, stirring and shaking the pan frequently, until golden, about 15 minutes. Pour in the vinegar, turn the heat to high, and simmer until the liquid is reduced by half. Pour in the turkey or chicken stock, and boil until the liquid is reduced by half.

5. Thinly slice the remaining cold butter. Reduce the heat to low and whisk the butter into the sauce a little at a time. Remove from the heat and stir in the cracked pepper.

6. Grill or broil the turkey slices less than a minute per side. (Or, as I did, cook them on top of the onion mixture in the pan.) Spoon the sauce over them, garnish with parsley and cilantro, and serve.

VARIATION
Skinless, boneless chicken breasts, sliced and pounded, are also delicious prepared this way. To save time, you can sear the chicken or turkey breasts in a tablespoon or so of vegetable oil in a skillet over high heat instead of grilling them.

Chapter 26

Bad Girl Makes Good

B oy, I must have been trouble when I was your student!" Nell Newman greeted me at the door of her simple clapboard house in Santa Cruz, California, on a drizzly day in April. I'd come to interview my former student, now all grown up, for a *More* magazine article.

At first I was too startled by Nell's appearance to respond. It was suddenly as if I were looking decades into the past: Nell had the same athletic figure and long, sun-bleached blond hair that she had the day she enrolled at Horizons, the high school where I had taught, and she kept brushing her hair out of her face, like she did back then. Nell's is a pretty face, one that combines the fine features of both her movie-star parents. She wore no makeup then, and she wore none now. Except for a few lines creeping up around her eyes, at forty-something Nell looked much the same as she did at fifteen. The only difference: It wasn't anger I saw in those mesmerizing blue eyes. It was joy.

"I didn't exactly peg you as the girl most likely to succeed," I finally said.

"Me neither!" Nell shot back. She said she regretted that she'd been a slacker at Horizons, but because she switched schools so often, she fell too far behind academically to catch up. "The truth? My teachers always let me slide because I was Paul Newman's daughter."

Nell and her proud papa.

Nell invited me inside, even though she said she didn't allow many journalists into her house. "But since you were my teacher . . ."

Nell's living room is decorated in a homey, unpretentious style: an old iron stove fills the fireplace; the mantel holds family pictures and photos of the falcons and hawks Nell once owned. It was her fascination with birds of prey that led her to go back to school and study biology in college. After graduating, she worked for a foundation to save endangered birds of prey whose eggs were being destroyed by DDT. "I realized that it would make more sense to run a business that gave its profits to foundations I cared about," she said, "like my dad did."

In 1993 Nell created the organic-food division of Newman's Own, Paul Newman's food company. The after-tax profits go to more than one hundred educational and charitable organizations. So far, that has translated into 1.4 million dollars. "A lot of people didn't think I could accomplish what I have in the past eight years," she added, "but I proved them wrong!"

It took some doing for Nell to persuade her father to let her start an organic division of Newman's Own. "Like most guys, Dad wasn't into organic foods," she explained. "He thought *organic* meant nut loaf with yeast gravy. He couldn't relate to it." To change his mind, Nell cooked the family's Thanksgiving dinner with organic ingredients. "After Dad cleaned his plate, I said, 'So, Dad, how did you like your organic Thanksgiving?' Finally I had his attention!"

Nell led me into the kitchen, a sunny room with yellow walls and white trim, to make lunch. She was proud that all of the food in her house was organic, as was everything she grew in her backyard. She has eaten organic food since college, but she made it clear that she was not a vegetarian. She is what she calls a "flexatarian."

Nell cut a loaf of whole-grain bread and spread honey-mustard sauce on several slices. Next she piled on gravlax that she had made from the salmon she caught the previous weekend. She learned to fish from her father, and she shares his love for it. Nell is like her father in other ways too: "We both like to do things that are fast— and dangerous," she said. "For him it's driving race cars. For me it's surfing. The bigger the waves, the scarier it is; but it's exhilarating."

I complimented Nell on the gravlax—it was intriguingly salty and sweet, and had a spicy kick. She credited the zip to coriander and cumin. "I love to experiment with new flavors. I love to cook, and I love to eat! If I gain weight, I just go surfing more till I lose it."

Nell was eager to discuss restaurants in Los Angeles, because she was headed there soon to accept an award from the Sierra Club, and she wanted to go out for dinner afterward. As I rattled off my list of favorites—Spago, Campanile, Chinois—I realized that she was listening to me with more attention than she had given me when I was teaching English to her at Horizons nearly three decades ago. I kidded her that it was too bad she wasn't interested in food and restaurants back then—we would have had common ground that may have led her to drop her resentment of me as her teacher and allowed us to be friends.

Nell unwrapped an angel food cake flecked with chocolate shavings from a Newman's Own Organics orange peel-chocolate bar, a product she developed because her father loved chocolate-covered orange peel. "He loves this cake," she said, offering me a slice. I took a bite; the cake was light, moist, and delicious.

Later that afternoon at the Santa Cruz organic farmers' market, Nell picked through a pyramid of glossy green organic artichokes that she planned to steam for dinner and serve with her father's salad dressing. "Not bottled Newman's Own—it's not organic," she said, explaining that she whips up her own version of his salad dressing with organic ingredients. "It tastes even better that way," she insisted. She wouldn't divulge the recipe: "If I did, I'd have to kill you!"

But because I was her old high school teacher, Nell gave me the recipe for her father's favorite angel food cake.

Paul Newman's Favorite Angel Food Cake

SERVES 12

You'll find Newman's Own Organics orange dark chocolate bars shelved with the candy, not the baking ingredients, at your local health food store. If you're a chocoholic, buy an extra one to eat.

FOR THE CAKE

1½ dark orange chocolate bars (3 ounces each) or
3 ounces Newman's Own Organics dark orange
chocolate bars
1¼ cups sugar
1 cup all-purpose flour

½ teaspoon salt

12 egg whites, at room temperature

1 tablespoon lemon juice

3 teaspoons vanilla extract

1 tablespoon orange zest (preferably from a blood
  orange)

FOR THE GARNISH

2 pints fresh strawberries, sliced

1 cup slightly sweetened whipped cream

1. Preheat the oven to 350°F. Grate the chocolate into a bowl using the large holes on a cheese grater. Set aside.

2. Onto a piece of waxed paper, sift ¼ cup of the sugar with the flour and the salt three times. (It's easier to pour into the sifter from the waxed paper.)

3. With an electric mixer, beat the egg whites until frothy, then add the lemon juice. Continue beating at high speed until the egg whites form soft peaks.

4. Sprinkle the sugar onto the egg whites a few tablespoons at a time, and at low speed, continue beating until the sugar is combined.

5. Sift the flour-sugar mixture, ¼ cup at a time, over the egg whites, blending well, then gently fold in all but ⅓ cup of the grated chocolate, followed by the vanilla and the orange zest. Save the ⅓ cup of grated chocolate to sprinkle on individual pieces.

6. Pour the batter into a clean, ungreased angel food cake pan. Bake for 45 minutes, or until the cake is lightly browned on top and a knife inserted into the center comes out clean. Do not slam doors while the cake is baking, or it may fall.

7. Remove the cake from the oven and invert the pan for ½ hour.

8. To serve, run a knife around the edges and center of the cake and transfer it to a serving plate. Use a serrated knife to cut it. Serve each slice with strawberries and whipped cream, then sprinkle with the remaining grated chocolate.

Chapter 27

Separation Anxiety Redux

One humid, hot day in early September 1996 I helped Julia move into her dorm for her first year at Princeton. When I went away to college, I had separation anxiety about leaving my mother. Now my separation anxiety—about leaving my daughter—was ten times worse.

Unpacking box after box of Julia's clothes, making her bunk bed with new sheets that didn't quite fit, and cleaning the dust and grime from the windowsills and closets—tasks that hadn't occurred to Julia or her roommate to do—left me exhausted. I was glad when Paul joined us for Parent-Student Orientation. It was the last event before we were to entrust Julia to the university—and the fates. When the meeting was over, Julia kissed us good-bye and melted into the crowd of freshmen marching into the gym. She didn't even look back.

I was okay until we hit the George Washington Bridge on our way from New Jersey to Connecticut, where we were going to stay at Joyce and Jim's house. Jim Seymore had been Paul's roommate at

Princeton and is now the managing editor of *Entertainment Weekly*. His wife is a chic blonde with alabaster skin, a curvaceous figure, and a great sense of humor and style. Her photography is shown in galleries, and she has decorated their American Colonial house in a style that would impress Martha Stewart.

Clutching a map, I navigated while Paul drove. When I saw the WELCOME TO NEW YORK sign on the bridge, it hit me that we were already one state away from Julia. When we returned home in a few days, there would be an entire *country* between us. I burst into tears: "Julia's gone! Her childhood is over! We'll never have her back!" I was inconsolable and lost track of where we were on the map. We ended up in the Bronx.

It took us an extra hour to make our way to Joyce and Jim's house. By that time, my chest had stopped heaving, but my eyes were red from tears. Joyce took one look and put her arm around me. "We'll have a glass of wine, we'll cook. You'll feel better."

Joyce and I had cooked together several times before. Once, when she and Jim came out to L.A. for the Oscars, we made pasta with fresh tomatoes that Joyce insisted were ten times better than the tomatoes available back east in March. On that trip I introduced Joyce to Nancy Silverton, who took us on a tour of her La Brea Bakery and even allowed us a glimpse into the inner sanctum, the room where the starters for their various breads are kept. The heady odor of yeast bordered on the rank, yet like the odor of fresh truffles, it was seductive.

Nancy gave us each a small plastic container of sourdough starter to take home. "Just make sure you feed it," she said, instructing us how to add water and flour each day. The starter languished in my fridge—I didn't have the time or the energy to nurture it, let alone use it to bake bread. After a week, I dumped it. Joyce, however, coddled her starter as if it were a puppy. A few weeks later she phoned me to report that she had baked three excellent loaves of bread with it, but that the starter was outgrowing its container and she feared it would take over her refrigerator, like Audrey II in *Little Shop of Horrors*. I reassured Joyce that it was okay to put the starter out of its misery.

In Connecticut a few years later, Joyce and I took our children to an all-you-can-pick peach orchard one morning. After we returned to Joyce's house, Joyce, Julia, and I set out to make peach pies. That's when I realized that Joyce is a very precise cook, totally the opposite of me: She caught me about to pour sugar from the box right into the peach-pie filling—who needed a measuring cup? She grabbed my arm: "Stop! You've got to stick to the recipe!" I measured the sugar. Joyce couldn't know that one day in the future we'd be cooking together *without* a recipe.

On the night of my good-bye Julia trauma, Joyce and I took our time preparing dinner and consumed several glasses of Chardonnay in the process. We both missed having Julia with us in the kitchen— she had always been an enthusiastic and skilled assistant. Talk turned to the mixed feelings that Joyce and I had when *we* left home for college, and the pleasures and the angst we experienced once we got there. Gradually, I regained my equilibrium. Who cared that we didn't sit down to dinner—leg of lamb with rosemary and garlic, roasted baby red potatoes with sea salt, and fresh vegetables from Joyce's garden—until almost midnight?

Part IV

Connections and
Reconnections

*A*t this stage of our lives, with the kids (more or less) out of the house, the women of my generation are finally finding time to concentrate on . . . well, us. Many of us have invested more of ourselves in our jobs. Even if we never got married or had kids, we are still working. There are a lot more things to buy than there were in our mothers' day, from Palm Pilots to DVD players to teeth-whitening treatments, and we need the money for them.

In the workplace we face competition from women a decade or two younger than we are, but that doesn't stop us. In fact, we look and dress pretty much the same as they do. When our mothers were our age, they wore matronly clothes. To this day, we're still wearing skirts that hit just above the knee or higher, tailored pantsuits, and slim-fit jeans. Our mothers only wore jeans—baggy ones, with rolled-up cuffs at that—when they gardened.

Many of us have gone through midlife crises and as a result have changed careers or shed husbands. As we've reassessed our lives, we've *reassessed our friendships. We have lost touch with some of our girl-friends over the years—because of a divorce or a move, or through our own negligence. We are even beginning to lose friends through death. It reminds us all the more just how precious friends are.*

Who are our girlfriends, anyway? The girls we've known since childhood? The ones we met in high school or college or when we were newlyweds? The women we met through our children or through work? How about our grown-up daughters? Now that we are ensconced in middle age, it's important to us to find out—especially after the horror of September 11, which suddenly made our world feel insecure and even frightening.

Are we too old to make new friends? Are we too old to sample a new dish or to try a new recipe? New tastes awaken our senses and motivate us to be open to other new experiences. The same can be said of new friends.

Chapter 28

Lost Friends Found

Ten years ago on a spring day, my mother called and said that my father wasn't feeling well and had gone to see his doctor. The doctor did tests and diagnosed liver cancer. It was too late for effective treatment; my father had six months to live. My father resigned himself to what fate had thrown his way. Within three weeks he took to his bed, and two weeks later he died.

During my father's illness, I flew to Seattle to visit. So did my sister Sheila. We made his favorite dishes—fresh Dungeness crab and baked salmon with my mother's Thousand Island dressing. Finally, all he could stomach was ice cream. Nevertheless, at his request, we helped him to the table each night so that he could sit down to dinner with his family. When he was back in bed, I lay down next to him and took his hand. My father had been a calming influence in my life. Even as he lay dying, he wasn't afraid. After his death, remembering his calm helped me see the pettiness of my insecurities and fears.

Every seat in the sanctuary was filled the morning of my father's funeral. My mother's best friends, including Mary and Edith, were there, of course, as were their daughters Gloria and Laurie, my best childhood friends. I was touched to see my old high school friends Robin, Laurie, and Shelley there too. I had lost contact with them over the years after I left Seattle. It was my fault. In trying to invent a new, grown-up identity, I had turned my back on the friends from my youth. Now, after my father's death, I felt an urge to reconnect with them. The friends who knew me the longest—who knew my family—became a source of comfort.

My bond with Laurie, my best friend from high school and college, became especially strong in the years that followed. In 1968 she had shed her first husband after less than a year of marriage and moved back to Seattle from Los Angeles. There she began dating a man she had known since she was fourteen and he was eighteen. It seemed inevitable, Laurie said in retrospect, that she would marry him.

They raised two daughters, and Laurie studied psychology and became a high school counselor. She had always been intuitive about people's feelings, and empathetic; she thrived in her new job. She grew to be much more self-assured and self-confident than she was when we were younger. It made it easier for us to be friends.

After her second daughter left home for college, Laurie's marriage fell apart. It was painful for Laurie to leave a relationship of twenty-something years, but she needed to do it. By e-mail and by phone, I became her confidante. It was a role I had played when we were teenagers, but now things were different. Laurie didn't rely on me for advice; I was a sounding board for her feelings while she made her own decisions.

Over the next few months, Laurie shared secrets about her life with me, secrets that I didn't share with Paul. It was the first time since we'd been married that I kept things from him. I didn't feel guilty. I was rediscovering something I had given short shrift to after I got married—an intense connection with a girlfriend.

A year later, Laurie married a man she had first dated in 1962, the summer before we went away to college together. They had been too young at the time to have a serious relationship. Now, when they both were in their fifties, they fell in love. Having known Laurie through dozens of boyfriends and two husbands, I could see that Garry was right for her. I was honored to be the matron of honor at their wedding. It was held on a summer afternoon at Canlis, in the private upstairs room where I'd had my wedding dinner. The Canlis salad was the first course.

A few weeks later Laurie told me that Robin, my other best friend from high school, was angry with me. Robin had shown up at my father's funeral and had spoken politely to me at Laurie's wedding, but both times she was not the warm, effusive Robin I had known and loved when we were teenagers. I decided to find out what Robin's gripe with me was. I e-mailed her in Sun Valley, where she spends part of each year with her husband, Terry. We arranged to meet in Seattle a few weeks later.

I t was a perfect spring day, and rhododendrons in neon pinks and purples brightened every street. The white sails on Lake Washington and the drone of speedboat motors brought me back to idyllic days just like this when I was growing up in Seattle.

A colorful mobile of two fish swayed in the breeze outside Robin's cozy, wood-shingled house. She was standing on the sidewalk, waving her hands in case I missed it. Wearing sweats, a T-shirt, and no makeup, Robin exuded the confidence of a woman who is comfortable with herself in middle age. I remembered that when we were teenagers, I had wished I possessed her self-confidence—or at least what appeared to me like self-confidence.

We hugged, and she took me on a tour of her house. I was struck by the vibrant colors in the living room, the overstuffed sofas and chairs that were slung with lush, silky mohair throws that Robin had knit. There was a view of the lake from every room, and throughout the house were objets d'art that she had picked up on travels with Terry. The house felt like a love nest, not one for a family with children. Robin long ago chose not to have kids. I would soon learn why.

Eager to clear up the bad blood between us, the first thing I asked when we sat down was what I had done to offend her. Never one to mince words, Robin's answer was blunt: "After you moved to California, you acted like your life there was better—more important—than my life here."

I admitted there was truth to what she said, that when I went off to college and later settled in Los Angeles, I left my hometown and friends behind and never looked back. One reason was that I needed to distance myself from the trauma caused by my sister's mental illness. Another was that I yearned to create a new persona for myself, something I felt wasn't possible if I continued to live in the close-knit community where I grew up.

I apologized to Robin if she felt I had snubbed her; it had been self-centered and arrogant of me. She forgave me even before I finished asking. "What's past is past," she said. "We're too old now not to forgive our friends."

Robin understood my need to distance myself from my family after Susan's nervous breakdown. For the first time she revealed to me the trauma in her own family, one she had kept a secret when we were best friends in high school: Her mother, the flamboyant, theatrical Janice whom I had admired, had physically abused her, and her stepfather, Gene, the bigger-than-life actor and theater director I had found so enchanting, had sexually abused her.

"Mother knew what Gene was doing," Robin said, gazing out the window as if it were too painful to say it to my face. "But she never intervened. If anything, she allowed it to go on. For years." The abuse continued until Robin moved out of their house in her early twenties. "Why do you think I rushed into my first marriage? I had to get the hell out of there!"

Laurie had told me bits and pieces of Robin's story some years back, but hearing it from her own lips was shocking. I had spent many days and nights at Robin's house when we were teenagers. I had adored her parents. Robin had certainly hid well what they were doing to her. "Now you know why I couldn't concentrate in school, why I got lousy grades," she said. "But I was terrified that if I told, my mom would do terrible things to me." Her pause was uncomfortably long. "And I was ashamed."

Robin explained why finally, when she was in her early thirties, she revealed the truth: Her sister Charlene was dying of cancer, and the pain and stress of Charlene's illness and death deeply affected her. "I went into an emotional tailspin, and it all came rushing out. Suddenly I had to tell everyone what Gene and my mother had done to me—I wanted the world to know! My mother's response to me was, 'So, what do you want me to do about it now? That was eighteen years ago.' Gene just said, 'Don't worry, Robin. I don't have that problem anymore.' " Robin vowed never to talk to either of them again.

Gene died many years ago. Janice was diagnosed with Alzheimer's disease and moved into a nursing home. Last year, after not seeing her mother for over twenty years, Robin decided to forgive her—that it would be better for both of them if she did. Robin's husband accompanied her to the nursing home. They walked into her mother's darkened room, to the foot of her bed. "Mother's eyes were closed, and I stood and stared at her for a minute," Robin recalled. "I composed myself and said, 'Mother?' She didn't respond, so I said it again in a very gentle voice, 'Mother?' She opened her eyes and looked startled."

Robin walked around to the side of Janice's bed, steadied herself, and leaned over close to her face and said, "It's Robin." Janice didn't respond. "A minute or two went by," Robin continued, "and I was just focusing on my breathing, trying to stay calm. Then I stroked her hair and said, 'Mother, I have come to forgive you for all of those years of abuse and neglect, and I forgive myself for the hurt my estrangement caused you.' She just continued to stare at me. I felt so strange. Then I said, 'Mother, you can let go now. Just be at peace.' After a minute, her eyes filled with tears; one rolled down her cheek."

Robin and Terry stayed for another few minutes, and Robin glanced around at the family photographs in her mother's room. There were none of her.

Terry took Robin's hand and led her outside. They sat on a bench in a garden that Robin's father had donated to the nursing home in memory of Charlene and of Robin's brother Charles, who had been killed in a car accident caused by a drunk driver. Robin burst into tears. "I felt so sad," recalled Robin. "To have lived in fear that caused such anxiety through most of my life, to have lived without the nurturing and protection from my mother that every child needs . . . and then to lose a sister and a brother . . ."

Robin changed the subject to the times she came over to my house during high school. "I was escaping my own house," she said. "Your parents made me feel safe, especially your father." We reminisced about the nights he tutored us in algebra at the kitchen table. "That huge freezer was right next to the table, and your dad said we could take anything we wanted—oatmeal cookies, Milky Ways, frozen marshmallows. We just dipped our hands in."

Robin and I discussed the role that denial played in our lives when we were growing up. My family failed to notice the subtle signs of Susan's mental problems. In Robin's case, it was a psychiatrist who was responsible. When Robin was eleven, she was asked to fill out a questionnaire for a family health-insurance policy. In response to the question "Do you ever wish you were dead?" she answered, "Yes." As a result, she was sent to a psychiatrist—a psychiatrist who happened to know her family. Robin broke down and told the psychiatrist that her mother and stepfather were abusing her. "I gave her exact incidents, the gory details, but she refused to believe me," recalled Robin. "She said I was imagining things, and warned me not to tell anyone."

Years later, after Robin told her friends and family about what her mother and stepfather had done to her, she went into therapy. In the course of their sessions, she revealed to her therapist that when she was eleven, the psychiatrist had denied what she told her. The psychiatrist had since become prominent in the Seattle mental health community. Robin's therapist knew how damaging the psychiatrist's negligence had been to Robin years before, so she confronted her about it. "The psychiatrist broke down in tears and admitted to my therapist that back then she had believed what I told her, but she was afraid to let it out," said Robin. "She gave some b.s. reason like she was at the beginning of her career, and she couldn't risk a scandal if she made claims about two well-known members of the community."

It was Robin's closeness to her sister, Maggie, and brother, Tom, and their families, and her wide circle of girlfriends, that helped her emerge from the nightmare of her childhood trauma. "Friends and family are very important to me," she said. "Whenever I get together with my sister's or brother's family, we cook gourmet dinners. I find cooking relaxing and creative."

Robin and Maggie are both excellent cooks, masters of eclectic dishes that run from Peruvian ceviche to frozen mocha mousse. "Our mother was a wonderful cook but a horrible teacher," Robin said. "Cooking must be in our genes, because we sure didn't learn how to cook from her!"

A decade ago, Robin, Maggie, and their sister-in-law Darcy put together a book of the family's favorite recipes, so that they could pass them down to Maggie and Darcy's children. Robin is very close to her nieces and nephews. I told Robin it was a shame she never had her own children—she would have been a wonderful mother.

Robin turned and looked me in the eye. "I couldn't take a chance having kids," she said. "I know that deep down, I am still my mother's daughter."

Chapter 29

Mother and Earth Daughter

On a warm spring day, I met Aunt Hannah for lunch on New York's Upper East Side. Her choice of restaurant was one of those chic neighborhood Italian places that looks and feels like it's in Milan and doesn't bother with credit cards. Customers pay cash or, if they're regulars like Hannah, sign on a house account. Now in her midsixties, Hannah still exudes the kind of ageless beauty she possessed when I met her over thirty years ago. Wearing Greta Garbo sunglasses and a black leather blazer, she looked more elegant than the other ladies who lunched here, many of whom greeted her with a double air kiss.

Hannah is not a "lady who lunches"—far from it. When she was in her thirties she may have been the consummate Beverly Hills housewife and hostess, but today she is an acclaimed writer, whose biographies of Queen Marie of Romania and Empress Frederick of Germany have garnered literary prizes. She took time out from work on her latest biography, of Madame Chiang Kai-shek, to reminisce about the days when she was my ideal of a housewife and a cook, around the time I got married.

"I didn't have a clue about how to cook when I got married myself," Hannah said. "I was only twenty; I hadn't even finished college!" When they returned from their honeymoon, her husband, Bob, Paul's late uncle, had to teach Hannah how to make coffee. Hannah's mother didn't cook and believed that her two daughters didn't need to learn, not when they were taking piano lessons and learning important social graces. "According to mother, cooking was something that *other* people would do for us."

When Hannah and Bob moved into their house in Beverly Hills, they had three children under three years old. Hannah was overwhelmed, and Bob hired a staff to help with the house, the cooking, and the children. When things were under control, Hannah decided to teach herself how to cook. She bought an armful of cookbooks and began experimenting. She enjoyed cooking but lacked confidence, so she would spend days trying to perfect a recipe. One that was particularly tricky was cabbage borscht. When she finally felt she had it right, she ladled some into a bowl, covered it, and carried it down the street to a friend's house. "Tamara Chapro was one of the Russian émigré artists who lived in our neighborhood, and she was a fabulous cook," Hannah recalled. "I handed her the borscht and said, 'Taste it, please! Is it okay?' Tamara took a sip, thought about it, and gave me her verdict: 'It's perfect!' "

It was uphill from there. In the sixties, few of the women in Hannah's social circle did their own cooking; they hired cooks and used caterers. Hannah was proud that she did everything herself. One time, some friends from New York were bringing Craig Claiborne, the food critic of *The New York Times*, over to Hannah's for dinner. "I planned out a menu based on recipes from *The New York Times Cookbook*—until I realized that they were all Craig's recipes!" said Hannah. "I had to change everything, because I didn't want to feed him his own food."

Another time, when Hannah was going to entertain Suzy, her college roommate, and her husband, Si Newhouse (the current owner of Condé Nast), she hit upon the idea of serving a first course that consisted of five hors d'oeuvres on one plate. "I thought it would look impressive, but it was so much work," she said. "One of the dishes was something you prepared in a chocolate-roll pan with creamed spinach and ham inside; it took hours to prepare. I don't know what I was thinking!" Beef Bourguignonne and ratatouille followed the first course. "I learned to make a great ratatouille, but I made it so often back then that to this day I can't even look at ratatouille."

Hannah became a master of dishes that could be prepared ahead of time, and she never served guests something that she didn't try out first on her family. "My husband was very patient with me," she said. "So were my kids."

Hannah's sister, Myra, who wrote children's literature, taught herself to cook too. "We were both obviously rebelling against our mother," said Hannah. "Mother was not thrilled that we were spending so much time in the kitchen. She had a similar reaction when I wrote my first book years later. The first words out of her mouth were, 'Why does everyone have to write a *book*?' "

Every January Hannah and Myra got together to bake a birthday cake for their mother—a Lady Baltimore cake that she remembered from her childhood. "It was a perfectly dreadful cake," recalled Hannah, "filled with a disgusting cream concoction that had all sorts of dried fruits in it. But Myra and I got stage fright about doing it right because Mother was a perfectionist. Every year the cake turned out worse. The last time we made it, Myra and I ended up standing in my kitchen, laughing hysterically." Thinking about her late mother, who lived to be ninety-seven, Hannah smiled. "Mother thought our cake was pretty terrible too! It became a family joke."

Hannah's sister and mother died several years ago. So did Hannah's second husband, Alan Pakula, in a tragic car accident. Hannah's friends were wonderfully supportive through her tragedies—more supportive than her friends were when she lost her first husband, Bob. "I guess it was because I was young when Bob died, and they thought I was going to try to steal away their husbands." She sighed. "Or maybe I just didn't pick the right friends. Now I'm never alone unless I want to be." There was a wistful look in her eyes. "Of course, it's not the same as having Alan."

I met Anna, Hannah's daughter, in a Los Angeles restaurant that was a far cry from the chic, Upper East Side trattoria where I had had lunch with her mother a week earlier. Jack Sprat's Grill is a noisy café that serves salads, veggie burgers, and assorted low-cal entrées to women watching their weight.

Anna burst in the door with her mother's self-confident stride. In her midforties, she has Hannah's long, graceful neck and mesmerizing gray-green eyes, and like Hannah, her chin is always raised, à la Katharine Hepburn. But in contrast to her chic mother, Anna wears no makeup, has multiple pierced earrings, and was outfitted in jeans and an oversized blouse. She wears her long brown hair down, just like she wore it when she was a teenager. Hannah described Anna as a "life giver." She is right; Anna is the ultimate earth mother.

After graduating from Yale in the seventies, Anna worked for a few years in Hollywood as a sound editor, then married Pieter Jan Brugge, a Dutch movie producer. Like Anna, Pieter is genuine and down-to-earth (in contrast to most movie producers), and he stood behind her decision to be a stay-at-home mom for their three sons. "When the boys are old enough to drive themselves around, I'll do some writing," she said. "Finally!"

Anna recalled how miserable she was in high school, around the time Paul and I stayed with her and her brothers while her mother was visiting Alan in Europe. "I was on these diet pills that made me wired," she said. "I smoked three packs a day!" She missed her father, who had recently died, and because she went to a girls' school, she never met boys. "My social life consisted of playing cards with my girlfriend Maria and taking my horse to horse shows."

We turned to the subject of food and cooking. Anna admitted that though she always loved food, she avoided cooking because her mother was so good at it. "Once in a while when I was a teenager, Mom would try to teach me a recipe, but she was very precise. If I didn't do a step exactly by the book, she'd freak—and I'd storm out of the kitchen."

Today Anna most enjoys cooking for the book club that she and her girlfriends started when they were in their twenties, called Read and Feed. At first some women brought food to the meetings, but there was never enough—especially because several of them— including Anna—were pregnant at the time and always famished. To encourage more women to bring food, they instituted a policy of preparing dishes that reflected the theme of the assigned book for that month. For *Brick People,* a book about early Los Angeles, everyone brought Mexican food. For *Smilla's Sense of Snow*, they brought smoked salmon. It was only when they read British novels that the system broke down. "How many times can you bring English food," said Anna, "whatever *that* is?"

Over the years, each book-club member has become known for certain recipes. Anna is the salad person, and she usually brings one that is some variation on endive, radicchio, pine nuts, and a pungent cheese like Gorgonzola. She is also known for her baking. "When I was in high school, I baked dozens and dozens of chocolate chip cookies," she recalled, "but today, who's got the time to bake all those batches?" Now she bakes brownies or bar cookies—whatever can be baked at one time in one pan. I asked if she precisely measures ingredients. She laughed: "No way! It's a rebellion against Mother."

Anna noted that like other moms, she often cooks out of obligation. "The other day, I promised to make brownies for Nico's soccer team," she said, "but I didn't realize until I picked up Jurri from school that I barely had one hour to preheat the oven, make the brownies, bake them, and remove them from the oven before I had to pick up my other two boys. I told Jurri that if he helped me, he could lick the bowl, the spoon, and anything else covered in batter except the Cuisinart blade. Did it, got there, but the brownies were a tad undercooked." I assured her that everyone likes brownies slightly undercooked anyway.

Anna counts among her closest friends the women she met through Read and Feed. "Beth was the dip person," she said, describing a dip Beth taught her to make in the Cuisinart with sun-dried tomatoes, walnuts, and cream cheese, and another with Kalamata olives, walnuts, and olive oil. Anna and other book-club friends gave Beth moral support when she went through a trauma. "Beth was eight months pregnant, and a man snuck into her house through a window, choked her, and raped her," explained Anna. "Her husband freaked out; he couldn't deal with it. After the baby was born, he left her." When the police caught the rapist, Anna and the women from the book club attended the trial with Beth. They shared her relief when the rapist was convicted.

Today Anna often cooks with Sandy, who continues to participate in the book club even though she moved fifty miles away a couple of years ago. "Sometimes I pile the kids into the car and drive up to Sandy's for the weekend," said Anna. "Other families show up, and all the mothers hang out in the kitchen, making food for whoever needs to be fed. Somehow we muddle through." She laughed that big, honest laugh of hers: "Sandy is a great cook. I'm content just being her sous chef."

Chapter 30

The Family
That Cooks Together . . .

'll do the turkey and stuffing, and Julia will do the pies—"

"And I'll make the sweet potatoes, mashed potatoes, and cranberry sauce."

My sister-in-law Leni and I have Thanksgiving down to a system. In fact, we have been alternating as hostess for so many years that last November neither of us could remember where the previous Thanksgiving dinner had been held. We had to consult the last annual "carving the turkey" photo to see whose house it had been taken in.

Every Thanksgiving three generations of Boorstins gather for a long weekend of catching up, eating, more catching up, and more eating. Like most families at holiday reunions, the women spend a lot of time together in the kitchen. One thing I'm thankful for on Thanksgiving is that both of my sisters-in-law are also my friends. (I know several women who aren't so fortunate.) Preparing meals with Jon's wife, Leni, and David's wife, Hope—and Julia, who

always bakes at least three pies—is one of the best parts of
Thanksgiving weekend.

I met a girl who looks like Goldie Hawn and plays in a rock
band in San Francisco," Paul's brother wrote to us the summer
of 1974 when we were living in the French Alps. We imagined that
Jon had fallen for a ditsy hippie wearing love beads and flowers in
her hair. As it turned out, Leni did look like a young Goldie Hawn,
but otherwise she was responsible, well organized, and down-to-
earth, not a flower child. She played the flute with Lawrence
Hammond and the Whiplash Band occasionally at night. By day she
was the music curator at the Exploratorium museum. After Jon
talked Leni into moving from San Francisco to L.A. and I got to
know her, I realized why he couldn't live without her. Leni is kind,
selfless, and empathetic, traits that make a good wife as well as a
good friend.

Leni attributes her creativity as a cook to our Thanksgiving
family reunions, but not because of all the times she has hosted
the dinner. It requires more imagination to figure out what to serve
the night before. The meal has to be simple, in contrast to the
next day's feast, yet celebratory, for Wednesday night is when the
whole clan first gets together and everyone is high on warm family
feelings.

One year Leni came up with a dish for dinner the night before
Thanksgiving, and she has repeated it often since—a sweet-and-
sour winter borscht made with cabbage and beef. She always makes
a nonmeat version as well, for those kids who might be vegetarians
that year. Leni learned how to make the borscht from Pat Shultz,
her best friend and roommate in San Francisco.

"I certainly didn't learn to cook from my mother," said Leni,
who was the youngest of four children. "My mother had no patience

whatsoever. Sure, I'd nibble on the crumbs of the cookies she baked to send to my older siblings at college, and she taught me rules like 'oatmeal is best made the night before,' but other than that she didn't want me in her kitchen."

Leni grew up on her mother's casseroles—hamburger casserole, zucchini casserole, tuna casserole—but they weren't dishes she wanted to re-create as an adult. In her twenties, when she roomed with Pat in San Francisco, they baked chocolate chip cookies together, made appetizers like poor man's (eggplant) caviar from *The Silver Palate Cookbook* and vegetarian dishes from *Diet for a Small Planet*. It wasn't until she got married, however, that she became serious about food and cooking. Like Paul and their brother, David, Jon equates a good meal with motherly/wifely love. "Jon was so appreciative of everything I served," said Leni, "it took him ten years to reveal that he hated broccoli."

Today Leni's interest in food centers around the Sunday farmers' market in Hollywood. "After our two kids outgrew Sunday school, Jon and I exchanged religion for food," she joked. "We go every Sunday morning. We run into friends and talk about everything from which vendor is selling the best artichokes to world events. It has become like a town square." Being a regular at the farmers' market has made Leni aware of the seasonality of food in a way that doesn't happen in a grocery store. "It makes me feel connected to the earth underneath the pavement."

Paul's brother David did not stay married to Molly, my horseback-riding and pheasant-roasting companion in England. I was sad because as so often happens after a divorce, Molly put her ex and her ex's relatives behind her, including me. It wasn't until the early nineties that David found Hope. An independent and sensitive New Englander—who also happened to be striking-looking—Hope was the perfect match for him.

Hope admitted that the first time she participated in a Boorstin Thanksgiving, she was overwhelmed by the amount of food. She grew up in a family of seven where every night at dinner there was barely enough to go around. It wasn't for budgetary reasons. Her mother misjudged how much food was needed. "At one point she had five children under the age of eight and it was a madhouse," Hope recalled. "Just getting dinner on the table was a major accomplishment." If guests showed up, the kids knew the rule: FHB (family hold back). They weren't to take seconds until the guests had their fill.

Hope's mother, Cis, freely admitted that she hated to cook; she thought of it as a chore, not a choice. As a result, she tried to find dishes that were easy to prepare. "One of Mom's favorites was what she called Stay Abed Stew," said Hope. "You throw stuff into a pot in the morning, go back to bed, and when you wake up, it's ready to serve."

Hope's parents taught her that food is fuel for the body, not a topic for conversation. "Maybe it was due to the hyper-Protestant ethic they grew up with," explained Hope. "Our family dinners were always lively, but we talked about what we did in school and current events, not about the food. My parents wouldn't have cared if they ate the same thing every night."

It wasn't until Hope went away to college that she began to enjoy cooking, especially when she prepared meals with her three sisters. "We were into feminism, so it never even occurred to us to cook to attract men," she recalled. "We were not particularly creative at it, but cooking was something fun that we could share."

Over Christmas the entire family gathered at their house in Woodstock, Vermont. "This was the seventies, and at any one time at least two of us were vegetarians, so we made huge salads," recalled Hope. "Lettuce and tomatoes were the least of it. Veggies, nuts, cheese, croutons, apples . . . we threw everything into the salad bowl." The dressing was Good Seasons—the little packets of ground-up herbs (and sodium) that you mixed with oil and vinegar.

Eventually they graduated to homemade vinaigrette, but they didn't use olive oil. "I don't think I knew what extra-virgin olive oil was until after I got married!"

After the Matthiessen children grew up and moved away from home, Hope's mother developed an interest in baking bread. During her twenties, on a visit home, Hope picked up her mother's penchant for it. Cis didn't follow a recipe for the bread she baked; she simply showed Hope how it was done.

Today Hope bakes bread with her six-year-old daughter, Rebecca, who enjoys the whole process—getting out all the ingredients, measuring, stirring the dough. "Rebecca's patience is limited only when it comes to kneading," said Hope. "When she gets tired, I don't mind taking over. I find the rhythm of it restful; it centers me. And when the bread is baked, I feel satisfied that I've produced something tangible, delicious, and nurturing to my family."

Leni's Night-Before Soup

SERVES 6

This is my simplified variation of the soup that Leni traditionally serves the night before Thanksgiving. I suggest making it the night before you intend to serve it, as the flavor intensifies over time in the refrigerator and you can skim off the congealed fat. The caraway seeds produce a tantalizing aroma. Serve the soup with warm, thick-cut rye bread to continue the caraway-seed theme.

FOR THE SOUP

> 1 tablespoon butter
> 2 to 2½ pounds beef short ribs
> 1 onion, peeled and quartered, with 1 whole clove
>   stuck in each quarter
> 4 cloves garlic, chopped

3 sprigs fresh dill

3 cups beef stock or bouillon

2 cups water

3 large beets, peeled and cut into bite-size cubes

2 cups shredded green cabbage

2 carrots, diced

1 leek, outer leaves removed, coarsely chopped

2 tomatoes, chopped

1 large potato, peeled and coarsely chopped

1 tablespoon tomato paste

5 cups chicken stock or bouillon

1 tablespoon tomato paste

1½ to 2 teaspoons caraway seeds, or more to taste

¼ cup chopped fresh dill

1 to 2 teaspoons sugar

Salt and pepper to taste

Juice of 1 lemon

FOR THE GARNISH

Sour cream

Fresh dill leaves

1. In a heavy frying pan, melt the butter and brown the ribs over medium-high heat for 12 to 15 minutes, turning often so that they are cooked on all sides. Remove the ribs from the pan and blot with paper towels to absorb the grease.

2. In a big soup pot, put the ribs, the clove-studded onion, the chopped garlic, dill sprigs, beef stock, and water, and bring to a boil. Lower the heat and simmer, covered, for 1 hour.

3. With a slotted spoon, remove the onion and cloves from the soup and discard. Add the remaining ingredients except for the chopped fresh dill, sugar, salt and pepper, and lemon juice, and return to a boil. Lower the heat and simmer, uncovered, for 1 hour. (If liquid reduces too much, add chicken stock or bouillon, 1 cup at a time.) Cool to room temperature.

4. Remove the bones from the soup and shred off the meat. Discard the bones, fat, and gristle, and return the shredded meat to the soup. Refrigerate the soup overnight or until ready to serve.

5. Before serving, with a slotted spoon, remove the beef fat that has congealed on the surface of the soup and discard. Bring the soup to a boil and add the remaining ingredients. Lower the heat to simmer and cook for 5 to 10 more minutes.

6. When serving, garnish each bowl with 1 to 2 tablespoons of sour cream and a sprig of dill.

Chapter 31

A Life in Food

Barbara Fairchild and I became friends over foie gras. It was at one of the food-related press events I am invited to every few months, in this case a particularly fancy dinner at the Hotel Bel-Air in Los Angeles. No matter how wonderful the food is, press dinners can be tedious unless you are seated with someone lively and interesting. That night I lucked out. Barbara and I were semisecluded at the end of a long table, and we talked nonstop about food, common friends, movies, the state of the world, and more food.

Barbara admits that her psyche has been focused on food her entire life. It was no surprise when, after twenty-three years at *Bon Appétit*, in 2000 she became the editor-in-chief. In her own words, she has "tasted just about everything there is to taste, and eaten just about everything there is to eat." Still, Barbara is not a food snob. She appreciates the French fries at In-n-Out Burger as much as she does the foie gras at the Hotel Bel-Air (well, *almost* as much). When we get together for dinner every few months, often we pick a new or trendy restaurant—as long as it is quiet enough for conversation.

Barbara and I agree that when we're dining with our girlfriends, it's not just about the food, it's about the friendship.

Barbara and Paul Nagle, the man she calls her "husbandlike person," live in a bungalow on a quiet, tree-lined street. The warm, cozy interior is decorated with vintage chocolate-ad posters (chocolate is one of Barbara's passions) and foreign-film posters (movies are another). The kitchen is small but *bon equipée*—meaning it features state-of-the-art appliances and cooking equipment for preparing the most sophisticated dishes.

When Barbara claims that she was "predestined" for a career in food, she is only half joking. In fourth grade, while her classmates were making papier-mâché state maps for their lesson in California history, she was making sourdough starter, like the forty-niners did during the gold rush. Barbara's mother, Ina Lieb, consulted *Mary Margaret McBride's Encyclopedia of Cooking* to figure out how to do it. They made the bread dough together, and Barbara's mother baked it after Barbara left for school in the morning. "There I was, giving my talk to the students about the history of sourdough," she recalled, "and suddenly my mother walks in with sourdough bread warm from the oven, and a stick of butter. I was the most popular girl in school that day."

Her mother's enthusiasm for cooking was an inspiration to Barbara. On Christmas they baked sugar cookies, rum balls, and minifruitcakes that she soaked with whiskey, which Barbara and her two sisters gift-wrapped and gave to friends and neighbors. "My mother's brownies are still *beyond*," said Barbara. "I don't think it's the recipe that makes them so good. She's been using the same pan since 1946, this beat-up old thing she calls her lucky pan. She knows intuitively when to take the brownies out of the oven so that they're crisp on the edges but still soft in the middle. And her matzoh balls . . . my mom is Lutheran, but her matzo balls are lighter and tastier than any that my father's Jewish relatives make!"

In the summers when Barbara was growing up in New York, her

family drove to Cumberland, Maryland, a little town in the Alleghenies, to visit her mother's relatives. "We were city people, and suddenly we were surrounded by aunts, great-aunts, and cousins who cooked down-home Southern food and put up watermelon-rind pickles and peach preserves," recalled Barbara. She rolled up her sleeves and joined in.

Later, after Barbara's family moved to Los Angeles, her mother got a job as a secretary at an electronics company (and quickly worked her way up to vice president). It was a big turning point for Barbara. "I was in junior high, and I was the only kid in class whose mom was in the workforce," she recalled. "It made me proud." Because now and then her mother worked late, Barbara—sometimes with her father's help—prepared dinner for the family. "I was taking home ec, and every day I came home and cooked what I had learned in class. Unfortunately, my best dishes were chocolate chip cookies, pizza, and muffins."

Barbara's interest in food developed further during high school. For family dinners, she was now making chili, macaroni and cheese, and roast chicken. One summer she bought a crate of peaches to make peach preserves, like her relatives did back in Maryland. Her sisters were reluctant helpers, but they washed the peaches and put them through a food mill. "It was a hundred and three degrees in the kitchen, and there was peach juice all over the floor," Barbara recalled. "We were sweating like pigs, but we got the job done. My sisters still tease me about all the grand cooking schemes I roped them into when we were teenagers."

When Barbara was eighteen she made her first *gougère* (a French cheese puff). By the time she was nineteen, she was a hundred pounds overweight. It took her a year, but through Weight Watchers she lost every pound, and she hasn't fluctuated by more than ten pounds ever since. "It's ironic that I was fat before I started working in food, not after," Barbara said.

After college Barbara got a job as an editorial assistant at a travel magazine. She married at twenty-three, and like other newlyweds in the early seventies, she and her then husband entertained often at home. She spent hours preparing dinner, and *Bon Appétit* was her "cooking bible." When a position opened up at the magazine, Barbara jumped on it. This was before computers, and her first job was typing recipes and running the recipe-testing kitchen. Soon she graduated to writing. "That's when I started my full-blown culinary education," she said, "at the University of *Bon Appétit*."

Barbara and I discussed how the style of entertaining has changed over the years since she began working at the magazine. "When I was younger, I prepared eight-course dinners," she said. "By the time everyone sat down, I was exhausted. Now, if people come over, I do something simple. I don't want to be stuck in the kitchen when everyone is in the living room or out on the patio, talking. I like being part of the party."

Today Barbara most enjoys cooking for family holiday dinners. "I used to get nervous on Thanksgiving," she said. "I insisted on preparing the entire dinner, and everyone expected a lot from me because I worked for the magazine. I knew if I blew it, we'd end up eating takeout from Koo Koo Roo." Barbara now makes the turkey and gravy according to one of her favorite old *Bon Appétit* recipes, and sometimes a soup from the current Thanksgiving issue. The stuffing recipe is her own creation—it calls for sourdough bread, sausage, apples, and lots of mushrooms; she bakes it in a buttered casserole dish, rather than using it to stuff the turkey. The guests bring the other dishes—based on *Bon Appétit* recipes.

Over the years Barbara has become close friends with other important women in the food world, including Julia Child. They first met in 1991, when they shared a car from the San Francisco airport to Napa Valley, where they were attending a food-and-wine event. "I'm not a person who is easily intimidated," said Barbara, "but at first I was so in awe of sitting next to the leading woman in American cooking, I was tongue-tied. I didn't want Julia to think I was interviewing her, so I decided not to talk about food. The whole way, we talked about everything else. Julia knew more juicy Hollywood gossip than I did!"

A few months later Julia invited Barbara to come to her home in Santa Barbara and join her for dinner at a friend's. "Paul and I picked up Julia to drive her to the host's," recalled Barbara. "Julia had prepared a whole cracked crab for the dinner and displayed it on a silver platter. She handed me the platter, and I climbed into the backseat, while she sat up front with Paul. The road was winding, and I was worried the crab would go flying."

The crab stayed put and the evening was terrific. "Julia's friends were very down-to-earth, people who enjoyed good food and wine, like we did."

Barbara has never cooked dinner for Julia. They meet at restaurants because they enjoy trying new places and revisiting the ones they love. Sometimes they discuss what food tells about a country's culture—how you can learn about France from French cooking, and about Italy from Italian. They agree that some chefs today put too many ingredients in a dish or on a plate, and it makes the food confusing. They also agree that the essence of good food is simplicity. Barbara and Julia agree about most things, except one: "Julia thinks that the fries at McDonald's are better than I do," said Barbara. "I prefer the fries at In-n-Out Burger."

Bon Appétit's Roast Turkey with Herb Rub and Shiitake Mushroom Gravy

SERVES 16

This is from the November 1994 issue of Bon Appétit. *Barbara has been using the recipe for her Thanksgiving turkey ever since then.*

FOR THE TURKEY

> 3 tablespoons chopped fresh rosemary, or
>   1½ tablespoons dried
> 3 tablespoons chopped fresh thyme, or 1½ tablespoons
>   dried
> 3 tablespoons chopped fresh tarragon, or
>   1½ tablespoons dried
> 1 tablespoon ground pepper
> One 20- or 21-pound turkey, neck and giblets reserved
> Fresh herb sprigs: rosemary, thyme, and/or tarragon
> 2 tablespoons vegetable oil
> 6 tablespoons butter, melted
> 4 cups canned low-salt chicken broth

FOR THE GRAVY

> ½ cup all-purpose flour
> ½ cup dry sherry
> 3 tablespoons butter
> 12 ounces fresh shiitake mushrooms, stemmed and
>   sliced
> 1 tablespoon plus 1 teaspoon chopped fresh rosemary,
>   or 2 teaspoons dried
> 4 cups (approximately) canned low-salt chicken broth
> ⅓ cup whipping cream
> 2 teaspoons chopped fresh thyme, or 1 teaspoon dried
> 2 teaspoons chopped fresh tarragon, or 1 teaspoon
>   dried
> Salt and pepper to taste

1. Make the turkey: In a small bowl, mix the first 4 ingredients. Pat the turkey dry with paper towels and place it on a rack set in a large roasting pan. If you're not stuffing the turkey, place the herb sprigs in the main cavity. Otherwise, spoon the stuffing into the main cavity. Tie the legs together loosely to hold the shape of the turkey. Brush the turkey with the oil, then rub the herb mix all over it. Place the turkey neck and giblets in the roasting pan.

2. Position the rack in the lowest third of the oven, and preheat to 425°F. Drizzle the melted butter all over the turkey, and pour 2 cups of the broth into the roasting pan. Roast the turkey for 45 minutes. Remove from the oven, and cover with foil. Reduce the oven temperature to 350°F, and return the turkey to the oven. Roast an unstuffed turkey 1 hour, a stuffed turkey 1½ hours. Remove the foil from the turkey; pour the remaining 2 cups of broth into the pan. Continue roasting the turkey about 1 hour and 40 minutes longer, basting occasionally with pan juices, until a meat thermometer inserted into the thickest part of the thigh registers 180°F or the juices run clear when the thickest part of the thigh is pierced with a skewer. Transfer the turkey to a platter and tent with foil. Let stand 30 minutes. Reserve the liquid in the pan for gravy.

3. Make the gravy: In a small bowl, mix the flour and the sherry until it forms a smooth paste. Melt the butter in a large, heavy saucepan over medium-high heat. Add the mushrooms and the rosemary and sauté until the mushrooms begin to soften, about 3 minutes. (This can be made up to 3 hours ahead and kept at room temperature.)

4. Discard the turkey neck and giblets, and transfer the pan juices to a large glass measuring cup. Spoon off the fat. Add enough chicken broth to measure 5 cups and add this to the saucepan with the mushrooms. Add the flour paste and whisk until smooth. Bring the mixture to a boil, stirring frequently. Boil until thickened to light gravy, about 10 minutes. Mix in the cream, thyme, and tarragon. Season with salt and pepper to taste, and serve with the turkey.

Ina's Brownies

Barbara says her mom's great brownies result in part from the old, beat-up "magic" pan she bakes them in. I didn't have a square 8 by 8-inch pan like the one Ina indicated, so I baked the brownies in a rectangular pan. My son was unimpressed with the results, so I went out and bought an 8 by 8-inch Pyrex baking dish and tried again. This time Adam said I nailed it. From now on, I will consider the square Pyrex baking dish that I bought for under ten dollars at Ralph's as my "magic pan."

3 eggs

1½ cups sugar

¼ pound butter, cut into pieces

4 ounces unsweetened chocolate, cut into pieces

1 cup flour

1 teaspoon vanilla extract

1 cup chopped walnuts (optional)

1. Grease an 8 by 8-inch pan, and preheat the oven to 325°F. In a mixing bowl, whisk the eggs and gradually add the sugar. Mix well.

2. In a saucepan set over simmering water or in the top of a double boiler, melt the butter and the chocolate together. (You can also do this in the microwave: 30 seconds at a time, mixing in between zaps.)

3. Add the melted chocolate/butter to the other ingredients and blend. Do not beat or overmix. Add the flour, ⅓ cup at a time, gently mixing after each addition. Again, do not overmix. Add the vanilla extract and the walnuts, and blend well.

4. Pour the batter into the prepared pan and bake for 25 to 35 minutes. Check after 25 minutes to see if they are done—a toothpick inserted into the center should come out clean. (However, if the sides are well baked but the center is still a bit sticky, remove from the oven.) Cool on a rack before cutting into squares.

Chapter 32

Julia and Freddy

What do you say when you're face-to-face with the icon of American cooking? When I walked over to Julia Child at Barbara Fairchild's birthday party, I introduced myself and told her that she so inspired my daughter, Julia, when she was in the sixth grade and taught cooking to kindergarteners with her girlfriend, that they called the class "Brooke and Julia's Child Cooking Class."

Still lively and focused at eighty-nine, Julia Child laughed that big, boisterous laugh that anyone who's ever seen her on TV knows so well, and patted my arm. "That's marvelous," she said. "I'm so flattered."

I wanted to interview Julia Child for this book, but Barbara's birthday party wasn't the time and place. Scores of people were crowded onto the back patio of Café des Artistes in Hollywood, and we were about to sit down to dinner. A few weeks later, after Julia returned to her house in Cambridge, Massachusetts, I e-mailed her assistant and asked when I could phone her. The assistant e-mailed me back and said she'd ask Julia and get back to me. The next day,

Famous food friends: Julia Child and
Barbara Fairchild.

as I was working away on my computer, the phone rang. I heard Julia's distinctive chortle. "Can we talk now?" she asked. "I'm about to go up to Maine with my family." When Julia Child calls, you drop everything to get a word with her.

I mentioned that Barbara had told me how they became friends through their common interest in food. "Yes, the nice thing about food people is we are always talking about food and there's so much to say!" she replied. I asked her to recall other women that she connected with because of food and cooking. She thought for a moment and then said, "Why, Freddy, of course!"

Frederica Child was Julia's sister-in-law, the wife of her husband Paul's twin brother, Charlie. Freddy was older than Julia, and she and Charlie married young. They lived in France during the twenties and thirties, and Freddy learned to cook there. After Julia married Paul, she and Freddy became close friends, and Freddy taught Julia lots of things about cooking.

It's hard to believe that Julia Child didn't learn how to cook until after she got married. "I grew up in Pasadena, and our family always had a cook," she explained. "My mother knew good food—Welsh rarebit, for example—but she didn't make anything but the occasional biscuits and pancakes. When I was about to get married and I asked her for cooking tips, she said things like 'Bring the bowl to the board, not the board to the bowl.' " Julia laughed, and I understood why: When she had her TV show in the sixties, she often missed the bowl when breaking an egg, or dropped ingredients on the floor. When she did, she simply shrugged and carried on.

After Julia's marriage and before she and Paul moved to Paris, they spent summers with Charlie and Freddy at the family's log cabin in Maine. "The cabin had an old wood-burning stove," Julia recalled, "and one day Freddy and I decided to make lobsters. We found this old galvanized-iron washbasin about two feet long—it was labeled HAPPY HOME LAUNDRY—and we scrubbed it down. We filled it with water and boiled the lobsters in it on top of the stove."

Julia's sister-in-law taught her how to cook potatoes and green vegetables—"Everything Freddy made was very simple but delicious," said Julia—and how to bake bread. "Freddy was very good at skillet corn bread," Julia recalled, "and she had an old bucket with a dough hook that we used to knead bread. This was before electric mixers, of course, and everything took hours."

Julia reminisced about how when she moved to Paris, she discovered French food. "Everything was so delicious, I decided, 'This is for me!' " She enrolled in the Cordon Bleu cooking school, and the rest, as they say, is culinary history.

But Julia didn't wish to talk about her life as a cookbook writer and TV personality. She returned to the subject of her friendship with Freddy: "In the fifties, Paul and I would meet Freddy and Charlie at the cabin in Maine during the summer, and Freddy and I spent all of our time in the kitchen. We didn't make anything fancy—stews, bread, lobster. Freddy was very much a trial-and-error cook, and we had our share of disasters." While Julia and Freddy cooked, they talked. "This was when the McCarthy hearings were going on, and we watched it on TV. We were positively horrified."

Freddy died fifteen years ago, but Julia remembered her fondly. "Freddy was a wonderfully vigorous woman. She had beautiful red hair and was about five feet five. I was six feet tall and I towered over her. Once, when we were young, Paul, Charlie, Freddy, and I went to Washington, D.C., to a cocktail party. A drunken English guest had heard that twins were coming—Paul and Charlie, of course—and he walked up and looked at Freddy and me and said, 'Oh, here are the twins!'" She laughed that big laugh of hers. "Freddy and I had great fun together."

Whole Boiled or Steamed Lobsters
From *From Julia Child's Kitchen* (Alfred A. Knopf, 1975)
I LIVE LOBSTER PER PERSON; I- TO 2-POUNDERS FOR SINGLE SERVINGS

Julia's recipe is suited for lobsters up to 20 pounds in weight, though I'm sure that even the queen of American cooking would have trouble wrestling such a behemoth into the pot. She suggests that home cooks boil or steam no more than four lobsters at a time—unless you have a very big pot and a powerful enough heat source to quickly bring the water back to a boil once you've put them in. In a note about the recipe, Julia says that although lobsters are a luxury, nothing need be wasted: After all is eaten, you can chop the discarded shells and boil them with a few chopped onions, carrots, and celery to make a fine fish stock.

1. If you are boiling lobsters, you need a very large kettle or wash boiler of rapidly boiling sea water, or tap water with 1½ teaspoons salt for each quart of water. If you are steaming them, you need a very large kettle or wash boiler fitted with a rack positioned 1½ to 2 inches above the bottom of the kettle, and 1½ inches of rapidly boiling sea water or salted water. You also need a cover (or tray) for the kettle, plus, if needed, a weight of some sort to make a tight fit.

2. If you are boiling lobsters: Plunge live lobsters headfirst and upside down into the boiling water; cover the kettle and weight the top down if necessary. As soon as the water comes back to the boil, remove cover, reduce heat so lobsters boil slowly but steadily, and begin timing (see below).

3. If you are steaming lobsters: Place lobsters on the rack, cover the kettle, weight down the top if necessary, and as soon as steam begins to escape, start timing (see below).

4. Timing: from the moment water boils again:

> 1- to 1¼-pound lobsters: 10 to 12 minutes
> 1½- to 2-pound lobsters: 15 to 18 minutes
> 2½- to 5-pound lobsters: 20 to 25 minutes
> 6- to 10-pound lobsters: 25 to 35 minutes
> 10- to 15-pound lobsters: 35 to 40 minutes
> 15- to 20-pound lobsters: 40 to 45 minutes

For lobsters 6 pounds or more, add 5 minutes to the boiling time if the shells are very thick.

5. When is a lobster done? Here are several ways to check. Some clever people are able to tell by looking at and feeling the underside of the tail section, which should be opaque and springy; I have had no success with this system. I do pull off one of the little legs close to the body, and break it open; the meat should come easily away from the shell. Or gently pull the shell up from the chest section and peer inside at the green matter, which should be just set, not liquid. Finally, you can take the lobster's temperature immediately after you remove him from the pot; use a small instant-type pocket thermometer and insert it through the vent hole at the end of the tail, an inch into the center of the meat—165°F is done.

6. After boiling, it is a good idea to drain the water out of the lobsters if you're going to serve them whole in their shells. Plunge a knife into the front of the head, between the eyes, to split the shell. Hold the lobster up by its tail and let the water drain out of the head; then you might hold it up by its claws to drain them, and again hold it by its tail in case more water is still to come.

7. Serving whole boiled lobsters: The most satisfying way to enjoy whole boiled lobsters is for each to have his own, served as a separate course with bowls of melted butter for each person, along with French bread, halved or quartered lemons, salt and pepper, finger bowls, and a large stack of paper napkins. Provide a plate for each lobster, and a communal bowl or individual ones for shell scraps. If you don't have lobster shears for everyone, have several sharp-pointed kitchen shears for the group, or nutpicks and nutcrackers. Oyster forks, or some such small instruments, are useful as well. Serve a dry white wine like Riesling, Pouilly-Fuissé, Muscadet, or Pinot Blanc, and you will not need much after the lobsters except perhaps a green salad or coleslaw, and a dessert of fresh berries or a fruit tart.

8. Eating whole boiled lobsters: One way of attacking a whole boiled lobster is to break off all the little legs. While the lobster cools, eat them one at a time, twisting them apart at the joints and drawing the pieces through your teeth to squeeze out the meat. Then break off the big claws and claw joints; cut or crack the joints to break the shell and get at the meat, lifting it out with nutpick or fork and dipping it into melted butter for each mouthful. For the claws, bend small end downward to break it away and draw its cartilage out of the main claw; dig meat out with nutpick. Cut or crack open the main claws to get their meat. Twist tail from chest, then break off end flaps from tail and push meat out of shell with your forefinger, from the end. For the chest meat, pull body out of chest shell; pull off and discard feathery gills on outside or chest. Scoop green matter onto plate and reserve for the finish. Pull out and discard stomach sack in head. Break chest in half lengthwise, and dig out tender meat between cartilages with pick or fork. All coagulated white matter inside chest shell is edible, as is all green matter and pink roe; eat with fork or spoon, or spread it on your French bread.

Chapter 33

Travels with My Julia

When a woman gives birth to a daughter, she hopes that her baby will grow up to embody all her own best traits and talents, plus the good ones that she failed to exhibit. She wishes that her daughter one day will be a strong and self-confident woman, smart and savvy and independent—and happy. Beautiful wouldn't hurt, but she will teach her daughter that beauty is unimportant compared with kindness and generosity, qualities that reflect an inner beauty and contribute to happiness. A woman also hopes that when her daughter matures, she will consider her not just a mother but a friend.

When I gave birth to Julia, I had such hopes and dreams for her. She is twenty-three years old now, a reporter for *Fortune* magazine in New York, and far along on the path to fulfilling them. Julia has always made me proud. As for the beautiful part, she always has been beautiful, outside and in.

Julia's success as a human being has resulted from her natural talent and brains, but I'd like to think that I had a little something to do with her strength, self-confidence, and independence. When she entered nursery school, her separation anxiety was so acute that even after all the other mothers had been "allowed" by their children to leave them on their own in the classroom, Julia burst into tears when I suggested that I go. The wise principal advised me to "sit my butt down on the floor in the corner of the classroom and sweat it out" until Julia was ready to be on her own.

When Julia was a teenager, I sweated out her occasional temper tantrums and rebellious outbursts of criticism. (Advice to women with teenage daughters: Never wear a terrycloth bathrobe when allowing them to vent their feelings. It will make you sweat even more.) To this day, Julia argues that I am too often impatient with her, that I am unable to give her my undivided attention when she needs it. She's right; the demands of my life often make it hard for me to focus on her needs. That is why I have always tried to plan time alone with her.

Cooking together in the kitchen has counted as time alone. So has traveling together. In fact, I think it is on the trips we have taken without Paul or Adam along that Julia has grown to know and trust me enough to think of me as her friend.

I am fortunate that I have been able to take Julia along on some of my travel-writing assignments. After her graduation from high school, we took scuba-diving lessons and went on a diving trip to Belize. After her first year in college we flew to New Zealand, where we went horseback riding among a herd of elk, and to Tahiti, where we snorkeled among sharks. Before she graduated from college, she met me in Lisbon for a cruise on which I was writing a story about Joachim Splichal, the consulting chef. The highlight of the trip was visiting the Malaga market with Joachim, where he introduced us to food items like *brandade*, the dried, salted fish that is a staple of Spanish and Portuguese cuisine, and sheep brains. Joachim got a kick out of watching Julia's face as he described the delicious taste of the slimy gray organ. "You slurp it right out of the skull!" he said.

In my travels with Julia, food has played an important role, for she shares my enthusiasm for exploring exotic markets and tasting intriguing dishes. I must say, however, that I didn't take Julia to Kenya with the intention of introducing her to new dishes and flavors. I assumed that as in India, where I had traveled with Paul before she was born, the food in Kenya would be unsafe to eat and that our diet would be confined to rice and bread. It didn't matter. I was taking Julia to Africa to show her the wonder of seeing wild animals in their native habitat, something I had experienced decades ago in India.

Our trip to Kenya turned out to be one of our most memorable. Seeing wildlife was the high point—especially when we rode horses among giraffes, zebras, and kudus—but to my surprise, food turned out to be an important part of the adventure.

It took over twenty hours of flying to reach the Laikipia Plain, but once we stepped out onto the dusty airstrip, I was glad we'd made the journey. The vista of rugged earth and cobalt blue sky extended for a hundred miles. I understood why they say that in this part of Africa visitors often feel as if their eyesight has improved.

I had been invited here to write a travel article about Laragai, a country estate built by Lords Valentine and Michael Cecil, whose great-great-grandfather was Great Britain's prime minister under Queen Victoria. The estate is located in the middle of a thirty-five-thousand-acre cattle and wheat ranch owned by the Dyer family, who were pioneers in this part of Kenya after World War I. Since the Cecil brothers do not get to Laragai often, they decided to rent it out to private groups.

Set on a cliff overlooking a vast plain, Laragai has a half-dozen enormous bedrooms, a drawing room with a forty-foot-high ceiling and two fireplaces, a swimming pool, tennis court, and two airplane hangars—one for each of the Cecil brothers' planes. From the moment I set foot on the estate, I realized it would please tourists seeking luxury in the African bush. Julia agreed but brought up a good point: "How can the food be good in the middle of nowhere?"

Our skepticism vanished with dinner. The creamy green soup distilled the essence of avocado; the salad was a toss of baby lettuces that Fuzz Dyer, the ruggedly handsome manager of Laragai, had picked that morning. With it came fresh-baked bread made with wheat grown on the Dyer ranch, slathered with butter made from the milk of the Jersey cows raised by Fuzz's mother, Rose.

Next up was succulent breast of duck with a bittersweet orange sauce. "My mum raises ducks on her farm too," Fuzz added. She was also the one to thank for the crisp sugar snap peas, baby carrots, and buttery litle potatoes. By the time dessert was served—a frozen whipped-cream bombe with crunchy bits of meringue hidden inside—Julia and I were determined to meet the cook. Fuzz pointed us toward the kitchen. "My wife's the best cook in Kenya."

A tiny blond who looks a lot younger than forty and lives in jeans and a T-shirt, Bindi Dyer has the slim, narrow-hipped figure of a long-distance runner—which she is. We complimented her on the fabulous meal, and I asked who had taught her to cook. Her tanned face broke into a grin: "Aunt Doodie, of course. Aunt Doodie cooked for the Churchills!"

Over the next few days, we watched—and helped—Bindi prepare everything from garlicky lamb patties to brownies studded with Kenyan macadamia nuts to cheesecake crowned with sweet Kenyan bananas. While Bindi cooked, she talked—about growing up in Kenya, about her short-lived chef's career in London, and about her two young sons who were away at boarding school in western Kenya. She missed them terribly, but because Borana Ranch is in the bush, boarding school was the only option for their education. When they are older, they will be sent to boarding school in

England, as Bindi and her sister were. Bindi also told us about her Irish aunt Doodie.

Born on an eight-thousand-acre ranch owned, like Borana, by descendants of Brits who pioneered in Kenya after World War I, Bindi and her twin sister, Delulu, were nicknamed by their African nanny. When they were twelve, the government of the newly independent Kenya reclaimed the land, so the family moved to Spain. They took over an old, deserted olive farm six miles north of Seville. Bindi learned to speak Spanish and, alongside her mother, how to prepare Spanish dishes like paella and gazpacho.

When she was thirteen, Bindi and her twin sister were sent off to boarding school in England. "Croft House was the most dreadful school," she recalled. "I absolutely loathed it! I couldn't wait for the weekend, when we'd take the train into London and stay with Doodie and our

Bindi Dyer, the best cook in Kenya.

cousins." Bindi described her aunt as a "tough bird." Doodie drove a jeep on an air base during World War II, and afterward she stayed in England, married Bindi's uncle, and had a family. "My uncle was perfectly foul to her and eventually walked out. Doodie was much better off without him."

Doodie supported her three children by working as a private cook for prominent families like the Churchills, and by catering. Whenever Bindi was off from school, she worked for her. Bindi fondly recalled times when they were frantic to get food to a party. "Aunt Doodie had a big yellow Labrador that rode everywhere in the backseat of her car. The problem was getting the damn dog hair off of the food platters!"

When Bindi was nineteen, she was in a terrible car accident. Her pelvis was broken in three places, and both her hips were dislocated. Since her parents lived in Spain, she phoned her aunt for help. Bindi spent several months recovering at Doodie's house in London. "Aunt Doodie was like a good mum to me," said Bindi.

Bindi joined Doodie's catering business after she finished school. For formal occasions, they hired an ex-butler from Buckingham Palace to serve, and Bindi found it all very exciting. She went on to cook in such fashionable London restaurants as Draycott's Wine Bar, Monkey's, and Menage à Trois, but she credits her aunt Doodie for inspiring her as a cook. "Auntie always pushed the boat out with her cooking," explained Bindi. "She started with the best ingredients; she never bought anything that was not top-quality. And she taught me to always add your personal touch. Auntie would say to me, 'If a recipe calls for strawberries but you've got good mulberries, use the mulberries instead.' "

In the kitchen at Laragai, Bindi offered Julia and me another slice of tonight's frozen bombe, explaining that it was a dessert her aunt often made for the Churchills. "Auntie would be cross with me because I didn't put hazelnuts in the meringue tonight," she said. "But she'd be pleased I found some mascarpone and added it to the double cream!"

Aunt Doodie's Avocado Soup

SERVES 4 TO 6

Bindi uses Kenya-grown Fuerte avocados. I used California-grown Haas avocados, and they worked just fine. This soup is simple to make, and it is creamy and delicious. Its pretty lime green color fades, however, so serve it within a few hours of when you make it—and serve it ice cold.

> 4 big, ripe avocados, Fuerte if available, peeled and
>   cut into chunks
> 8 ounces cream cheese, cut into pieces
> Juice of 1 big lemon
> 2 pints chicken stock
> Salt and pepper to taste
> Watercress or parsley for garnish

1. Put all the ingredients except the garnish into a food processor, and mix until smooth and creamy, about 1 to 1½ minutes.

2. Refrigerate for 2 to 3 hours, and serve garnished with watercress or parsley.

Chapter 34

The Champagne Queen

After the disaster on September 11, I e-mailed Mireille Guiliano, a friend who lives in a penthouse apartment on West Fourteenth Street in New York, to see how she was. Several times when I had visited Mireille, we had stood on her roof terrace to watch the sunset, which was glorious from that vantage point. On a clear day, the last rays of the sun gilded the Statue of Liberty and glimmered golden in the windows of the World Trade Center.

Mireille e-mailed me back to say that of course she was devastated by what had happened. Every time she glanced out her window, the hole in the skyline where the towers had been reminded her of the horror and the tragedy. She couldn't bring herself to climb the steps to the roof terrace to watch the sunset.

Mireille's sadness was particularly poignant because she is usually cheerful and optimistic, and her job revolves around promoting the celebratory moments in life. Mireille is the president and CEO of Clicquot Inc., the person responsible for turning Veuve Clicquot champagne into a leading prestige brand.

A trim, petite brunette with the smooth, ageless skin that fashionable French women always seem to have, Mireille wears only moisturizer, a hint of eyeliner, and no lipstick—she lacks the patience for it. The last time I visited her, she prepared Sunday supper for her husband, Edward, and me in their tiny kitchen.

I met Edward and Mireille several years ago when Edward, who now is the president of the New York Institute of Technology, wrote restaurant reviews for a guidebook I edited. Restaurants are Edward and Mireille's passion, and they eat out nearly every night. That's why, on Sunday nights like this one, Mireille was happy to stay home and cook.

Mireille grew up in a small town in eastern France in the fifties, and Sunday was the one day of the week that her mother wasn't working, so she cooked for the family. "My mother taught me that cooking can be both relaxing and rewarding," Mireille explained. Her mother got up early and baked cinnamon cake, brioche, or a fruit tart for breakfast. "The delicious smells would wake everyone up, and we'd go down to the kitchen in our bathrobes and eat, while mother was already cleaning the sweetbreads or peeling potatoes for lunch." Sunday was also the only day the children in Mireille's family were allowed to drink a little wine. "My mother gave me my first taste of her favorite champagne when I was six—it happened to be Veuve Clicquot!"

Mireille's mother owned a little shop that Mireille described as the Dean & DeLuca of its time. "Reps came with samples of the finest chocolate and champagne," she recalled. "On top of that, my mother and my aunt were fabulous bakers. The other kids in our neighborhood ate bread, but we ate croissants!"

Later Mireille attended the university in Paris, where she found the cafeteria food so bad that she could barely eat it. When she went home for the weekend, she discussed recipes with her mother and watched her cook. This was when Mireille started to think about what went into cooking, and the importance of technique. "I wrote down my mother's recipes, but I didn't cook much when I got back to school," she said. "It was too complicated and time-consuming, and I didn't enjoy cooking just for myself."

In Mireille's kitchen, she sprinkled fennel seeds on three halibut steaks, wrapped them in foil, and slid them into the oven. She eats so many rich meals in restaurants that she likes to keep it simple when she cooks at home. Even though the halibut recipe is low-calorie, Mireille never diets. Instead, she uses self-discipline: "The secret is yoga every morning, a good breakfast but little lunch, lots of mineral water, and lots of walking," she said. "And very small portions."

Mireille met Edward on a bus in Istanbul in 1973, when they were both graduate students traveling on vacation. "It wasn't love at first sight," she reminisced, "but close to it." Soon she joined him in New York, where she worked as a translator at the United Nations. "Edward was in for a surprise when I moved in with him. The myth about French women being great cooks didn't quite apply to me, even though my mother kept telling me that *l'amour de l'homme passé par l'estomac.* My first year in New York, Edward cooked most of the time. I was embarrassed about it because where I came from, men didn't cook unless they were professional chefs."

One day Mireille stopped by a cooking school in the West Village and signed up. At the end of the first lesson, the teacher, Lydie, a Frenchwoman married to an American, took Mireille aside and said she couldn't let her pay for the class because it was obvious that she already knew how to cook. Mireille told Lydie about her experiences with food when she was growing up in France. Lydie concluded that she must have learned to cook just by being with her mother in the kitchen. She advised Mireille not to waste her money on cooking school. "Lydie said, 'Go out and buy yourself Julia Child,'" recalled Mireille, "'and start practicing.'"

Mireille and Lydie became friends, and Mireille called her whenever she couldn't figure out a recipe. In the meantime, Mireille started reading cookbooks like novels and marking those recipes that hit her fancy. Within a year or two Mireille was cooking for dinner parties that she and Edward held, but she only prepared French food, and she made everything from scratch. "These were the late seventies, and you couldn't find good bread in New York, so I baked my own," she said. Mireille often cooked all day to prepare a dinner for four or six guests. "I made elaborate dishes like terrines. My husband's friends were very impressed because their girlfriends couldn't cook."

Mireille pulled a bottle of Veuve Clicquot from the refrigerator along with a jar of caviar. "Champagne and caviar," she said. "Is there any better first course?" Standing in her kitchen, we ate the caviar on blinis that she had bought in a plastic vacuum pack and steamed until they were warm.

The halibut was perfectly cooked and redolent of fennel seeds and champagne. "Veuve Clicquot, of course," she said. As we sat down to dinner, I kidded Mireille that as savory as the dish was because of it, I would never advise anyone to waste such good champagne on cooking fish.

Mireille's Halibut in Champagne

SERVES 4

Mireille uses Veuve Clicquot when she prepares this dish, but I make do with white wine ordinaire *and it tastes just fine. Veuve Clicquot— or any such fabulous champagne—I save for drinking. If you are not a halibut fan, substitute another thick fish like Chilean sea bass, mahimahi, swordfish, or salmon. Rice is an excellent side dish.*

2 teaspoons extra-virgin olive oil, or olive oil cooking
   spray
Four 4-ounce fillets of halibut, mahimahi, Chilean sea
   bass, swordfish, or salmon
½ cup champagne, sparkling wine, or white wine
8 sprigs fresh thyme
8 thin lemon slices
2 teaspoons fennel seeds or more to taste
8 sprigs fresh parsley
Salt and pepper to taste

1. Preheat the oven to 350°F. Tear aluminum foil into 8 squares large enough to wrap a fish fillet with room to spare. Double up the pieces of foil, creating 4 packets, and lightly brush each with olive oil or spray with olive-oil cooking spray.

2. Place one fish fillet in the center of each foil square. Drizzle with the wine. Put 2 thyme sprigs, 2 lemon slices, ½ teaspoon fennel seeds (or more to taste), and 2 parsley sprigs on each fillet. Season with salt and pepper to taste and seal each foil into a packet, leaving room for steam to build up within. (You can do this in the morning and refrigerate the packets until dinner. Remove them from the refrigerator and let warm to room temperature before baking.)

3. Place the packets of fish on a baking sheet and bake for 10 to 15 minutes. Do not overcook or the fish will be dry.

4. To serve, set one packet on each plate and have each diner carefully open it. Steam will escape as the packet is opened. Guests should spoon the juices over the fish.

Chapter 35

More Pheasant Follies

Susan, how about coming over tomorrow tonight and helping me roast a pheasant?"

On the other end of the phone, my friend Susan laughed. "Why on earth do you want to roast a pheasant?"

"I need a pheasant recipe for my book because I once roasted pheasants with my ex-sister-in-law in England, and you and I roasted one in the early eighties—"

"We nearly incinerated that poor bird with Jack Daniel's!"

"Besides, you're moving to New Mexico. How many more chances will we have to cook together?"

Susan was one of my best friends in the late seventies and early eighties, when she and her husband, Al, were our closest "couples friends." They were our favorite restaurant-reviewing partners—Susan is as passionate about food and cooking as I am—and because their daughter, Katy, and Julia were such good friends, our two families got together often. When Susan and Al announced that they were getting divorced, Paul and I were shocked and upset. Al emotionally withdrew from us, but we remained close to Susan.

I saw Susan often and I fixed her up with single men. A beautiful woman in her early thirties, she had no trouble attracting them. At one point, in fact, there were two vying for her attention, like knights in a medieval tale: Tom, an English professor like her former husband, and an equally tall, equally handsome Hollywood screenwriter. Eventually, Susan chose Tom. Paul, Julia, and I attended their wedding in Santa Barbara.

As so often happens when a friend remarries, Paul and I never became as close "couples friends" with Susan and Tom as we had been with Susan and Al. It wasn't that we disliked Tom; we enjoyed his company. But Susan started a new life with Tom that included his circle of friends, and as our daughters grew older, they too grew apart, so we saw each other less often as families.

It wasn't until both our daughters were nearly finished with college that Susan and I began seeing each other for an occasional glass of wine, a ladies-only dinner, or an evening out with our spouses. As we moved into our fifties, both of us began to appreciate the importance of female friends. However, because we devoted most of our nonfamily time to our work, it was hard to find time to get together.

When Susan recently revealed that she was accepting a job in Albuquerque, I was happy for her. It was a good position, one with a promising future, and she and Tom had always fantasized about moving to New Mexico. Still, it hit me how much I would miss her.

Susan and I always had an easy friendship, built around a common enjoyment of—and issues with—our daughters, and our shared interest in food, cooking, swimming, and literature. Susan is calm and easygoing, never envious or critical; I don't think we have ever had an argument. Every time I'm with Susan, I learn something. On this particular Saturday night, I wanted to learn how to cook a better pheasant.

When Susan and Tom arrived at our house, Tom handed over a bottle of California Pinot Noir to go with the pheasant. Paul uncorked it, then Susan and I shooed the men into the living room while we huddled in the kitchen. I handed Susan an apron to put on over her red blouse and what our daughters would describe as "flood-length" pants. In her midfifties, Susan is still a head turner. I reminded her how in the eighties, when she and Al joined Paul and me for restaurant-reviewing dinners, I got a kick out of going to the ladies' room with her. When we walked through the restaurant, every cute guy turned to look at her.

Susan unloaded several old cookbooks from a satchel. She had bought them in the late sixties in England, when Al and she were on their way to live in France for a year. One was an English cookbook, its cover torn and its pages yellowed with age. Susan carefully pieced together several sheaves of pages from an old French cookbook.

The pheasant recipe in the English cookbook called for lots of butter and bacon, and gravy made from the pan juices and more butter. We agreed that that sounded too rich for '01 tastes. The pheasant recipe in the French cookbook was pretty much the same, loaded with fat and calories. In one of my Italian cookbooks, however, I discovered one that we liked. We decided to create our own variation on it.

Susan powdered the pheasant with Wondra flour, then sautéed it in olive oil in a heavy pan. The skin still looked pale and pasty. This bird sure didn't brown easily. Susan reminded me that that was the reason we had doused the last pheasant we cooked with Jack Daniel's and set it aflame. I checked my cabinet: no Jack Daniel's.

We stuffed Kalamata olives and fresh sage into the bird's cavity, draped bacon strips over the breast, added white wine to the pan juices, and boiled it down, then added chicken stock and popped the pan into the oven.

Next we debated whether to make an English bread sauce to go with it. I deferred to Susan. The idea of bread cooked to mush in milk and butter did not appeal to her. She suggested that we make rice instead. Since the only rice in my cupboard was Italian arborio, she mixed it with mushroom and onions sautéed in butter, chicken bouillion, and Parmigiano-Reggiano, and whipped up a rich, creamy risotto.

Susan admitted that since she married Tom, she has switched her allegiance from French cooking, which she had favored when she was married to Al, to Italian. "With Al, I cooked elaborate, formal dinners," she recalled. "French classics that took hours, like duck with Bing cherries, or pork with bourbon, mustard, and prunes. But with Tom, I go for dishes that are easier and more casual—pastas and Sicilian chicken dishes that are ultimately warmer and more fun." She laughed. "Maybe the two cooking styles reflect the kind of men I've been married to."

Susan reminisced about the trips she and Tom have taken to Italy and their love especially of Sicily and its food. "I make this really great Sicilian swordfish recipe—"

"Next time we'll make swordfish," I promised, opening the oven to baste the pheasant. The skin still looked wan. I suggested pouring on some brandy in lieu of Jack Daniels, but Susan said it would only scald it.

When the roasting time was up, I transferred the bird to a platter and surrounded it with watercress. Carving was difficult—the joints didn't seem to want to come apart—and the breast meat was dry.

We sat down to dinner with Paul and Tom. Tom took a bite of the pheasant, then of the rice. "Great rice!" he said. It was luscious and creamy.

Paul was more forthright. "I think this pheasant needs something." I rummaged in the fridge and pulled out a jar of Newman's Own Pineapple Salsa. It helped. A little.

The pheasant was a wash, but Susan and I weren't fazed. These things happen. I turned to Susan. "So tell me about this great Sicilian swordfish recipe of yours . . ."

Susan's Sicilian Swordfish

SERVES 6

This takes time to prepare, but it is a savory change from plain swordfish. The sauce is one that Susan created to serve with broiled swordfish, but it works deliciously with the stuffed swordfish too. Because the sauce is not cooked, it is really more of an Italian "salsa" with a bright, lemony flavor.

FOR THE FISH

    1½ pounds fresh swordfish, cut into 6 thin slices
        (ask the butcher to cut two ¾-pound pieces into
        3 thin fillets each)
    Juice of 1 lemon
    ½ teaspoon coarse (kosher or sea) salt
    Olive-oil spray
    12 bay leaves

FOR THE STUFFING

    1 small onion, minced
    2 cloves garlic, minced
    1½ tablespoons extra-virgin olive oil
    ½ to ⅔ cup grated Fontina or Asiago cheese
    2 eggs, beaten
    Juice of 1 lemon
    ½ cup finely chopped Italian parsley
    ½ cup finely chopped fresh basil
    1 tablespoon capers

1 tablespoon pine nuts, chopped

1¼ cups fresh bread crumbs (make in a food processor
    from Italian bread with crust removed)

1 tablespoon currants or chopped white raisins
    (optional)

FOR THE SAUCE

1 cup finely chopped fresh basil

1 cup finely chopped fresh Italian parsley

¼ cup capers

2 cloves garlic, minced

Juice and zest of 1 lemon, or more to taste

⅓ cup extra-virgin olive oil

Salt and pepper to taste

1. Put the swordfish fillets in a Pyrex baking dish and cover with cold water. Add the lemon juice and sprinkle on the salt. Let sit at room temperature for 30 minutes. Dry the swordfish fillets, place each one between pieces of waxed paper, and gently flatten with a rolling pin. Refrigerate until ready to stuff.

2. Make the stuffing: Brown the onion and garlic in the olive oil over medium heat until the onion is opaque, about 8 to 10 minutes. Put paper towels in a container to absorb the oil and spoon in the onion mixture. Cool to room temperature.

3. In a bowl, mix the drained onion mixture with the other stuffing ingredients, using only ¼ cup of the bread crumbs and reserving the rest. Blend well and set aside.

4. To make the swordfish rolls, spray the bottom of a Pyrex baking dish with olive-oil spray (or lightly grease it with olive oil). Divide the filling into sixths and spread each portion on one side of a fillet.

Carefully roll up each fillet and place it, seam side down, in the dish; secure it with 2 toothpicks. Place the swordfish rolls close together and insert 2 bay leaves between each roll. Refrigerate until ready to bake, then bring to room temperature.

5. To make the sauce: Mix all the ingredients and season to taste. Put in a small serving bowl and leave at room temperature for at least 2 hours. Mix well before serving.

6. Preheat the oven to 350°F. Sprinkle the remaining bread crumbs over the swordfish rolls and spray lightly with the olive-oil spray (or gently brush with olive oil). Bake for 15 to 25 minutes, until the fish is cooked through. Place one swordfish roll on each plate and spoon the pan juices over it before serving. Pass the sauce separately.

Chapter 36

Losing a Friend

One Thanksgiving morning a few years ago, Julia and I were making pumpkin pies in the kitchen when Brad phoned. "Happy T-Day!" I said, for we always exchanged good wishes on Thanksgiving with Mary Ann and Brad. But Brad wasn't calling to wish us well. He revealed that he had done something terrible to Mary Ann, though he wouldn't be specific: "She is going to need the support of all her friends."

I never found out exactly what Brad did to Mary Ann—it had something to do with money. Nevertheless, we rallied to Mary Ann's side and lent moral support as she broke up with the man she'd been with since she was fourteen and for the first time in her life tried to make it on her own.

My friendship with Mary Ann deepened during the months that followed. We'd always been friends as part of couples. Now we became friends on our own. A few years earlier Mary Ann and I both had discontinued screenwriting with our husbands to pursue other interests—mine was journalism; hers was interior decoration.

The fact that we were no longer in competitive careers made it easier for us to talk openly with each other. If Mary Ann chose not to reveal the details of her split with Brad, though, I understood. Some things remain private, even between good friends.

I gave Mary Ann advice and support as she embarked on her new career; her fantastic sense of style made her a natural as a designer. She gave me advice and support about how to deal with my children. She had studied child psychology and had raised her own daughter, Jessica, who is ten years older than Julia.

A year or so after Mary Ann's breakup with Brad, she became involved with another man. Fred gave her love and security, and she seemed happy. They bought a house—Mary Ann's dream house—that she decorated with modern furniture, striking paintings, black-and-white photographs, and the dozens of metal wind-up toys that she collected.

A few months later Mary Ann developed ovarian cancer. She bravely battled the disease, methodically enduring every form of chemotherapy available. Though she was often nauseated and worse, she never discussed her illness in a negative tone. When I called to see how she was feeling, she spent one minute reporting on whether she'd had a good day or a bad day, then she asked how my kids were.

My children had grown up going to Mary Ann's for swimming and barbecues in the summer, for Halloween in the fall, and for Christmas dinner. She always brought them gifts on their birthdays. She had had a profound impact on Adam's life, for she was the one who introduced him to fencing: "Adam loves weapons; he'll love fighting with swords," she had suggested. She was right; Adam became a nationally ranked saber fencer. The day he won a championship in Louisville, Mary Ann was the first person I called with the news.

Several times Mary Ann's cancer went into remission, and she and Fred were able to travel to Europe. For three years in a row, they threw a Christmas Day bash that our family attended. The festivities always ended in an explosion of poppers, a symbol of Mary Ann's irrepressible childlike streak.

Last Christmas, as at every dinner at Mary Ann's house, I spent time with her in the kitchen. Cooking was only an excuse. This was our private time. Mary Ann didn't have to tell me that she sensed her battle with cancer was coming to an end. I read it in her eyes. She said she wished we had spent more time together without our men, that we had made it a point to go out to dinner, just the two of us. She regretted the fact that she hadn't nurtured more female friendships in her life. I understood, for I shared her feelings. We had both married young, in a time when women were expected to devote themselves to their husbands. As a result, we didn't develop as many strong female friendships as our "liberated" daughters have.

A few months later, Fred called us to say that Mary Ann only had a few weeks to live.

Before the last time I went to visit her, she warned me on the phone, "I look scary." When I saw her sitting in her living room, bundled up in sweats, a bandanna on her head, she looked gaunt and frail but not scary. She was smiling and joking—the same Mary Ann I'd known for thirty-five years. She said not a word about her death sentence.

She could no longer eat—her stomach wasn't working, she said—but she insisted that Paul and I help ourselves to the deli food laid out on the kitchen table. Jessica was there too, and I asked if her mother had shown her the article I had written for *More* in which I mentioned our friendship and Mary Ann's grapes brûlée recipe. Jessica hadn't seen the story. Mary Ann apologized for forgetting to show it to her—she blamed it on "chemo brain."

"What was the recipe of mine you included? Grapes brûlée? What the hell was grapes brûlée?"

I described it—grapes, sour cream, and brandy, with caramelized brown sugar on top.

"I remember that recipe," she said. "I made it for the dinner party when I got burned by the fondue. Is that what it was called?"

Jessica wrinkled her nose. "It sounds so seventies."

"It *was* the seventies!" Mary Ann turned to me. "It's too bad that Jessica doesn't like to cook, like we did."

"Who's got time?" Jessica replied. She explained that before she got sick, her mother had decorated her new duplex, and she had stocked the kitchen shelves with cookbooks. "Mom said, 'If a guy walks in, he's got to believe you can cook! How else are you ever going to find a husband?'"

Though Mary Ann teased Jessica, I knew that she was worried about her. Jessica had devoted so much of the past three years to caring for her mother, she had had no time or emotional energy for a relationship with a man. Mary Ann feared that after her death, her daughter would find it hard to start one.

It wasn't until the memorial service for Mary Ann that it sank in: One of my best friends was gone. I would never again hear her slow, gravelly voice on the phone, or bend down to give her tiny body a hug. I embraced Jessica, who is as petite as her mother was and has the same dark, expressive eyes, the same pretty face. Neither of us spoke. We clung to each other, weeping.

The living room was crowded with Mary Ann's friends and family. Many were young people, who, like my children, had been nurtured by Mary Ann as they grew up. The guests who gave

Julia with Mary Ann, who was tiny in size but big in spirit.

eulogies all mentioned Mary Ann's playfulness, her outspokenness, her creativity, and her loyalty.

In the more than thirty years I knew her, Mary Ann was a better friend to me than I was to her. She always remembered the small things, and she taught me a lot about how to be a mother. By the way she faced her final few months of life with such dignity, she taught me a lot about how to die.

After the memorial service, I turned on my cell phone to call Julia in New York and share my grief with her. I saw that I still had "Mary Ann" programmed on the automatic dial. Julia did too. It reminded me of just how much a part of my everyday life she had been. I did not erase her name or her phone number; I never will. And I will never forget the good times we spent together at her dinner table and at mine—and in both of our kitchens.

Chapter 37

My Dinner with Suzy

Lightning streaked the slate sky over Paris, a dramatic counter-point to the thousands of lights that sparkled like glitter on the Eiffel Tower. Standing beside me on the rooftop terrace of the Meurice Hotel, Suzy Kalter Gershman, the woman I had met when she wrote a *People* story about me and my roller-skating book over twenty years ago, looked out at the mythic city skyline and sighed: "I still can't believe I live here."

After Suzy moved to Connecticut from Los Angeles in the mid-eighties, we had lost touch. I read her articles in magazines, though, and bought her expanding series of *Born to Shop* guidebooks. Suzy traveled extensively for research and garnered a reputation as the "shopping lady," an expert on where to find everything from antiques in Hong Kong to lingerie in Cannes. Her wit, cleverness, and out-there personality shined through in her writing, and I was happy when a magazine editor gave me Suzy's e-mail address a couple of years ago. We met for lunch when I was in New York.

One hug, and suddenly it was as if we'd just seen each other the week before. She brought me up to date on her career and her family: After her son left for college, Suzy became a consultant for Galeries Lafayette and now divided her time between Connecticut and Paris. She and Mike, her husband of twenty-plus years, toyed with the idea of moving to Paris permanently.

After that, we stayed in close touch. One day, an e-mail arrived that was in stark contrast to the funny, chatty messages Suzy usually wrote: Mike had been diagnosed with a brain tumor.

Mike died three months later, and Suzy eventually moved to Paris alone. After a year and a half there, she was beginning to feel as if she belonged. I was glad that I could visit her on my way to Italy, to get a peek into her new life. In our thirties we had never been best friends, but with similar careers now we had more in common, and our e-mails had brought us closer.

Like Auntie Mame, this tall, attractive woman with a daring style and bigger-than-life personality stands out in a crowd. After laser eye surgery a few years back, Suzy put away her thick glasses; she wears two gold watches on her wrist—one set to Paris time, the other to New York time; and her once-brunette hair is red. For this Fourth of July gathering of American journalists at the Meurice Hotel, she had added a jaunty chignon and had gelled wisps of hair to stand straight up on her head. Wearing a flowing green organza dress, she described her overall look as "Statue of Liberty."

Suzy knew most of the guests at the reception, introduced herself to those she didn't, and invited six for dinner *chez* Suzy the next evening. "I go after interesting characters who will add something to the party," she confided to me, "but I also try to have a good balance of personality types."

Suzy enjoys hosting dinner parties for friends who have become what she calls her "Paris family." Just as when she entertained in Los Angeles years ago, her parties often have a theme. "Last August, I threw a Princess Di memorial dinner," she said. "Everyone wore black, and we lit candles in Diana's memory. Tomorrow night our theme will be 'Suzy and Sharon cook in Paris.'"

The next morning we were up early to shop at Poncelet, the cookbook author Patricia Wells's favorite open-air market in Paris, a short walk from Suzy's apartment. I marveled at the jewel-like wild strawberries and the deep purple cherries nearly the size of apricots. Stalls beckoned with Technicolor produce, succulent rotisserie-roasted chickens, and pyramids of pink langoustines. They reminded me why Paris is still considered the culinary capital of the world.

At Suzy's favorite wineshop the proprietor was friendlier than the cliché Parisian shopkeeper. In other words, he was amused rather than annoyed by my bumbling attempts to communicate in French. He insisted that we taste a new aperitif from Provence that contained the juice and pulp of melon and was scented with almond. We bought a bottle not just because of the intriguing taste but also because of the name: Melopepo. Suzy enjoys surprising guests with amusing products they've never seen before, so we decided to start our dinner with melon, prosciutto, and Melopepo.

Suzy's apartment is decorated with Paris flea-market furniture, plus paintings, posters, and tchotchkes that she picked up on research trips for her *Born to Shop* guidebooks, primarily the one she wrote on China after her husband died. She didn't bring over any furniture from her old house in Connecticut. "I guess I didn't want to live surrounded by Mike," she explained. "It was too painful."

As we set the table, using pretty floral china from a service for twenty-four that cost Suzy seventy-five dollars at the Paris flea market, she recounted how frightening it was to start over in a new city without her husband: "I knew many people in Paris, but some of those I thought were friends turned out not to be, while others I never imagined would care have looked after me."

One such caring friend was Alain Ducasse, the famous chef who owns restaurants in Monte Carlo, Paris, and New York. They had met in Monte Carlo ten years earlier, when Suzy interviewed him for *Born to Shop France*. Since she had heard Alain liked unusual things, she showed up with a sand pail loaded with weird goodies: a jar of honey with nuts suspended in it, from Sicily; a shish kebab skewer holding candied walnuts, from Vienna; and a teapot that rested on its side, from a hotel in Munich. "Alain was so amused by everything, we became friends," she said. "To this day, whenever I come across fun new products, I bring them over to show him."

I'm not surprised that the kitchen is one of the biggest rooms in Suzy's apartment. "I would have put my office in here, but there was no way to run a phone line in," she said, popping a CD of vintage Dean Martin into the player. "Dean Martin is very retro, very in," she announced.

Martin belted out "Volare" as we unloaded the groceries and discussed how entertaining has changed since the late seventies and early eighties, when we were friends in Los Angeles. "In those days, I had ten matching Pierre Deux tablecloths, I knew the balloon man by his first name, and I drove all the way downtown to pick up flowers at the wholesale flower mart," recalled Suzy. "I always freaked out before a party, and Mike hated it. I never freak out anymore. I wish Mike were here to see that."

Suzy doesn't cook French food for guests. "French food is much too serious, and there's too big a chance that I'll blow it," she explained. "I don't want anyone comparing the way I make something to the way it's supposed to be done." Instead, Suzy prepares dishes she describes as "quasi American," but always with her own unique twist.

One time she made the enchiladas she learned from Maggie, her Texan friend, for Alain Ducasse. "Instead of Cheddar cheese, I played around with French cheeses," she said. "The chèvre worked pretty well, but the Roquefort was dreadful." Maggie accompanied Suzy to China when Suzy was doing research for her *Born to Shop China* book, and they talk on the phone often. Recently, Maggie was diagnosed with cancer. "There's not much the doctors can do, but Maggie is still cheerful. We joke that the only thing that will cure her are enchiladas."

The one French dish that Suzy says she felt she had to master was *tarte tatin*. "Somehow, I felt that if I could make this classic French dessert, it would signify that I really lived in Paris," she explained. Suzy added her own touch: Texas pecans that she brought back from a visit to her father in San Antonio, and white raisins soaked in cinnamon syrup.

While I peeled Granny Smith apples for the *tarte tatin,* Suzy flattened chicken breasts for a recipe she discovered in a French magazine at the beauty parlor. "I didn't have anything to write with at the time, so I memorized it," she said. "Of course, I changed a few things once I tried it." She rattled off the ingredients, but she didn't indicate the measurements. "How much of each?" I asked, taking notes.

Suzy shrugged. "My grandma Jesse used to come from Florida to visit when I was growing up, and I'd watch her cook," she said. "She never measured. 'You just *shit* a little sugar, you *shit* a little flour,' my grandmother would say."

"*Shit* as in *shiterein*?" I pointed out that my grandmother and my mother were *shiterein* cooks too.

"It's one thing to be a *shiterein* cook," Suzy joked. "Just as long as you're not a *shitty shiterein* cook!"

To go with the chicken, Suzy made a French version of her grandmother's potato pancakes. She used chives instead of onions, olive oil instead of butter, and chèvre instead of sour cream on top. Since it was a muggy summer day, as Suzy stood over the stove frying the potato pancakes, she stripped down to her panties and an apron.

Suzy insisted on preparing everything in advance so that we wouldn't be stuck in the kitchen once the guests arrived. By the time we had the food under control, I'd not only learned how to make three terrific dishes, but we'd discussed hormone replacement therapy, mood elevators, dealing with aging parents, Suzy's adjustment to living in Paris, and our postmenopausal sex lives. We had never discussed intimate subjects when we were younger, but it was easy now.

Suzy in Paris: It was too darn hot.

Because we were older? Because we had nothing to hide from one another? Whatever the reason, it felt good to talk so openly.

That night, when I became acquainted with Suzy's "Paris family" around her dinner table, I began to imagine myself moving to Paris with Paul in a year, after Adam left home for college. *Hmmm.* Suzy's friends, including Giuseppe, a Venetian photographer and playwright, and two journalists from San Francisco, were gracious and stimulating, and they argued that they'd grown intellectually and emotionally by living here. Life was good—and quite cheap— and the food was *definitely* better than in the States.

A footnote: While I was in Paris, often I thought of Mary Ann, for she loved to travel, and whenever I went on a trip I brought her back something oddball that I knew she'd find amusing, such as the rubber squeaky toy shaped like a nun that I found once on Manhattan's Lower East Side. From my trip to Paris, I would have brought her back a bottle of Melopepo.

When I was packing to leave, cramming all the French food and wine products that I'd bought into my suitcase, I heard the "click" of something falling onto the floor from the heap of clothes, shoes, and purses on Suzy's guest-room bed. I hunted under the bed for what had fallen. Among the dust mites, I saw something sparkle. I was surprised to pull out an antique silver-and-amethyst pin that Mary Ann had given me for my fiftieth birthday. I had looked for it after she died and was distressed when I couldn't find it. Now I realized that I must have taken it off several years ago, and stashed it in my dressy purse, which I had brought to Paris for the gala dinner at the Meurice Hotel.

I told Suzy about the incident and how it made me feel Mary Ann's presence in a place—and with a friend—that Mary Ann would have liked.

"You have an angel," was Suzy's response.

Suzy's Beauty Parlor Chicken

SERVES 8

Suzy gave a Mediterranean twist to a recipe she discovered in a Parisian beauty parlor. I don't go to the trouble of making a side dish of potato pancakes like Suzy did when we cooked it in Paris. Couscous or rice work even better with this ultra-lemony chicken.

8 skinless, boneless chicken breasts, pounded between
    sheets of waxed paper to flatten
Salt and pepper to taste
½ cup olive oil
4 or 5 cloves garlic, minced
2 onions, finely chopped
Juice and zest of 5 or 6 lemons
½ cup white wine
One 6-ounce jar pitted Kalamata or green Italian olives

1. Sprinkle the chicken breasts with salt and pepper. In a heavy frying pan, heat ¼ cup of the olive oil and brown the chicken breasts over medium-high heat until they are cooked on both sides, 3 to 4 minutes per side. Remove the chicken breasts to a plate covered with paper towels to absorb the grease.

2. Scrape any remaining bits of chicken from the pan and discard. Add the remaining olive oil and sauté the garlic and onions, stirring frequently, until the onions are opaque, about 6 to 8 minutes. Add the lemon juice and zest and white wine and bring to a boil. Lower the heat and simmer, uncovered, until the liquid reduces by half, about 20 minutes.

3. Add the chicken breasts and the olives to the pan and mix well. Simmer on low, covered, for 10 minutes. Remove the cover, turn over the chicken breasts, and cover with the sauce. Cook for 10 minutes more, uncovered.

4. You can prepare the dish up to the last cooking stage an hour or so ahead of time. When the pan has cooled, cover it and keep at room temperature. Reheat just before serving.

Chapter 38

Cooking the World's
Biggest Mushroom

The recipe calls for bay leaves. What's the Italian word for bay leaves?" Joyce asked as we wandered through the farmers' market in Panzano, an ancient hill town a short drive from the house she and Jim had rented in Tuscany. Paul and I had come to visit, and this was a fantasy come true for Joyce and me—to shop for fresh ingredients and then cook a fabulous meal in Italy.

The only problem was that the roast-pork-marinated-in-red-wine recipe that Joyce had brought from home called for bay leaf, and we didn't see the herb among the bundles of fresh basil, sage, rosemary, and oregano displayed at the produce stand. Joyce drew a sketch of a bay leaf for the vendor. "No *alora*," he said with a shrug. I was ready to give up—what difference would it make if we skipped the bay leaves in the recipe, anyway? But Joyce, who had once chided me for pouring sugar from a box instead of measuring it for a peach pie, was determined to follow the recipe to the letter.

We walked down the cobblestone street to the butcher shop. Front and center in the butcher's case was a snowy white mound of lard topped with a red rose. It's ironic that Italians, who have one of the most delicious and sophisticated cuisines in the world, and cook with healthful olive oil, eat *lardo* in pastas, on bruschetta, and even plain, sliced, as an antipasto.

Branches of greenery decorated the butcher case. Joyce immediately recognized what they were: *alora!* In words that were as close to Italian as she could manage, Joyce asked the proprietress if we could buy ten *alora* leaves from the display-case decoration. It took the pretty, dark-haired woman a while to figure out what Joyce meant. When she did, she smiled broadly, reached into the case, and grabbed a laurel branch. She wouldn't hear of us paying for it. That's Italians for you.

Built of ancient gray Tuscan stones, the house that Joyce and Jim were renting was bordered by lavender bushes that hummed with bees and attracted butterflies that looked like delicate blossoms when they alighted. The site couldn't have been more ideal: a hillside overlooking a checkerboard of Chianti vineyards toward Badia a Pasignano, a picturesque village with a medieval abbey whose bells echoed across the valley.

The house had been built from a disintegrating stable by its English owners. Joyce and I prepared dinner in the whitewashed kitchen that boasted a massive old fireplace but modern appliances. While the pork marinated—bay leaves and all—we reminisced about other dinners we'd cooked together, and she told me how she fell in love with cooking in the first place.

J oyce grew up during the fifties in Florida, in a house where dinner was typically pot roast with canned carrots, or spaghetti and meat sauce. Her mother wasn't experimental, and she didn't want Joyce messing up her kitchen. "She'd say, 'The best way to learn to cook is to learn how to clean up first,' " Joyce recalled. It wasn't until Joyce was twelve that she had her first taste of gourmet food. On a family trip to Quebec, they had dinner in a French restaurant, and Joyce ordered escargots and crêpes. "I felt beyond sophisticated."

Joyce moved to New York in the mid-sixties and became hooked on Julia Child. She bought cookbooks by her, Craig Claiborne, and James Beard. "The first time I invited my boyfriend to dinner, I made fish with grapes," she recalled. "I thought I had to impress the man who might become my future husband." Indeed, Joyce married her boyfriend (not Jim) in 1967, and started giving dinner parties. "I made dishes like Cornish game hens stuffed with cream cheese, and lamb chops stuffed with Gorgonzola, dishes that are much too rich for today's tastes."

Joyce also took cooking classes, something she still enjoys doing. That's how she learned Chinese cooking. "This was in the days when to get fresh ginger, you had to take the subway all the way down to Chinatown," she said. "I used my wok more than any other pot in the kitchen." When Joyce and her husband moved to San Francisco, their apartment had an electric instead of a gas stove. "The wok didn't work on electric, so I gave it away. I really miss that wok!"

Soon it was time to make the pasta, our first course for dinner. Joyce pulled out the porcini mushroom we had bought at the market. *Ta-da!* At over eight inches long and with a stem nearly two inches thick, it had to be the world's largest porcini. The mushroom man had insisted that the porcini would be as big in flavor as it was in size, but Joyce and I were skeptical. Perhaps he was just putting one over on gullible Americans. I almost felt guilty when I took a knife to the phallic-looking thing.

Joyce was nervous about making the pasta without a recipe. I convinced her that we could wing it. We debated whether to sauté the mushroom slices in olive oil or butter. I chose olive oil—we were in Italy, after all—but Joyce opted for butter, and since she was a better cook than me . . . The aroma that wafted from the big iron pan as the porcini cooked made my mouth water.

Size matters.

I'd brought a three-pound wedge of genuine Parmigiano-Reggiano cheese from Parma, where I had traveled to do research for a magazine article before coming to Tuscany. I grated the cheese on the drained (but not rinsed!) wide papparadelle noodles while Joyce tossed them with the porcini. Grating was difficult, and a little does not go a long way, so soon I was tossing Parmigiano-Reggiano shavings into the pasta and passing around little chunks for everyone to eat solo. As I learned in Parma, this pungent, buttery cheese—the only genuine Parmesan because it's made in the city of Parma—all but melts in your mouth, especially when paired with a robust Chianti Classico. Jim pulled the cork from a bottle of the ruby red wine.

The Chianti Classico also matched well with the *fegato* we'd picked up at the butcher shop in town. I call this Tuscan antipasto that you spread on toast rounds "Italian chopped liver" because it reminds me of the chopped liver my grandmother often made when I was growing up. Instead of the chicken fat (schmaltz) she used when sautéing chicken livers, however, the Italians use olive oil—and that makes a big, delicious, difference.

For dinner, we moved outside to a long marble-topped table set under a grape arbor and bordered by pots of geraniums. As we dined, the sunset tinged the distant medieval village pink; it looked like the picture on a postcard you'd send to someone you wanted to make jealous.

The pappardelle with porcini was lusty and seductive. Butter had been the right choice. We barely had an appetite for the pork roast that followed. Even though it was aromatic with bay leaves and fork tender, it didn't leave as memorable an impression as the pasta. Perhaps the mushroom man was right. When it comes to porcini mushrooms, size matters.

Italian Chopped Liver (*Fegato*)

SERVES 8 TO 10 AS AN HORS D'OEUVRE

After tasting this heavenly appetizer at every restaurant we visited in Tuscany, I pored over recipes for it in Italian cookbooks and figured out one of my own. The chopped-fig part I picked up from Cibreo, one of the best restaurants in Florence. They add a bit of a sweet surprise.

2 cloves garlic, minced

1 onion, minced

2 tablespoons extra-virgin olive oil

1 pound chicken livers

4 to 6 fresh sage leaves, chopped, or 1½ teaspoons dried

½ cup Marsala wine

1 tablespoon capers

1 anchovy, or 1 teaspoon anchovy paste

1 egg yolk

4 to 5 dried figs, finely chopped

½ to 1 teaspoon salt, or more to taste

Pepper to taste
Thin slices of Italian bread that have been brushed
with olive oil or sprayed with olive-oil cooking
spray and toasted in a 350°F oven for 10 to 15
minutes. Alternatively, use crackers.

1. Sauté the garlic and onion in the olive oil over medium-high heat until the onion is opaque, about 5 minutes. Add the chicken livers and sauté, breaking up the livers with a spatula and stirring frequently for 7 to 8 minutes, until they lose their pink color. Add the sage, wine, and capers and turn the heat up to high. Cook, stirring frequently, until the liquid has evaporated, 8 to 10 minutes. Let cool slightly.

2. Put the mixture into a food processor along with the anchovy or anchovy paste and egg yolk. Pulse a few times, scraping down the sides of the container with a spatula after each, until the mixture is creamy with little lumps in it. Do not overmix or it turns into paste! Transfer the mixture to a bowl, add the chopped figs, salt, and pepper, and blend well. If you love capers, add another teaspoon.

3. To serve, spread on rounds of toasted Italian bread, or put it in a bowl with the toast or crackers on the side.

Pappardelle with Porcini

SERVES 4 TO 6

Alas, it is hard to find fresh porcini mushrooms in the United States, and when you do, they're expensive. Dried porcinis are expensive too, but a little goes a long way.

1 stick butter

3 shallots, minced

1 pound fresh porcini mushrooms, sliced, or 8 ounces
    dried porcinis, plumped in water for 1 hour

¼ cup white wine

1 pound pappardelle or other wide pasta

½ to ¾ cup grated Parmigiano-Reggiano cheese

Salt and pepper to taste

½ cup chopped Italian parsley

1. In a heavy pan, melt the butter and sauté the shallots until soft. Add the porcinis (if using dried mushrooms, add the water they've been plumped in too) and the wine. Continue cooking over medium heat until the mushrooms are soft and the wine has evaporated, about 20 minutes.

2. Cook the pasta according to package directions and drain. Remove the pan from the heat and add the drained pasta to the mushrooms. Toss until the sauce is evenly distributed, then toss in the grated cheese. Add salt and pepper to taste.

3. Garnish with the parsley and serve immediately. Pass the pepper grinder and more grated Parmigiano-Reggiano cheese.

Chapter 39

Reconnecting

How ironic that the sister of the man I almost married introduced me to the man I *did* marry. In the process, however, I ended up losing a girlfriend. Writing this book inspired me to reconnect with Ellen, my almost-husband Justin's sister. I hadn't seen her in over thirty years.

A girlfriend from my Berkeley days filled me in on bits and pieces of Justin's life: He had married the woman he was fooling around with when we were engaged; he later divorced her to marry someone else. Justin had also become a psychiatrist. Yes, the guy whose shrink called me to break off our engagement became one himself.

My friend reported that Justin had dabbled in food—he studied cooking and opened a short-lived restaurant. An irony, given that I had become a restaurant critic. He had also become fat and bald. I had seen his e-mail address at the top of a mass e-mail joke she had sent me. I decided to e-mail him and ask about Ellen's whereabouts.

Justin was shocked to hear from me. For a few days there was a flurry of e-mails between us. I filled him in on all the good—no, make that *fabulous*!—things in my life since I last saw him—Paul and our wonderful marriage, our perfect kids, my satisfying career.

Justin apologized for having hurt me deeply three decades ago. He hoped I wasn't still angry with him. *Angry?* I hadn't given him much thought since I met Paul. Now could I please have Ellen's e-mail address?

Julia insisted on coming along with me to the SoHo Grand Hotel to meet Ellen for tea. It was not just that I had told Julia what a remarkable woman Ellen was. Julia was intrigued by the concept that if Ellen had been my sister-in-law, she never would have been born.

Ellen looked like a slightly older version of her twenty-year-old self. She was plumper, as she had described herself in her e-mail, and there were a few wrinkles at the corners of her big brown eyes, but she had the same permanent dimples in her cheeks and she radiated tremendous spiritual energy. She was wearing unpretentious artist's clothes: paint-spattered jeans, clogs, and an oversize beige silk blouse that revealed—unintentionally, I'm sure—a glimpse of cleavage. The first thing out of my mouth: "Paul always thought you were sexy. You still are."

Ellen embraced me and studied my face. I remembered that she looked at people very closely when she was a teenager, as if she were boring through whatever protective emotional barriers they had, to see their essence.

Ellen reported that her mother, Dorothy, had died from lung cancer some time ago. "Did you know she ended up writing cookbooks? One was only about purple food—she loved the color purple," said Ellen. I wasn't surprised to hear it. Dorothy had owned scores of cookbooks, and she was a gourmet cook before gourmet cooking was fashionable.

Ellen never became an enthusiastic cook like her mother. "I didn't want to have to live up to her reputation," she said. She recalled that when she was a student at Berkeley, a boyfriend asked her to bake him an apple pie. She didn't have the faintest idea how to do it, so she called Dorothy, who said that she'd take care of it. "A couple of days later I got a package from Mom that contained apples that had been sweetened and sautéed, premixed piecrust dough, a pie tin, and instructions," said Ellen. "All I needed to do was add water to the crust mix, put it in the tin, add the apples and the top crust, and pop it into the oven. My boyfriend thought I was a brilliant cook!"

After Berkeley, Ellen earned a Ph.D. in literature and visual arts, studied art on various fellowships in the United States and abroad, and moved to San Francisco to paint. There she met her future husband. "Mom knew Steve was the one the weekend we drove down to see her and Dad in L.A.," said Ellen. "We didn't get in until two A.M., and Mom had laid out all this food on the table: filet mignon, French fries, Caesar salad, and her homemade onion rings. Steve shoveled it all in. My mother was happy he loved her food."

Ellen pulled out a catalog from one of her recent art exhibits. Her works are reminiscent of ancient illuminated manuscripts; many feature whimsical depictions of animals as well as people. They are not only ravishing; they exude the spiritual depth I would expect from Ellen's art. Ellen said that she thinks her love of color came from her mother's love of purple.

Ellen's mother was with her when Nyssa, Ellen's daughter, was born. Ellen recalled the horror of what followed: When the doctor started to extract what was left of the placenta, he didn't realize it was still attached to her uterus. "He literally pulled my uterus inside out," she said. Hemorrhaging ensued, and Ellen went into cardiac arrest. She was put on artificial life support and hovered between life and death for nine hours. When she recovered enough to walk, days later, the doctors explained that the only reason she had lived was through sheer willpower. "I refused to die. I couldn't let my daughter come into the world without a mother."

For the next year or so, Ellen suffered from what is known as

Lazarus syndrome. "That's what they call the perceptual phenome-
non that happens to people who come back from death," she
explained. "I could barely see, barely walk, and if I turned on a
faucet, I didn't understand the relationship between my action and
the water coming out. I didn't recognize that it was my hand at the
end of my arm. It was so scary."

After the trauma, Ellen had to relearn to paint, and she had to
learn to love her baby. "Steve had to be the mother and the father
for months," she said. She attributes her recovery to Eva, a nutri-
tionist who became a dear friend. "Eva is a healer. She said I had
lived to paint and to raise my child, and that's what I must make
myself strong enough to do."

Eva prescribed a special diet for Ellen. During the day, she drank
Swedish bitters with hot water and ate salads with eight different
vegetables and grated fresh beets, along with fresh fish, chicken,
and brown rice. "At four every afternoon, I had to drink grape juice
spiked with cayenne pepper," she recalled. "It tasted awful!" At
night, Ellen ate all the fruit she wanted. "Eva's regimen worked. The
doctors couldn't believe how fast I got well."

It was getting late, and Ellen had to leave to meet her daughter
at the subway. Julia and I went with her.

Nyssa is a pretty sixteen-year-old with reddish blond hair and a
fair complexion, unlike Ellen, who has dark hair and olive skin. But
Nyssa's almond-shaped eyes are definitely her mother's. "This is my
greatest achievement," Ellen said, hugging her.

Nyssa wanted to know my past connection to her mother. I tried
to explain how I had almost married Ellen's brother and that Ellen
had introduced me to my husband, who was Julia's dad, and that Julia
wouldn't have existed if all that hadn't come to pass. It was too much
for Nyssa to grasp in the moment before she and Ellen had to go.

"It doesn't matter how we were connected in the past," Ellen
said, giving me a hug. "What matters is, we're friends, and we've
found each other again."

Chapter 40

A New Friend
from a Past Life

Once in a great while you meet a woman you immediately connect with on a deep level. She doesn't have to be similar to you in background, culture, or tastes. There is no explanation, but you feel a kinship. It's almost as if you must have been best friends in a former life. I felt that way five minutes after I met Nikki Tesfai. I had gone to her office to interview her for a story that had nothing at all to do with food. Yet ultimately, it was our shared interest in food that brought us closer.

A beautiful forty-seven-year-old Ethiopian woman whose dark, sparkling eyes hint at her inner strength, Nikki is the founder and director of the African Community Resource Center, the only refugee center in L.A. that aids people who have fled from African as well as European and Asian countries. ACRC is also the only refugee center in the United States that has a residential shelter for battered refugee women.

I visited Nikki in her office a few weeks after the September 11 horror, and she was sad about the lives that had been lost. Her faith in America as a safe haven had been shaken. After all, this was the country that had welcomed her after she was abused and tortured in Africa.

Nikki was born and raised in Addis Ababa, where her family attended the Coptic Christian Church but secretly celebrated Yom Kippur because they were Jewish. Her father saved his money so that he could send her to school in Switzerland. When she did so well that she won a scholarship, he was able to pay for her younger brothers to go to school in the United States, where she eventually joined them. At the Southern college she attended, Nikki was targeted by the Ku Klux Klan and narrowly escaped.

Nikki returned to Ethiopia and joined the Eritrean liberation forces. At first they welcomed her support, but when she criticized their cruel treatment of women, they arrested her. It was hard for Nikki to talk about the nightmarish year she spent in an Eritrean prison. She stopped and took several slow, deep breaths, like the Lamaze breathing technique I learned years ago to take my mind off pain, before she could continue.

After a year in prison, Nikki was released, and she set off on foot across the desert to Khartoum. There she was put into a refugee camp that was almost as horrific as the prison. Because she spoke English, French, and Italian as well as several Ethiopian dialects, she got a job with a United Nations relief organization. Her boss sent her to a UN conference in Italy even though she made it clear to him that she had no intention of returning.

In Italy she married a fellow refugee, and they moved to Houston, where her brother lived. Nikki bore two children, but when her husband became abusive, she packed the kids into her car and drove to Los Angeles. The police directed her to a refugee center.

Nikki soon realized that the refugee centers in L.A. do not welcome Africans. They deal mostly with Hispanics and Vietnamese and contend that they can't help Africans because they lack staff who speak their languages. In 1984 Nikki established a refugee center that did.

I spent three hours with Nikki discussing the counseling, employment placement, and English-language classes that ACRC provides for refugees. Then we turned to more personal issues: Nikki has two sons around the same age as my children, and we shared proud stories. I invited her to come to my house for dinner. She said that she loved to cook, and she insisted on bringing Ethiopian food—something I had never tasted.

Nikki, my best friend in a former life.

Nikki arrived with enough food for a dozen people, even though our guests included only my friend Irma and Paul's friend Nick Clapp, who had been to Ethiopia recently to research his book about the queen of Sheba. Nikki explained that she wanted us to enjoy an Ethiopian feast.

She had picked up some of the dishes at an Ethiopian restaurant run by one of her friends; others she had made herself, including *wat,* an orange-hued chicken stew with hard-boiled eggs poking above the surface. It was a dish that her mother taught her how to make when she was five years old. "Girls were taught to cook at an early age because it was one of their duties in the house," she explained. "My brothers were gone a lot—they played outside, but my sister and I helped my mother in the kitchen."

Nikki's mother, Tesge, had never been to school, and she was proud that her own children were able to get an education. Every morning she made pita bread that the family ate with tea, and she had bread and tea ready for Nikki, her siblings, and their friends when they came home after school. The family sat down to dinner together every night, sometimes with neighbors as their guests. "My mother loved to feed people—anyone who came into the house," recalled Nikki. "When I was little, she fed my friends and me with her fingers."

Cleanliness was very important to Tesge, and after she picked out a chicken from her flock and slaughtered it, she spent hours cleaning the skin. "The chickens ran around outside and ate all sorts of things besides the grain my mother fed them," explained Nikki, "so their skin was tough and dirty." Tesge soaked and scrubbed the chicken first in vinegar and water, then in lemon juice and water. To this day, Nikki still cleans chickens the same way, even though she buys plump free-range birds at Whole Foods. "When I make *wat,* I want to be able to pick up the lid and smell the spices, not the chicken."

Cooking *wat* requires several hours. Nikki explained that she minces the onions—six or seven big ones—into tiny pieces, just as her mother taught her to do. She fries them in vegetable oil and water until they turn reddish and soft, then she adds Ethiopian spiced butter and *awazze,* the ground red pepper that gives the dish its vibrant color and its spicy kick. While it cooks, she adds fresh tomatoes, tomato sauce, the chicken, and finally the hard-boiled eggs. *Wat* is a lusty dish, with layers of flavors and textures.

Another Ethiopian speciality that Nikki brought us to sample was *tebes,* chicken and beef kebabs rolled up with mixed vegetables in *injera* bread, like an Ethiopian wrap. *Injera* bread is a story in itself: Each piece looks like a big round spongy tortilla with little holes in it. It takes three days to make; the dough must ferment before it is baked. Ethiopians tear off pieces of *injera* and use it to scoop up *wat* and other stews—no forks and knives required. Nikki showed us how it was done, and we quickly got the hang of it. She was sorry that she hadn't had time to bake *dabo,* a sweet whole wheat yeast bread with raisins that her mother made on special occasions when Nikki was growing up in Ethiopia.

Nikki was proud to share her country's food with us, and we lingered over dinner, savoring the array of new flavors and discussing the world's problems. I couldn't help but marvel at the fact that just days before, Nikki and I had been interviewee and interviewer, conversing in a formal setting. Now, having broken bread together, we were friends.

Chapter 41

Mom's Best Friend

My mother and I have grown closer through the years; we are good friends now. During the course of raising my children, I began to understand the difficulties she must have gone through while raising my sisters and me. Perhaps you have to be a mother yourself to truly understand—and appreciate—your own mother.

I have allowed my children to criticize me—to express anger toward me—far more than my mother allowed her children to do. To this day, "Honor thy father and thy mother" is a lot more loosely interpreted in our house than it was in my parents'. I'm of two minds about whether that is a good thing or a bad one. Paul and I sometimes joke that if our children go into therapy someday, they will whine to their shrinks about how insensitive and even unloving we were to them when they were growing up. We wish that we could be there to give the therapist *our* side of the story, which would undoubtedly differ greatly from theirs. It makes me wonder how much of what I said to my own shrink about my mother's insensitivity toward me when I was growing up was simply not the case at all.

My mother's perseverance, determination, and competence have served her well in old age. The entire fifty-three years she and my father were married, she never balanced a checkbook—she didn't note the checks that she wrote, let alone subtract them in her check register. My father was in charge of the money in our household, and he liked it that way. After he died, she was anxious about taking over the task, but she quickly mastered it. She even made money in the stock market, something my father did rarely (if ever).

My mother didn't wallow in her loneliness as a widow. She took solace in her family and friends; she has many close friends, many whom she has known her entire life. When all the other widows began talking about Albert Miller, an eligible octogenarian widower, my mother made a play for him. Albert was smitten, and he was soon off the market.

Albert adores my mother; a day doesn't go by when he doesn't tell her how beautiful she is, or how young she makes him feel, or how much he loves her. At first I felt awkward seeing my mother with a man other than my father. But soon I realized that she was lucky to have found a good partner so late in life, and someone so good to her. After a few months of "living together," she insisted that they get married. Even at their age, she felt that cohabiting without being married "just wasn't right."

A few years ago my mother was diagnosed with liver cancer. The doctors said that they would operate and then make a prognosis. The morning of her operation, my mother refused to allow Sheila or me to give her a ride to the hospital. In her typical stubborn fashion, she insisted on driving herself. The doctors removed a lot of stuff from inside my mother, but they gave her a clean bill of health. When it was finally time for her to go home from the hospital, she was in pain and could barely walk, but she was prepared to take the wheel. Sheila and I had a hard time persuading her to let one of us drive.

Today my mother lives each day as it comes. She is in good health, but she has aches and pains and so does Albert. She worries about him; she takes care of him. She has always been a worrier and a caretaker.

At eighty-three, my mother still plays bridge with "the girls" at the club. She laughs when she calls her little group "the girls," and laments that it gets smaller each year—that she goes to more funerals than weddings. "We're all so old," she says. "Cherry, it's depressing to be old."

My mother takes pride in her children and her grandchildren, but we don't live close by, and though we talk to her every other day, we don't see her nearly enough. It is her friendships with women that nurture her on a daily basis. She lives a block away from her sister, my aunt Rosie, and two blocks from Mary, her best friend.

D on't be shocked when you see Mary," my mother warned. "She's been in and out of the hospital." Years ago, when I was dating Chester, their son, Mary and Harry's house was brand-new and the height of modernity, with cedar-paneled walls, terrazzo floors, and floor-to-ceiling windows overlooking a marsh thick with blueberry bushes. The family room was the most lived-in; the living room and dining room were used only when guests came. It is still the case.

I was not alarmed when Mary opened the door. She looked the same as she always has—just older and smaller. Mary is in her late eighties and has all the ailments you'd expect of a woman her age. But she was wearing a smart pants outfit, earrings, and a necklace, and she had on a touch of lipstick, as if she were about to step out in public. Her hair was thinning and gray—she'd finally allowed it to go gray—and she was tentative on her feet. Her mind, however, was sharp, and she exuded the personality and self-confidence that she did when I was a little girl and her daughter's best friend—and later a teenager and her son's girlfriend.

Mary and my mother sat down next to each other on the living room sofa, so close that their bodies were touching. "Your mother

Mom and Mary in the fifties: Best friends for more than sixty years.

and I are best friends," said Mary. "We've been best friends for sixty years."

"I met Mary at the university," added Mother. "I played the violin at her wedding."

"Your mother and I have never fought. Never!"

"We talk on the phone every day."

"We go out for dinner together at least twice a week."

"We have a favorite Chinese restaurant."

"I like our Greek restaurant better."

Their banter reminded me of the touching scenes in the movie *When Harry Met Sally* of old married couples talking to the camera, proudly explaining how they met and why they stayed together so long. Just as in the movie, it was obvious just from watching these two why they were longtime friends.

Mary reminisced about the parties she and my mother gave in the forties, when they were newlyweds: "We'd go to the bakery and buy what was called a 'sandwich bread loaf.' It was cut horizontally down the middle. We'd fill it with corned beef, or maybe your mom's tuna salad, then slice it on the bias—big slices for the men, smaller slices for the ladies."

In the fifties, after the women in their social circle had kids and their husbands began to prosper, entertaining revolved around bridge parties, golf games at the country club, and charity luncheons. "We held lots of luncheons," said Mary. "The women wore suits and hats and looked their best. It was always important to look your best."

In those days women talked about their children, their husbands' jobs, and their social life, but they never discussed two subjects: sex and money. "You never revealed how much your husband was making," explained Mary. "And no one we knew got divorced."

I noted that all of their close friends, the couples who came to our house for Fourth of July barbecues and cocktail parties on New Year's Eve, had stayed married for over fifty years. "Divorce wasn't an option," Mary explained. "Besides, we were couples who really loved each other."

Mary was the only one of my mother's friends who worked when her kids were growing up; she helped her husband, Harry, in their drugstore. "I also did writing for all the charity groups I belonged to—"

"Mary is a great writer," my mother added.

Mary's housekeeper, Mrs. Ekberg, did most of the cooking, and Mary still has her recipes. She found them at the back of a cabinet after the housekeeper left. I offered to get the recipes from the kitchen, but Mary insisted on doing it herself. I knew there was no use arguing with her.

She got up slowly from the sofa and retrieved a notebook of handwritten recipes, some so faint I could barely read them: the

Lazy Daisy Cake; caramel popcorn balls; and beet mold made with lemon-lime Jell-O, julienned canned beets, and crushed pineapple.

"We all made Jell-O molds in those days," said my mother. "Edith's were always the best. She had the patience to make layered ones in two or three colors."

Mary showed me photographs of Gloria and her husband, and of Gloria's three sons and their new babies. "I'm a great-grandmother three times over," she said proudly. If ever there was a strong matriarch, it is Mary.

Gloria is still best friends with my other best childhood friend, Laurie, Edith's daughter. Over the years their interests and to some extent their social circles have gone in different directions, but they are more emotionally connected to each other than to any other women. According to Gloria, she and Laurie are more like sisters than friends. I don't see them often, but when I do I feel a warm bond that comes from having known them—and their families—my whole life. Like me, Gloria and Laurie have stayed married to their husbands for over thirty years. Perhaps we all inherited the "stay married" gene from our mothers.

Mary showed me photographs of Chester's daughter and two sons but none of him. Chester had become the high-profile trial lawyer he'd dreamed of being since he first saw *Inherit the Wind,* a movie he took me to when we were teenagers. But the golden boy also became the black sheep of the family. Troubles with wives, work, and the law ultimately stacked up against Chester. When he was fifty-eight, he died of a sudden heart attack.

When I was in my thirties, I had had dinner with Chester—Chet was his grown-up nickname. He still was strikingly handsome and fit, with a tan that rivaled George Hamilton's. He still exuded charisma and smarts, and I had a warm spot in my heart for him; I could understand why he had been my first true love. But I sensed that he was self-destructive, that he recklessly tempted fate. When he was a teenager and ran into problems, he had charmed his way out of them. He tried to do that as an adult, perhaps, but it no longer worked. The unraveling of Chester's life was as tragic as what happened to my sister Susan.

My mother once told me that Mary rarely confided in her about her problems with Chester, just as my mother kept her problems with Susan to herself. She said they didn't have to talk about them. "I could always sense when Mary was upset, and she knew when I was," she said. "What's important is that we were there for each other."

Before we left, I gave Mary a gentle hug, and I could feel how fragile she was. Mary and my mother pecked each other on the lips and traded their usual "Get some rest," "I'll call you later," "I love you."

I wondered if, when I reach my eighties, I will have as close a friend as Mary is to my mother. How fortunate I will be if I do.

Chapter 42

Domestic Chaos and Bliss

Sheila and Victor had come to L.A. for a visit, and they were staying at Judy's house. Paul, Adam, and I were invited for dinner, but I drove over to Judy's ahead of them. I couldn't wait to see my sister and her three-year-old son.

My fifty-something sister has a three-year old son? Let me explain.

After the summer when Sheila visited Paul and me in the French Alps, she went on to have a successful yet often frustrating career as a composer. She won various prizes and fellowships, earned a Ph.D., and became the composer in residence at SUNY (State University of New York) at Stony Brook.

My parents took pride in Sheila's success and attended performances of her music in New York, San Francisco, and Seattle. I attended many of them too. Each time, I was amazed and proud that my little sister, the kid I'd slugged with a broom when she wouldn't give me the roller skate key, could create such beautiful music.

Over time Sheila's music increasingly reflected her various spiritual phases—and sometimes there was a man involved. When she was studying yoga, for example, she came under the spell of the yogi and nearly became a Sikh, white turban and all. The close encounter with Sikhdom didn't result in a husband, but it led her to compose an opera, *The Thief of Love.* She based the libretto on an ancient Indian myth about a princess who vows only to marry a man who is smarter than she is.

Later she became fascinated with Orthodox Judaism, went to Israel, and returned with an Orthodox Jewish boyfriend. Though no marriage ensued, her involvement in Judaism resulted in a lyrical string-orchestra composition entitled "The Song of Sarah." The piece reflected the biblical story of Sarah, who was sad that she couldn't have a child, prayed to God for one, and finally conceived Isaac.

As in the opera she composed, Sheila eventually found a man who was as smart as she was (it would have been difficult to find one who was smarter). She married John at a small ceremony in my parents' house, and I was the matron of honor. In the weeks before the wedding, my mother made several hundred cheese blintzes and stored them in the freezer. A French caterer prepared sophisticated fare for the reception—even a croquembouche wedding cake—but Sheila had insisted on serving blintzes too. After the wedding, just as my mother had predicted, there was French food leftover, but no blintzes.

Sheila and John lived the artist life, with John making films and Sheila composing. In 1997 Sheila got her long-wished-for moment in Carnegie Hall—a Russian virtuoso performed her powerful piano concerto. After you've played Carnegie Hall, what else is there? Sheila still longed for the one thing that she had missed out on in life: a child. She had suffered a couple of miscarriages after she married John—the doctors said she was too old to have a baby—so they decided to adopt. I argued that she wouldn't have the energy for a baby at her age and that she was nuts to give up her independence.

Sheila was so incensed at my negativity, she threatened to stop speaking to me.

Several of Sheila's girlfriends had adopted Romanian babies through a woman they said had a magical ability to match an orphan with prospective parents even without meeting them. Sheila spoke to Vivi in Romania on the phone several times and had total faith in her. "She's a very spiritual woman," Sheila told me. Spirituality is very important to my sister.

When Vivi's call finally came, Sheila was caught off guard by the baby she had picked for John and her. They had requested a baby girl. Victor was a two-year-old boy. Sheila called me for advice. I argued that if Sheila trusted Vivi and Vivi said that Victor was the child for her, Sheila should trust her.

Sheila was in love the minute Victor peeked out at her from behind the door of the five-story walk-up apartment where he lived with a foster family in Romania. He was the fulfillment of Sheila's vision when she composed "The Song of Sarah."

When I met Victor, an impish boy with sandy hair, wide brown eyes, and a trusting smile, I was overwhelmed with emotion. I apologized to Sheila for opposing the adoption. She instantly forgave me.

And maybe it's true, as my mother-in-law, Ruth, says, that babies bring good luck. Last year, Sheila's opera, *The Thief of Love*, was performed in New York—twenty years after she composed it. My mother was unable to attend the performance, but Julia and I sat in the front row, and before the last act I called her in Seattle on my cell phone. I asked if she wanted to hear the music. "Maybe for a minute or two," she said. I held up my phone so that the music carried over it until the final curtain. I knew my mother would listen to the whole thing—and she did. "Are they giving her a standing ovation?" she asked afterward, thrilled to hear the applause. I was happy to report that they were.

hen I arrived at Judy's, a Spanish-style townhouse in West Hollywood with towering twin palm trees in front, Victor was sitting on the porch, waiting for me. "Auntie Cherry!" he shouted. "Mommy, Auntie Cherry's here!" Sheila had told me that Victor was fascinated that my family nickname is that of a fruit. He was also intrigued by the fact that Sheila and I sound and look so much alike, which we do more and more as we get older.

I had seen Victor in New York a few weeks earlier, and he hadn't talked much. Now words came tumbling out of his mouth as if they'd been there all along but he just hadn't been ready to say them. He let me pick him up. Feeling Victor's smooth cheek next to mine, hearing his little-kid voice, and smelling his distinctive kid smell—a blend of milk, orange juice, and chocolate—made me remember why I had had my own kids. Sheila beamed at my pleasure in her son.

The proud new mom at fifty: My sister, Sheila, with Victor.

Victor squirmed out of my arms and dashed into the living room, where Judy had piled pillows near the sofa. The kid had not taken a nap all day, and he was wired. He leaped off the sofa onto the pile of pillows and knocked a bowl of popcorn all over the rug. Judy's shaggy black mutt was running around the room, barking. Ike had never encountered a three-year-old. Victor had never encountered a dog as rambunctious as Ike. They were meant for each other.

Judy didn't mind the chaos. She reveled in it. "Judy," I said, "you would have been a great mother!"

She grabbed Victor in a bear hug. "Now I'm old enough to be a *grandmother!*"

After living in L.A. for several years, Judy had moved to New York to work first as a reporter at *People,* then as a talent booker for the *Today* show. Along the way, she fell in love with Harold Hayes, a man seventeen years her senior, who had been the editor of *Esquire* magazine in its heyday.

Harold was movie-star handsome, Judy a darling, tiny thing who didn't even reach his shoulders. After they got married, they moved to L.A., where Harold became editor of *California,* a quasi reincarnation of *New West,* the first magazine I wrote for. Sheila was sorry to see Judy leave New York. I was thrilled to have her living close by again.

Judy and Harold entertained often at their cozy ranch-style house. Judy's dinners always were memorable—even better than before she moved to New York—for she had fallen in love with Italian cooking. "I learned to cook from Charlotte [Judy's mother] and Marcella [Hazan, the famous Italian cookbook author]," she explained.

Judy's life was idyllic—until Harold was diagnosed with a brain tumor. In the months that followed, until he died, she rarely left his side. That was well over a decade ago. To Judy, I think it will always seem like just yesterday.

I have eaten dinner in every one of the eight or so houses and apartments that Judy has lived in—first in Los Angeles, then in New York, then back in L.A. Each time I have been comforted by the aromas of cooking—usually garlic and basil from one of Judy's lusty Italian dishes. Today, however, her house smelled like garlic and something else. "Soy sauce," Judy explained. "I'm into an Asian phase."

A crowd was gathered in Judy's kitchen: Sheila, Victor, and I, plus Paul and Adam, who had just arrived. Under ordinary circumstances my teenage son may have weaseled out of dinner at a friend of his mom's, but not when it was Judy. He was captivated by her buoyant charm, her sense of humor, and her ability to focus on him as if he were the most interesting person in the world. Besides, Adam loved Judy's cooking.

Judy offered us fresh shrimp punched up with dill, lemon juice, and a touch of mayonnaise. Adam wolfed his down. Victor took a cautious taste, then fed the shrimp to the dog.

Judy ran through tonight's menu: fresh salmon done with an Asian twist; a "power" rice dish with vegetables and little bits of egg-white omelet based on a dish served at Xi'an, our favorite Chinese restaurant in Beverly Hills; and a spicy corn-and-tomato salsa made from a recipe she found in *Bon Appétit*. Of course, there was also a big salad.

"Judy makes the best salad dressing in the world," Sheila told Adam.

"It took me years to come up with one that's better than Canlis's," Judy said, pouring vinaigrette on the baby greens, fresh asparagus tips, marinated artichoke hearts, and little clumps of feta cheese. She tossed the salad, skewered a forkful, and handed it to Adam.

Adam took a taste. Impressed, he turned to me: "Why can't your salad dressing taste this good?"

I asked Judy for her recipe. "I'll never tell!" she said. "I'm saving it for the cookbook I'm going to write someday."

Sheila and Judy reminisced about the dinners they made together when Judy was attending Stanford and Sheila was at UC Berkeley, where she lived above a bookstore that was torched in a student protest. Adam wanted to hear the details of the torching. Judy and Sheila had clearer memories of what they ate.

Judy recalled driving up to Sheila's for Passover one year with a brisket in the backseat. "It was my mother's recipe; I'd never make anything that salty today."

Sheila had made a potato kugel that was also from a recipe of Judy's mother, with lots of sautéed onions and butter. "Today I make it with sun-dried tomatoes and olive oil," she said.

Judy recalled that they had chocolate mousse for dessert, but she didn't remember who made it.

"Not me," said Sheila. "I didn't know how to make chocolate mousse. I didn't know how to make chicken soup either. I learned after I moved to Boston. You know what the secret is? You put cloves in the onions."

"Cloves of garlic, or *cloves* cloves?" I asked.

"Cloves as in those spicy little round things that people stick in hams." Sheila recounted how she picked up the chicken-soup recipe from the girlfriend of a colleague of hers, who was jealous that Sheila spent so much time talking music with him.

Sheila began to describe how she made chicken soup, but Adam wanted to hear stories about when Judy, Sheila, and I were kids, growing up together.

Judy launched into a description of the freezer we had in our kitchen: "I was so short, I had to boost myself up over the lip of the freezer so I could reach inside. One time I fell in!"

Sheila added that once she broke her finger in the freezer: "I was hunting around in it one night for frozen marshmallows. I heard someone coming and I slammed the lid shut, right on my pinkie!"

"Speaking of fingers . . ." Judy held up her left index finger, which was wrapped in several layers of Band-Aids. "I was chopping tomatoes for the corn salsa, and Ike was snuffling around at my feet. I glanced down and the knife slipped."

Judy couldn't change the bandaging without help, so I gave her a hand. "Just for that," she said afterward, "I'll give you the recipe for my salad dressing."

Judy's Salad Dressing

SERVES 6 AS A SALAD

This is a cinch to make. It works well on a salad of baby lettuces, endive, marinated artichokes, and hearts of palm, or simply on chopped romaine. If you add goat cheese, blue cheese, or feta cheese to the salad and toss well, the dressing becomes wonderfully creamy. Adam dubbed this the best salad dressing he has ever tasted—even better than the dressing on a Canlis salad.

¼ cup extra-virgin olive oil
3 tablespoons lemon juice
1 tablespoon sherry wine vinegar, or a mixture of
    balsamic and red wine vinegar
1 tablespoon anchovy paste
Scant 1 tablespoon Dijon mustard
Scant 1 tablespoon Worcestershire sauce
Dash of Tabasco sauce
1 or 2 cloves garlic, minced
Salt and ground pepper to taste

In a small bowl, whisk all the ingredients together.

Sheila's Chicken Soup

SERVES 8

The soup requires patience—make it over a couple of days, letting it cool down overnight. Sheila uses kosher chickens—they are saltier— and she says you cannot cook this soup too long. If the level gets low, add water.

6 quarts water

2 small or 1 large roasting chicken

2 large onions, quartered, with 8 whole cloves (1 per
   onion quarter) stuck in them

5 bay leaves

8 stalks celery, cut into 1-inch pieces

8 large carrots, peeled and cut into 1-inch rounds

4 medium parsnips, peeled and cut into 1-inch rounds

Salt and pepper to taste

1. Fill a large heavy soup pot with the water. Clean the chickens and put them into the pot. Bring the water to boil and cook for 30 minutes. Skim the scum off the top of the water. Cover the pot and cook over low heat for 3 to 4 hours.

2. Add more water if it is needed to cover the chicken, add the vegetables, and bring the soup back to a boil. Turn down the heat, cover the pot, and simmer for 2 hours, until the meat is falling off the bone. If necessary, add more water to keep it soupy.

3. Strain the soup through a colander into another pot, and when the meat is cool, pick the bones and bay leaves out of the colander and discard.

4. Add as much of the chicken and vegetables as you like back into the soup—some like their chicken soup clear—and reheat before serving. Add salt and pepper to taste. Egg noodles or matzoh balls are a good addition.

Judy's Asian Salmon

SERVES 4

This is a foolproof marinade not just for salmon but for sea bass, halibut, or any type of thick fresh fish.

1 pound fresh salmon (or other firm-fleshed fish) fillets

FOR THE MARINADE
    ¼ **cup low-sodium soy sauce**
    1 piece fresh ginger, peeled and finely chopped
    ½ **cup sherry or Marsala wine**
    2 or 3 cloves garlic, chopped

Freshly ground pepper to taste

I. Place the salmon, skin side down, in a small baking pan.

2. Mix the marinade in a small bowl. Pour it over the fish and add the pepper. Marinate the fish at room temperature for 30 minutes.

3. Preheat the oven to 400°F. Bake the fish uncovered for 15 to 25 minutes, or until it is still slightly pink in the middle when pierced with a fork. (Cooking time varies according to the thickness of the fish.) Serve with the pan juices drizzled on top.

Chapter 43

The Reunion

It was one of those achingly beautiful summer days that makes me wonder why I ever left Seattle. Puffy white clouds threw shadows like ink blots on Lake Washington as I drove across the Floating Bridge into the city. On the southern horizon, Mount Rainier loomed so large compared with everything in the foreground that I felt as if I were gazing at a landscape painting in which the sense of perspective was askew.

Earlier in the day I had driven north to Bellingham, a picturesque old logging town near the Canadian border, to visit my sister Susan. She lives in an apartment building occupied by mental patients who, like herself, were released from a state institution because they were deemed capable of coping with life on the outside. Susan has lived there with a roommate, bolstered by weekly visits from a counselor, for over ten years. She is proud that she can do simple, everyday tasks—shop for groceries, clean house, cook—without being terrorized by the voices in her head. The voices will never go away—she accepts that—but the dozen or so pills a day that she takes keeps them under control. When they do spook her, if she can't reach her counselor, she calls 911. The 911 operators know Susan by name and reassure her that what she senses as danger is only in her head.

Today, as we do the several times a year that I come to see Susan, we sat on her porch, where she and her roommates smoke and drink coffee (the meds make them sleepy; nicotine and caffeine keep them awake), and played with her cat. Susan reminisced about the experiences we had growing up. I wasn't surprised that many of her favorite memories have to do with food: picking blackberries near the lake; eating our mother's tuna fish sandwiches after a swim; rummaging in the freezer for our uncles' oatmeal-raisin cookies and frozen marshmallows. I vividly remember them too.

For brunch I took Susan, her roommate, and Susan's guy friends—Vietnam vets—to IHOP. They deliberated about what to order, then wolfed down every morsel of their pancakes, eggs, and hash browns. Afterward, we stopped at the grocery store, where Susan picked out a value pack of T-bone steaks, something she couldn't afford on her food stamps and her small allowance, and I paid for them. Since the weather was warm, she and her friends planned to barbecue steaks for dinner. They found pleasure in discussing what to serve with the steak and what to have for dessert.

Before I left, Susan apologized that she was sick and couldn't be a better sister. I reassured her that she is a good sister, and that she has nothing to apologize for; she should be proud of her ability to be so independent. She apologized too for looking ugly. The meds had caused her to gain weight. For many years Susan wore thick eyebrow pencil and eyeliner, and red lipstick that bled over the edges of her lips. She was just trying to look pretty, but the effect was just the opposite. Today she wore only a trace of makeup. I told her she looked prettier without it.

I pointed out that though she is two and a half years older than I am, she has far fewer wrinkles than I do and only one or two gray hairs. "That's part of the joke God played on me," she said. As she smiled, I caught a glimpse of the dazzling beauty queen she was so many years ago.

"Take care," we said to each other, hugging. "I love you."

Shelley, Robin, and I had planned dinner at Laurie's, and I was the first to arrive. Her spacious red-brick house commands a 180-degree view of Seattle, the lake, and the distant Cascade Mountains. With its floor-to-ceiling windows, white walls, and playful modern art, the house is bright and cheerful. It's a Laurie house, uncluttered and welcoming.

Several years into her marriage to Garry, Laurie is happy and content. Garry makes her feel loved and secure and has brought out her spirit of exploration, a trait that was buried in her previous marriage.

Robin arrived next. She was wearing a loose silk blouse that on a big woman like her added to her regal bearing. She carried a frozen mocha mousse she had made from her sister's recipe. "You have Maggie to thank for all the calories," she joked as she stashed the dessert in the freezer.

Robin, Laurie, Shelley, and I hadn't been together as a foursome since the summer of '66, when we trooped through Europe ogling monuments and men and sampling new foods. Tonight we planned to cook together. I'd brought the fresh salmon. It was Copper River salmon season, and I'd been astonished to find that the savory, deep-orange-fleshed fish that goes for upward of $20 a pound in California was selling in Seattle for $7.99. I also couldn't resist buying fresh Oregon shrimp for $3.99 a pound, about half their price in Los Angeles.

I hunted in Laurie's fridge for some exotic sauce to slather on the salmon and spotted a bottle of Washington State Chardonnay. Laurie gave up alcohol in her twenties, but she keeps wine in the house for guests. I enjoy sampling Washington wines that are unavailable in California, but Robin suggested that we not drink tonight. Shelley, who has had repeated run-ins with alcohol, was on the wagon, and Robin didn't want to tempt her. While we were debating whether to uncork the bottle or not, Shelley breezed in, kicked off her sandals, and announced that she would never allow us to deny ourselves on her account; she could handle it.

Always the most athletic of the four of us, Shelley looked fit in her tight black pants and a black T-shirt, but she complained that she couldn't keep up with the younger women on the tennis court anymore. We made a pact: Tonight, no discussion of fifty-something aches and pains.

Shelly unloaded the makings for a Canlis salad—romaine lettuce, a bowl of freshly fried bacon crumbles, fresh-toasted croutons, and a lemon-and-olive-oil vinaigrette smoothed with coddled egg and pepped up with fresh oregano and mint from her garden. She passed out printed recipes for the salad that she had picked up the night before at Canlis, where she and her husband, Doug, went for his birthday dinner. The printed recipe looked a lot snazzier—a gold C Canlis crest at the top—than the oil-stained version from the fifties that I had in my old recipe notebook.

Shelley exclaimed that the food at Canlis had been fabulous. She described the dishes they ordered, then went into the details of the restaurant's recent remodeling. Robin, Laurie, and I worried that they had changed our favorite restaurant too much. Shelley assured us that it was more beautiful than ever.

As she prepared the salad, we gathered around the marble island in Laurie's kitchen and played the remember game:

"Remember when we went to ski school, and ate warm apple pie for lunch?"

"It was swimming in cinnamon sauce."

"Remember the guy who was the best skier?"

"Bob! He always had a little crust of dried spittle at the corners of his mouth."

"Yeah, but he was a good kisser!"

"*You* made out with Bob? I did too!"

Talk turned to the Sweet Sixteen party that Robin, Laurie, and I gave. We couldn't remember what food we served. Hot dogs? Fried chicken? Laurie phoned her father, who at eighty-four has a phenomenal long-term memory even though he can never remember where he put his glasses. George claimed it was fried chicken, but I disagreed: "My mother never would have bothered with fried chicken. Too messy."

"All I remember is the birthday cake," said Robin. "We ate the leftovers out of your freezer after the party."

"Why does birthday cake taste better frozen?"

We moved on to the year that Robin and Shelley spent living in San Francisco.

"For breakfast, we had coffee, a frozen Hershey bar, and a diet pill," Robin recalled. "That was the year Shelley taught me how to light a cigarette and smoke it while walking down the street."

"That was the year we wore big ladies' suits and had big hair!" Shelley added.

Now we were up to our grand tour of Europe. Robin recalled cutting herself on a broken wineglass in a Left Bank café. "The owner was a typical French asshole. His response to my pain and blood was to kick us out!"

Shelley recalled the first dinner she made after getting married: "By mistake I put cayenne pepper instead of paprika on the chicken, and I dumped a package of frozen peas on a plate. I didn't know you had to defrost them! I just wanted to please my husband."

"That's what we all were raised to do."

Time for dinner. I slid the Copper River salmon into the oven, and we sat down at the table in the dining room. Out the window behind us, the summer dusk was settling over the lake. We complimented Shelley on the Canlis salad. "It's the fresh oregano that makes it work," she insisted. Robin argued that it was the fresh mint.

Somehow, the subject changed to how we lost our collective virginities. It's a topic we never discussed in our teens or even our twenties, and I was surprised at the ease with which we did so now. Confessions—and jokes—popped up all around. It emboldened us to move on to an even more hush-hush topic: illegal abortions. The four of us had become sexually active in the mid-sixties, before birth control pills and legal abortions. When we were teenagers, we didn't share our horror stories—shame, I guess. Now we had nothing to hide from one another. One illegal abortion took place in a little town east of the Cascade Mountains, and the other was at a doctor's office in the heart of downtown Seattle, where other teenage girls sat staring at the floor in the waiting room with their mothers.

It was an easy jump from there to confessions about the men we slept with before we got married. Among the four of us, we came up with one Qantas Airline steward, one former high school basketball star, one two-timer who today is a senior executive at Boeing, a medical student who was engaged to be married, and one Austrian with neo-Nazi tendencies.

The salmon was ready, but we were not. We were marveling that we could be so open and honest with one another. Who needed salmon anyway? Instead, we opted for seconds and thirds of the Canlis salad, sprinkled liberally with fresh Oregon shrimp.

By the time we got around to "What choices do you regret making in your life?" we had skipped to dessert. Laurie regretted her first, short-lived marriage. Shelley regretted her troubles with alcohol. Robin said she didn't regret a thing—even having her tubes tied so that she wouldn't be able to have children.

I regretted that I crammed five years of college into four years at three different schools, and that I wasted a year of my life on Justin. I sort of regretted that I got married at twenty-three and didn't have much of a chance to explore life as a young single woman. On the other hand, I felt fortunate that the life I've shared with my husband has been good—and that he turned out to be a keeper.

I also regretted that I didn't put more effort into maintaining my friendships with women—especially them. If it's true that a woman is the sum of all the friends she's had in her life, I concluded that for me, Robin, Laurie, and Shelley were not just tiny slivers but one big, delicious slice of the pie (or should I say cake?).

Robin and Maggie's
Frozen Mocha Mousse

SERVES 12

This rich creamy dessert requires time to make, but it's worth it. Eat before it melts!

FOR THE CRUST

> 8 ounces chocolate wafer cookies
> 6 tablespoons unsalted butter

FOR THE MOUSSE

> 1 tablespoon dry instant coffee
> ½ cup boiling water
> 1¼ cups sugar
> 2 cups semisweet chocolate chips
> 4 extra-large eggs, separated
> 3 cups whipping cream
> Pinch of salt
> ⅛ teaspoon cream of tartar

1. To make the crust, preheat the oven to 375°F. Separate the bottom from the sides of a 9 by 3-inch springform pan; butter the sides only and put the pan back together. Crumble the cookies in a food processor or blender until they are fine crumbs. Melt the butter and stir it into the crumbs until thoroughly distributed. Pour two thirds of the mixture into the prepared pan; tilt the pan to about a 45-degree angle, and with your fingertips press a layer of the crumbs against the sides while rotating the pan. Then pour in the remainder of the crumbs and press them over the bottom of the pan. Bake 7 to 8 minutes. Remove the pan from the oven and cool completely.

2. In a 2-quart saucepan, dissolve the coffee in the water. Add ½ cup of the sugar and stir over moderate heat until the sugar is dissolved. Lower the heat and add the chocolate. Stir until it is melted and smooth. Remove the pot from the heat and cool. Add the egg yolks, one at a time, stirring with a wire whisk. Set aside and cool completely.

3. Using an electric mixer or a handheld egg beater, whip the cream until it holds a shape but is not stiff. Set aside.

4. In a small bowl, use a mixer to beat the egg whites until foamy. Add the salt and cream of tartar, and continue beating until the whites hold a soft shape. Gradually add the reserved ¾ cup sugar. Increase the speed of the mixer, and beat until the meringue is quite firm but not stiff or dry. Gradually fold most of the chocolate into the whites and fold the whites into the remaining chocolate.

5. In a large mixing bowl, fold together the whipped cream and the chocolate mixture.

6. Pour the mousse into the chocolate cookie–crumb crust, smooth or form a swirling pattern on top, and place the pan in the freezer. After an hour, cover the top with several layers of plastic wrap so that it is airtight. Freeze overnight or for up to 2 weeks.

7. Remove the pan from the freezer up to a day before serving. With a firm, sharp, heavy knife, cut around the sides of the crust, pressing the blade firmly against the pan as you cut. Release and remove the sides of the pan. Insert a firm metal spatula carefully under the crust and ease it around to release the dessert completely from the bottom of the pan. Transfer to a serving dish. Wrap the mousse airtight in plastic wrap, and return it to the freezer until ready to serve. Serve as is or covered with whipped cream.

Chapter 44

All Grown Up

Julia hadn't been home since Christmas, eight months ago. The first thing she did when she walked into the house was to open the refrigerator and peruse what was inside. *"Raspberry barbecue sauce? Dijon mustard with red bell peppers?"* The tone of her voice implied that she wasn't just impressed—she was upset that she had missed out.

Next she went to the pantry and started moving things around on the shelves. She said she was neatening up the mess, but I knew it was just an excuse to touch the boxes of sugar, the sacks of flour, and the jars of capers and olives and even Miracle Whip that she always found there, familiar ingredients for making the comfort foods she associated with home.

She rummaged through my collection of cookbooks looking for new ones. When she was in high school, Julia and her best friends, Julie and Hilary, spent hours browsing through my cookbooks. These girls didn't just bake chocolate chip cookies, like my friends and I did when we were their age. They made ambitious dishes like stuffed grape leaves, gnocchi, and floating-island meringues with soft peaks like the cowlicks on a baby's head. One New Year's Eve they even made a croquembouche. I had warned them how hard it was to pull it off. They worked all day baking and filling the cream puffs, stacking them in a pyramid, and gluing the whole thing together with sticky caramel. It looked—and tasted—as good as one at a French bakery.

Now that Julia shares a tiny apartment in New York with a minuscule kitchen, she rarely cooks. She misses it. She complained that one time she and her roommates tried making meringues, but they didn't have an electric mixer or even a wire whisk. She e-mailed me: "Have you ever tried beating egg whites stiff with a *fork*?!"

Julia is twenty-three, the age at which I got married, but marriage is the farthest thing from her mind. She enjoys her work, savors her independence, and even though she has a boyfriend, she maintains a wide network of girlfriends. They include young women she has known since high school, those she met in college, and some she has met since she moved to New York. She is still in touch with her best childhood girlfriend, Brooke. They are all women who value their friendships with other women as highly as they value a relationship with a man.

Even before she unpacked, Julia and I planned the dinners we intended to cook during the week she was home. She rattled off some possibilities: Chicken La Cassine; pasta with tomatoes, basil, and fresh mozzarella cheese; focaccia; plus a couple of promising recipes in this month's *Bon Appétit*. We knew that when we went to the farmers' market on Sunday, however, we would undoubtedly spot some enticing fresh produce that we hadn't considered, and change the menu accordingly.

And we did. For Sunday dinner, instead of a Canlis salad, we made an Israeli couscous salad with cucumbers, tomatoes, and shiny green bell peppers, to go with chicken baked with lemon juice and Parmesan cheese, a favorite old standby of mine.

One of our dinner guests was Mary Lou Malphus, who was Julia's kindergarten teacher and Brownie troop leader eons ago.

With her blond hair, melodious voice, and cheerful demeanor, Mary Lou reminds me of a fairy godmother; all she's missing is the magic wand. Mary Lou and her husband, Eddy, never had children, but Mary Lou has stayed in close touch with her favorite students over the years, so that today she has a dozen or so young adults whose lives she touches and whose accomplishments make her proud. One of them is Julia.

It hit me that until recently, I had thought of Mary Lou more as Julia's friend than mine, but in fact our common interests in food, restaurants, swimming—and Julia—have brought us closer. These days I see Mary Lou not just when Julia comes to town but other times as well. I guess just as I now have friendships with women that don't necessarily include Paul, my friendship with Mary Lou doesn't depend on the inclusion of my daughter.

As Mary Lou carefully unwrapped the chocolate layer cake she had brought for dessert, she explained its origins: "Jane, my roommate in college, got this from her grandmother, who said, 'Men can get sex from any woman, but not a good chocolate cake. And this one is good enough to get you a husband!' "

Mary Lou and Julia ice the husband-catcher cake.

Julia laughed at the idea that women once looked on cooking as a way to catch a man. Mary Lou paraphrased the *Cosmo* article she read back then. "It said a girl should always have good things in her refrigerator because the morning after a guy sleeps over, he will open it looking for something to eat. If he only finds bottled water and celery sticks, he'll never come back. So you should always keep fried chicken in the fridge and a yummy chocolate cake, like this one!"

Mary Lou advised baking this cake the day before it's served. "That's true of any cake made with buttermilk," she said, "and frost it just before serving so the frosting stays shiny and smooth." She handed a bag of chocolate chips to Julia, who melted them for the frosting.

The frosting recipe called for corn syrup, so I climbed up on a kitchen stool to locate an ancient bottle of Karo on the top shelf of a cabinet. I hadn't used it in years. The bottle was sticky and difficult to open, but the syrup still tasted sweet. She added it with water and a touch of Kahlúa to the melted chocolate chips, then she and Julia frosted the cake. "It's easier to bake this chocolate cake in a bundt pan, but let's face it," said Mary Lou, "the cake—and the baker—look better if it's a layer cake. Once you're married, you can let standards slide and use the bundt pan." Julia rolled her eyes. "Just kidding," Mary Lou added.

Mary Lou went to college in New Orleans, where she learned that in the South everyone has their favorite recipe for chocolate cake like they do for fried chicken. "There's even supposed to be a recipe for chocolate cake made with chicken fat," she said.

"Chicken fat?"

"I've never seen the recipe or tasted the cake, so maybe it's just a legend. I can remember my Southern aunts baking with lard, but not chicken fat. Maybe it's because they raised pigs but not chickens."

Julia urged Mary Lou to tell her about the parties that she and her roommate, Jane, gave when they roomed together. "We always planned the menu around dessert," explained Mary Lou. "And everyone got all dressed up. No guy would dare show up at our dinner table in cutoffs."

Jane's mother gave the girls a recipe for perfect rémoulade—the secret was Zatarain's Creole mustard. "When we were feeling flush, the first course was shrimp rémoulade," said Mary Lou. "If we were broke, we served the rémoulade over halved hard-boiled eggs."

Mary Lou and Jane are still close friends, even though Jane lives in the South and Mary Lou lives in California. "Whenever Jane comes to visit me, she brings five pounds of fresh Gulf shrimp," said Mary Lou. "And she always finds rémoulade and a chocolate cake in the fridge."

Another night when Julia was home, our dinner guest was Jessica, Mary Ann's daughter. I vividly remember the day in 1969 when Mary Ann cradled baby Jessica in her arms while we watched the first man walking on the moon, and the night in 1979 when ten-year-old Jessica helped Julia cut the cake on Julia's first birthday. Now, at thirty-two, Jessica is a vice president at MTV. It's a powerful job for a woman who is less than five feet tall and still looks like a teenager. Like her mom, Jessica may be tiny, but she's a dynamo.

Jessica revealed that she had a new boyfriend and that she had been cooking dinner for him. I was surprised—this is the young woman who a few months before had professed to have no interest in cooking. "I don't know why, but suddenly I got the urge to cook," she said. "I bought a Cuisinart, and I've been going through all the cookbooks Mom bought for my kitchen, experimenting with dishes. It's actually fun!"

I could picture a little smile on Mary Ann's face.

Among the things that Mary Ann left Jessica was a journal she had kept during the long hours she was undergoing chemotherapy in the hospital. "I couldn't bear to read it until about a month ago,"

Jessica admitted. "It was too painful. Now it gives me comfort. I savor reading what Mom wrote to me, page by page."

In the journal Mary Ann relayed how proud she was of Jessica, and how she hoped that after she died, Jessica would go on with her life—meet a man, get married, have children. She also wrote down her favorite recipes and her mother's favorites, recipes that she wanted Jessica to have. "Mom pasted in a recipe for a Jell-O mold with condensed milk and Philadelphia cream cheese that is in my grandmother's handwriting," Jessica said. "And one for chicken that she used to make when I was little, with sesame seeds and Kitchen Bouquet."

Julia had never heard of Kitchen Bouquet. I explained that it was a brown liquid that cooks used to brush onto meat and chicken to make them look brown. She thought it was gross. It was a fifties thing, I said.

Mary Ann's journal also included her recipe for *lavosh* sandwiches filled with sliced roast beef, lettuce, and horseradish cream cheese. I reminisced about the day I helped Mary Ann prepare dozens of the sandwiches for Jessica's high school graduation party, which was held in their backyard. The secret was wetting the large rounds of Armenian cracker bread so that they were soft enough to roll up. If we wet them too much, they turned to mush.

The memory of that sunny June day in Mary Ann's yard flooded back. Friends and family were mingling on the patio, congratulating Jessica and shaking their heads about how quickly time had passed since she was born. Julia, who was eight, was all dressed up and acting like a perfect little lady. Adam, who was three, was all dressed up and playing in the dirt. Mary Ann had piled stones there for him, knowing he would like building with them.

I reminded Julia and Jessica of what Barbara Lazaroff had said about shared food memories: We long remember what we ate and how we felt on important emotional occasions, especially those that mark the passage of time.

It was so quiet in the kitchen, I could hear the hum of the refrigerator and the *chop* each time I brought my knife down on a cucumber for tonight's salad. Julia had returned to New York that morning, and I missed her. During her week at home, it had been like old times, the two of us gabbing away, *La Bohème* on the CD player, as we cooked together. Our partnership in the kitchen had been smoother than ever, each of us performing several tasks at once (for better or for worse, Julia inherited my multitasker gene) and bickering about whether or not a dish needed more seasoning or more time in the oven.

I am fortunate that my daughter shares my passion for cooking, and that she finds it a creative and nurturing act. Perhaps someday she will bring her own daughter into my kitchen to cook with us. I will teach my granddaughter to make the dishes that Julia grew up with, like Grandma Fan's stuffing, Wolfgang's matzoh, and Mary Ann's grapes brûlée (but with raspberries instead of grapes). And my granddaughter will use the same utensils that Julia and I used, including my mother's dented old metal colander that she gave me when I moved into my first apartment, and the wooden spoon with the etching of a kiwi bird on the handle, a souvenir from the trip Julia and I took to New Zealand.

I walked over to the Federal desk in the living room and pulled out my old recipe notebook from when I was a newlywed. It was time to add the recipes that Julia and I prepared together, so that she and her future daughters will have them.

And when I give Julia my old recipe notebook, what will I tell her about female friendships?

One thing I will tell her is that though most women love only one man at a time in their lives, they can love many girlfriends. Julia might ask what the magic formula is—why we end up being closer friends with some women than with others. It isn't just how long you've known them or what experiences and ordeals you've shared. I think instinctively Julia knows the answer to the question: Between women, as there is between women and men, sometimes there is just a chemistry.

Julia's Focaccia

MAKES ONE 10 BY 13-INCH RECTANGULAR FOCACCIA

Julia has been making this dense Italian bread since she was about ten years old, and we never tire of it in our house. She likes to vary the toppings—from kosher salt to caramelized onions.

> 1 envelope active dry yeast
> Pinch of sugar
> 1⅛ cups warm water
> 2½ to 3 tablespoons extra-virgin olive oil
> ½ teaspoon salt
> About 3¾ cups unbleached all-purpose flour, or a
>   combination of all-purpose and bread flour
> ½ tablespoon chopped fresh rosemary
> ¾ to 1½ teaspoons coarse (kosher or sea) salt

1. In a large bowl, combine the yeast, the sugar, and the warm water. Stir and set aside until dissolved, about 5 to 10 minutes. Stir in 1½ tablespoons of the olive oil and ½ teaspoon salt.

2. Put in a food processor or the bowl of an electric mixer and gradually add the flour, mixing until it becomes hard to mix (you may not need all the flour).

3. Turn the dough onto a lightly floured surface, and knead until smooth and elastic, 5 to 7 minutes. The dough should be soft but not sticky. Place the dough in a lightly oiled bowl and cover the bowl tightly with plastic wrap. Set aside to rise in a warm, draft-free place until doubled in bulk, about 1½ hours.

4. Turn the dough out onto a lightly floured surface, then gently pull and stretch with your fingers to form a 9 by 13-inch rectangle. Transfer to a 9 by 13-inch baking pan that you've greased with olive oil or olive-oil spray. Cover with a damp towel and set aside to rise in a warm, draft-free place until almost doubled in bulk, about 1 hour.

5. Preheat the oven to 400°F. Dimple the dough with your fingertips. Brush with the remaining olive oil. Sprinkle water on the surface, then the rosemary and the coarse salt.

6. Bake in the middle of the oven for 20 to 25 minutes, until golden brown, spraying or sprinkling with water three times during the first 10 minutes. Immediately transfer the focaccia from the pan to a rack to cool slightly, so that the bottom won't get soggy.

TOPPING VARIATION
Instead of rosemary, chop an onion and sauté it until soft in 1 tablespoon olive oil and 1 teaspoon balsamic vinegar. Sprinkle on top of the focaccia before baking.

Mary Lou and Jane's Rémoulade
SERVES 8 AS AN APPETIZER DIP

I found Zatarain's Creole mustard among the exotic mustards at Pier 1 Imports. It adds zing to this New Orleans sauce, and it's good on shrimp or even plain hard-boiled egg.

> 6 tablespoons extra-virgin olive oil
> 2 tablespoons white vinegar
> 1 tablespoon paprika
> 4 tablespoons Creole mustard (Zatarain's)

½ teaspoon red pepper flakes
½ teaspoon salt
1 celery heart, minced

Mix all the ingredients well. Refrigerate before serving.

The Husband-Catcher Cake

SERVES 12

*Mary Lou told me that our common friend Susan (of the pheasant fol-
lies) always adds more chocolate than a recipe calls for. With that in
mind, the second time I made this cake I added three rather than just
two squares of unsweetened chocolate. It tasted even more delicious
that way.*

FOR THE CAKE

2 sticks butter, softened
1 box brown sugar
3 extra-large or 4 large eggs
3 squares unsweetened chocolate, melted
2 teaspoons vanilla extract
1 teaspoon baking soda
½ teaspoon salt
2¼ cups White Lily flour or sifted all-purpose flour
1 cup buttermilk

FOR THE FILLING

6 ounces apricot or raspberry preserves, or orange
    marmalade
⅛ cup fruit-based liqueur to match the above
    (i.e., apricot brandy, raspberry eau de vie, or
    Grand Marnier)

FOR THE FROSTING
> 3½ tablespoons light Karo corn syrup
> ½ stick butter
> 2 tablespoons water
> 1 tablespoon Kahlúa, brandy, coffee liqueur, orange
>   liqueur, or vanilla extract
> 1 cup semisweet chocolate chips

1. Cream together the butter and brown sugar until light and fluffy. Add the eggs one at a time, beating well after each, then the chocolate and the vanilla. Mix well.

2. Preheat the oven to 350°F. Add the baking soda and salt to the flour and mix. To the chocolate mixture, alternate adding the flour mixture and the buttermilk, a little of each at a time, beginning and ending the process with the dry ingredients. Do not overmix.

3. Pour the batter into 2 greased and floured or nonstick round cake pans, and bake for 30 to 35 minutes, or until a toothpick inserted into the middle of each cake comes out clean. Cool the cakes on a wire rack.

4. In a small saucepan, over boiling water, mix the filling ingredients well. Cool. Invert one cooled cake layer onto a serving plate, then spread on the cooled filling. Carefully top with the other layer. Cover gently but tightly with plastic wrap covered by aluminum foil and refrigerate overnight. Bring the cake to room temperature before icing.

5. In a medium saucepan, mix the Karo corn syrup, butter, water, and liqueur or vanilla and bring to a boil. Stir in the chocolate chips. Let cool and stir until the frosting is the consistency of whipping cream. Frost the top and sides of the cake.

Good Enough to Eat:
Notes on Recipe Testing

You're *not going to put that recipe in your book, are you?"* My teenage son, Adam, rolled his eyes and said that to me at least a dozen times during the months I spent testing recipes. Adam had a point. Several of the recipes were *not* good enough to be included (and they weren't), and many I had to test again and again—sometimes only with slight variations—until they *were* good enough. And then there were those that I tested, tasted, tested and tasted again, and dumped. No matter how many times I tried, for example, I couldn't get excited about "Aunt Myra's Pickled Salmon—Sort Of," a recipe that Hannah's sister had made in the seventies that calls for salmon cooked with sautéed onions, ketchup, and chopped sweet pickles and is served chilled.

I have always thought of myself as a good cook, but it was not until I was forced to measure, adjust ingredients, time, and adjust again while testing the recipes for this book that I realized there is a big difference between a good cook and a *pro*. A pro I am not. But I did get to be a better cook from the recipe-testing ordeal—and it was a hoot!

I emerged from the experience with a few cooking tips to offer:

- Always wear an apron, tie the strings in front, and tuck in a towel. When your hands become covered in flour, batter, or dough, wipe them on the towel—not on your jeans.
- Never go barefoot unless you enjoy the feel of raw eggs or squashed grapes between your toes. Chef's clogs, or sandals with high clunky soles like those the Spice Girls wear, give you better arch support than flats.
- Nonstick pans are preferable to old rusty *stick* pans.
- *Tasting* while you're cooking is okay—even necessary—but if you want to keep the pounds off, forget about licking the bowl the way you did when you were a kid. And *never* cook when you are hungry.

Throughout the months that I tested recipes, my kitchen constantly looked like the aftermath of a cooking class for kindergarteners, and my tiny pantry overflowed with oddball ingredients ranging from brined peppercorns (I mistook them for capers in the store) to unsulphured molasses. I also experienced a series of humorous kitchen disasters.

The first testing dinner I served to Paul and Adam the night before I was to leave for Paris and Tuscany, I bit down on a chicken bone (as in Chicken La Cassine) and cracked one of my back teeth. During the middle of the night my toothache was so painful that instead of getting on a plane to Europe the next morning, I went to the dentist and had the tooth pulled. He sent me off to Europe a day later with a swollen cheek and a gaping hole that showed every time I smiled.

A few weeks later my sister Sheila e-mailed me her recipe for chicken soup. One of the steps read: "2 big onions, cut in quarters and each quarter stuck with cloves (6 to 8)." I interpreted that to mean I should stick 6 to 8 cloves into each onion quarter. So, my eyes streaming with onion tears, I did just that. An hour later, as the soup bubbled away on the stove, the house began to smell like the clove gum I chewed in elementary school. I phoned Sheila: "Did you mean six to eight cloves per quarter onion?" I asked, "Or six to eight cloves, *total?*"

Sheila did the math. *"You put sixty-four cloves into my chicken soup?"* (Dummy.)

I hung up, ran to the kitchen, and began fishing cloves out of the soup. It was like picking ants out of a sugar bowl—and it was too late. Adam walked in, sampled the soup, and grimaced. "What's that *weird* taste?" Rather than explain, I dumped the pot and started over again.

Another time, my friend Susan rattled off her favorite Sicilian swordfish recipe while we were sipping iced lattes at Starbucks. The lengthy instructions, which I noted on a napkin, began, *"First you soak the swordfish fillets in milk . . ."*

I bought all the ingredients and spent several hours making the dish. The swordfish was delicious, so I phoned Susan to report: "First I soaked the swordfish fillets in milk—"

"Who told you to soak the fish in *milk?*"

"You did."

"Where in the world did I get *that* idea?"

Susan and I rummaged through our cookbooks for Sicilian swordfish recipes. The Sicilians soak swordfish in ice water.

Off I went to buy more ingredients to test the recipe again. With swordfish going for $17.95 a pound, it was an expensive exercise. And guess what? In the end, the swordfish soaked in milk tasted identical to the swordfish soaked in ice water.

There were other problems too. The oven door broke, and every time I slid something inside, I had to tape the door shut with electrical tape. Still, I could feel heat escaping into my already stifling hot kitchen. With six bands of electrical tape holding the door closed, it was hard for me to check on what was happening inside;

until the repairman showed up a few days later, every dish burned. I explained this to the guy as he replaced the broken door hinge for two hundred dollars including parts and labor. He looked at my mess of a kitchen and said, "Lady, don't blame bad cooking on the oven."

And then there was—or, I should say, *is*—the mouse (he may be a rat, but I prefer to picture him as a mouse) who paid nocturnal visits to the drawer below the oven, leaving little souvenirs behind. I tried those sticky tented mouse catchers. I tried saucers of Clorox and ammonia in the hope that he'd hate the fumes. I think he got high on them, for he left behind more evidence of his visit.

I thought of putting my cat in the drawer for the night, but at almost twenty-five pounds, Kitty Boorstin wouldn't fit. Finally, I bought an old-fashioned mousetrap and baited it with peanut butter. He took the bait—and the trap. The saga continues . . .

The capper occurred when I was kneading dough for Julia's focaccia. Though Julia always made it look easy, I was working up a sweat, so I opened the kitchen window to let in fresh air. A yellow-jacket flew inside and zapped me on the finger. *Yeoow!*

Because I'm allergic to bee stings, I panicked about the possibility that I might go into anaphylactic shock. I gulped down two Benadryl capsules, rummaged in my purse for my Epi-Pen (a prepackaged syringe of epinephrine to be administered in an emergency), and yelled for Paul. I handed him the Epi-Pen with instructions to jab it into my thigh if I fainted or stopped breathing. If he didn't, I might die. Paul insisted on taking me to the E.R. I begged him to wait—the focaccia dough wouldn't rise unless I finished kneading it.

I was still standing ten minutes later, so Paul returned to his office and I returned to my kneading—despite the fact that my afflicted finger had swelled to the width of a frankfurter. Then the Benadryl kicked in. My eyes drooping, I chucked the focaccia and crawled into bed.

The next morning my entire hand was so swollen, the skin was stretched as tight as the skin on a grape. It reminded Adam of one of those battery-operated rubber hands with wiggly fingers that kids stick in the ground on Halloween, so that it looks like a corpse crawling out of its grave. At Paul's insistence, I zoomed off to the doctor's.

"Yep, that's a bad allergic reaction, all right, " said Dr. Koblin, my kindly Beverly Hills doctor to the stars, including Antonio Banderas, who stepped into the adjoining examining room. (Antonio is shorter than you'd think but still gorgeous.) Dr. Koblin injected me with steroids, handed me mega-antihistamines to swallow, then advised me to listen to my husband the next time I get stung and go to the E.R.

As for my husband, Paul deserves a lot of credit—and not only for putting up with bee stings, mice, and a messy kitchen. I often slapped him with shopping lists that sent him on a treasure hunt in Ralph's, searching for rapid-rise (not regular) yeast; corn syrup (*what's corn syrup?*); unsweetened, not semisweet, dark, white, or milk chocolate; beef short ribs as opposed to beef long ribs or pork baby back ribs; and parsnips, those root vegetables, I explained when he didn't have a clue, that look like carrots, only they're white. ("And I bet they taste bad," he added.)

Paul and Adam were always willing guinea pigs, and I thank them for suffering through testing dinners that sometimes included the likes of German pancakes, focaccia, swordfish, fudge, and Aunt Myra's sort-of pickled salmon—on one menu. I appreciated their candor about the recipes that didn't work and their praise for those that did. "You finally *nailed* it!" Adam said almost with relief the day I finally made brownies from scratch that tasted better than Betty Crocker's.

Thanks to the taste testers and cooking helpers among my friends—and of course to all the women who so generously shared their food memories and recipes with me. I am also grateful to my editor, Cassie Jones, for knowing, even without tasting them, which recipes were the best.

Acknowledgments

Thank you again to all my friends and relatives who shared their colorful food memories and delicious recipes with me. I also want to thank Stephanie Woodard and the other editors at *More* for encouraging me to write an article about the discovery of my old recipe notebook for the magazine; my publisher, Judith Regan, for encouraging me to expand the article into a book; my agent, Liv Blumer, for helping me shape my ideas for the book; and my editor, Cassie Jones, for being an always upbeat sounding board, adviser, and cheerleader.

If you have your own fond food memories and recipes to share, I'd love to hear from you: sharonboorstin@aol.com.